Europäisches Wirtschaftsrecht
European Commercial Law

Founded by

Prof. em. Dr. Dr. h.c. Jürgen Basedow
Prof. em. Dr. Dr. Dr. h.c. Klaus Hopt
Prof. em. Dr. Wulf-Henning Roth

Edited by

Prof. Dr. Thomas Ackermann, LL.M.
Prof. Dr. Christian Heinze, LL.M.
Prof. Dr. Patrick C. Leyens, LL.M.
Prof. Dr. Rupprecht Podszun
Prof. Dr. Wolfgang Wurmnest, LL.M.

Volume 73

Katrin Silja Kurz

Innovation Competition

The novel theory of harm in the Dow/DuPont merger and its application in the scope of Article 101 and 102 TFEU

Nomos

C.H.BECK

First supervisor: Prof. Dr. Jörn Axel Kämmerer
Second supervisor: Prof. Dr. Joachim Jickeli
Day of the oral examination: 23.11.2021

The Deutsche Nationalbibliothek lists this publication in the Deutsche Nationalbibliografie; detailed bibliographic data are available on the Internet at http://dnb.d-nb.de

a.t.: Hamburg, Bucerius Law School – Hochschule für Rechtswissenschaft, Diss., 2021

ISBN 978-3-8487-8769-2 (Print)
978-3-7489-3336-6 (ePDF)

British Library Cataloguing-in-Publication Data
A catalogue record for this book is available from the British Library.

ISBN 978-3-8487-8769-2 (Print)
978-3-7489-3336-6 (ePDF)

Library of Congress Cataloging-in-Publication Data
Kurz, Katrin Silja
Innovation Competition
The novel theory of harm in the Dow/DuPont merger and its application in the scope of Article 101 and 102 TFEU
Katrin Silja Kurz
287 pp.
Includes bibliographic references.

ISBN 978-3-8487-8769-2 (Print)
978-3-7489-3336-6 (ePDF)

Onlineversion
Nomos eLibrary

1st Edition 2022

Dedicated to Sven Rissmann

Acknowledgements

This thesis was completed in April 2021 and accepted as a dissertation by the Bucerius Law School in September 2021.

I would like to express my sincere thanks to my supervisor Prof. Dr. Jörn Axel Kämmerer for his continuous support, encouragement and patience. His openness to the topic and his always excellent advice made this work possible. I am indebted to Prof. Dr. Joachim Jickeli for the rapid preparation of the second opinion.

A big thank you goes to my friends Alexander Iken, Johanna Weschke and Jonas Botta for helpful discussions and valuable input as well as benevolent guidance during the process of writing this thesis.

Finally, I would like to thank my family and all those who accompanied me during my doctoral studies and supported me with words and deeds.

Berlin, January 2022 *Katrin Kurz*

Table of Contents

List of Abbreviations and Acronyms

Legislation, legislative materials and decisions

AEUV	Vertrag über die Arbeitsweise der Europäischen Union = TFEU
Annex 4	Case M.7932, *Dow/DuPont*, Annex 4 to the Commission Decision, Implications of the economic theory on mergers, competition and innovation in light of the features of the Transaction.
Annex 7	Case M.7932, *Dow/DuPont*, Annex 7 to the Commission Decision, Commitments to the European Commission.
ARC	German Act against Restraints of Competition (GWB), 26.6.2013, BGBl. I p. 1750, 3245.
AstraZeneca/Novartis Decision	European Commission, Decision of 26.07.2000, OJ L 110, 16.04.2004, p. 1-72, Case No COMP/M.1806, *AstraZeneca/Novartis*.
Bayer/Aventis Decision	European Commission, Decision of 17.04.2002, C(2002) 1462 final, OJ L 107, 15.04.2004, p. 1-136, Case No COMP/M.2547, *Bayer/Aventis Crop Science*.
Ciba-Geigy/Sandoz Decision	European Commission, Decision of 17.07.1996, OJ L 201, 29.07.1997, p. 1-47, Case No IV/M.737, *Ciba-Geigy/Sandoz*.
CFR	Charter of Fundamental Rights of the European Union, OJ C 326, 26.10.2012, p. 391-407.
Deutsche Börse/NYSE Euronext Decision	European Commission, Decision of 01.02.2012, C(2012) 440 final, OJ C 254, 05.08.2014, p. 8-18, Case No COMP/M.6166, *Deutsche Börse/NYSE Euronext*.
Dow/DuPont Decision	Commission Decision of 27.3.2017, C(2017) 1946 final, OJ C 353, 20.10.2017, p. 9-19, Case M.7932, *Dow/DuPont*.
ECHR	Council of Europe, European Convention for the protection of Human Rights and Fundamental Freedoms, as amended by Protocols No 11 and 14, 4.11.1950.

EC Merger Regulation	Council Regulation (EC) No 139/2004 of 20 January 2004 on the control of concentrations between undertakings, OJ L 24, 29.1.2004, p. 1-22.
EC Treaty	Treaty establishing the European Community, OJ C 325, 24.12.2002, p. 33-184, or previous versions, respectively.
EGV	Vertrag zur Gründung der Europäischen Gemeinschaft = EC Treaty
EUV	Vertrag über die Europäische Union = TEU
FKVO	EU-Fusionskontrollverordnung = EC Merger Regulation
FuE-GVO	Gruppenfreistellungsverordnung für Forschungs- und Entwicklungsvereinbarungen = R&D BER
GC, Deutsche Börse	General Court, Judgment of 09.03.2015, Case T-175/12, ECLI:EU:T:2015:148, *Deutsche Börse/Commission*.
GE/Alstom Decision	European Commission, Decision of 08.09.2015, C(2015) 6179 final, OJ C 139, 04.05.2017, p. 6-13, Case No M.7278, *General Electric/Alstom (Thermal Power – Renewable Power & Grid Business)*.
Glaxo/Wellcome Decision	European Commission, Decision of 28.02.1995, OJ C 65, 16.03.1995, p. 3, Case No IV/M.555, *Glaxo/Wellcome*.
Glaxo Wellcome/SK Beecham Decision	European Commission, Decision of 08.05.2000, Case No COMP/M.1846, *Glaxo Wellcome/SmithKline Beecham*.
GRC	Charta der Grundrechte der Europäischen Union = CFR
Horizontal Cooperation Guidelines	Communication from the Commission - Guidelines on the applicability of Article 101 of the Treaty on the Functioning of the European Union to horizontal co-operation agreements, OJ C 11, 14.1.2011, p. 1-72.
Horizontal Merger Guidelines	Guidelines on the assessment of horizontal mergers under the Council Regulation on the control of concentrations between undertakings, OJ C 31, 5.2.2004, p. 5-18.
Market Definition Notice	Commission notice on the definition of the relevant market for the purposes of Community competition law, OJ C 372, 9.12.1997, p. 5-13.

Non-Horizontal Merger Guidelines	Guidelines on the assessment of non-horizontal mergers under the Council Regulation on the control of concentrations between undertakings, OJ C 265, 18.10.2008, p. 6-25.
Novartis/GSK Decision	European Commission, Decision of 28.01.2015, C(2015) 538 final, OJ C 95, 21.03.2015, p. 14, Case No COMP/M.7275, *Novartis/GlaxoSmithKline Oncology Business*.
Priority Guidance	Communication from the Commission – Guidance on the Commission's enforcement priorities in applying Article 82 of the EC Treaty to abusive exclusionary conduct by dominant undertakings, OJ C 45, 24.2.2009, p. 7-20.
Protocol No (27)	Protocol No (27) to the Treaty on European Union and the Treaty on the Functioning of the European Union, OJ 115, 09.05.2008, p. 309.
R&D BER	Commission Regulation (EU) No 1217/2010 of 14 December 2010 on the application of Article 101 (3) of the Treaty on the Functioning of the European Union to certain categories of research and development agreements, OJ L 335, 18.12.2010, p. 36-42.
Regulation 1/2003	Council Regulation (EC) No 1/2003 of 16.12.2002 on the implementation of the rules on competition laid down in Articles 81 and 82 of the Treaty, OJ L 1, 4.1.2003, p. 1-25.
Remedies Notice	Commission's Notice on Remedies acceptable under Council Regulation (EC) No 139/2004 and under Commission Regulation (EC) No 802/2004, OJ C 267, 22.10.2008, p. 1-27.
Stellungnahme 9. GWB-Novelle	*Podszun, Rupprecht*, Deutscher Bundestag, Ausschussdrucksache 18(9)1092, 19.01.2017, Stellungnahme als Sachverständiger im Wirtschaftsausschuss des Deutschen Bundestages zur Vorbereitung der Anhörung am 23.01.2017, Die 9. Novelle des Gesetzes gegen Wettbewerbsbeschränkungen (GWB).
Syngenta/Monsanto Decision	European Commission, Decision of 17.11.2010, C(2010) 7929 final, Case No COMP/M.5675, *Syngenta/Monsanto's Sunflower Seed Business*.

Technology Transfer BER	Commission Regulation (EU) No 316/2014 of 21.03.2014 on the application of Article 101 (3) of the Treaty on the Functioning of the European Union to categories of technology transfer agreements, OJ L 93, 28.3.2014, p. 17-23.
Technology Transfer Guidelines	Communication from the Commission - Guidelines on the application of Article 101 of the Treaty on the Functioning of the European Union to technology transfer agreements, OJ C 89, 28.3.2014, p. 3-50.
TEU	Treaty on European Union, OJ C 326, 26.10.2012, p. 13-390.
TFEU	Treaty on the Functioning of the European Union, OJ C 326, 26.10.2021, p. 47-390.
U.S. Horizontal Merger Guidelines	DOJ and FTC, Horizontal Merger Guidelines, 19 August 2010.
U.S. Intellectual Property Guidelines	DOJ and FTC, Antitrust Guidelines for the Licensing of Intellectual Property, 12 January 2017.
U.S. JV Guidelines	DOJ and FTC, Antitrust Guidelines for Collaborations among Competitors, 7 April 2000.

Other abbreviations

Abs.	Absatz = Section
AI	Active ingredient
Art.	Article
BGBl.	Bundesgesetzblatt = Federal Law Gazette
BT-Drs.	Deutscher Bundestag Drucksache = German Parliament Document
Cf.	Compare with
CFI	Court of First Instance of the European Union (since 01.12.2009: General Court of the European Union)
Commission	European Commission
DJ COMP	Directorate-General for Competition
DOJ	U.S. Department of Justice
ECJ	European Court of Justice
Et al.	And others
Et seq	And following
EU	European Union
FCO	German Federal Cartel Office
Fn.	Footnote
FS	Festschrift = Commemorative publication
FTC	Federal Trade Commission
GC	General Court of the European Union (former Court of First Instance)
No	Number
OJ	Official Journal
P.	Page(s)
Para	Paragraph
R&D	Research and development
VO	Verordnung = Regulation

I) Introduction

Innovation has long been considered one of the main drivers of economic and social welfare. It is also an important parameter of competition. In the recent *Dow/DuPont* merger decision ("Dow/DuPont Decision")[1], the European Commission ("Commission") based a far-reaching remedy on a theory of harm relating to the general innovation capacity of the two merging parties independent of identifiable products. In addition to overlaps in existing product markets and forthcoming pipeline products, the Commission focused on the mere innovative power of the two chemistry companies Dow and DuPont and the impact of the transaction on innovation competition in the crop protection industry. The Commission concluded that the merger would lead to a significant impediment to effective competition due to immediately reduced incentives to continue with innovation efforts in overlapping "*innovation spaces*".[2] Furthermore, the transaction would reduce innovation competition at industry level.[3] The Commission's theory of harm was widely considered to be novel.

One may wonder how the Dow/DuPont Decision fits into the concept of the internal market. Based on the objectives of the Treaties, might the Commission incorporate abstract innovation considerations into competition law decisions; moreover, is it even obliged to do so? And if innovation is an important parameter of the internal market as well as competition policy: Is the approach in the Dow/DuPont Decision valid?

In this context, one may question whether innovation can in fact be treated like price or quality of goods. What are the preconditions for drawing a link between market concentration and innovation? And what precisely is the novelty of the innovation competition approach in *Dow/DuPont*? Might innovation effects insufficiently be covered by means of existing theories and approaches?

In the first part of this thesis, I will put the Dow/DuPont Decision into context within the concept of the internal market, innovation and competition aspects in the Treaties. I will also elaborate and classify the

1 Commission Decision of 27.3.2017, C(2017) 1946 final, OJ C 353, 20.10.2017, p. 9-19, Case M.7932, *Dow/DuPont* (hereinafter „Dow/DuPont Decision“).

2 Dow/DuPont Decision, para 3297.

3 Dow/DuPont Decision, para 3297.

underlying rationale of the Dow/DuPont Decision, and analyze whether it is in line with fundamental principles of European merger control. I will place a special emphasis on the treatment of outweighing factors and efficiencies.

Even more far-reaching is the question of whether the novel theory of harm in *Dow/DuPont* may not only be used in merger settings but also with respect to cooperation or abuse of dominance. At first sight, the three main pillars of European competition law – prohibition of restrictive agreements according to Article 101 TFEU, prohibition of abuse of dominance according to Article 102 TFEU and merger control – seem to rest upon the same fundamental principles. Based on that finding, I analyze two examples of incorporating the innovation competition approach in *Dow/DuPont* into the setting of Article 101 and 102 TFEU.

With respect to Article 101 TFEU, one may ask what would have happened if Dow and DuPont had, instead of merging, set up a research and development cooperation. Must the principles set out in the Dow/DuPont Decision apply accordingly? And what would have happened had DuPont decided to license its entire patent portfolio to one downstream research company, refusing to deal with any other company in that same downstream market? This behavior is likely to be considered an abuse of dominance in the case of market dominance. But could the same result apply considering that DuPont does not have high shares in existing product markets, but is rather an important innovator?

In the second part of this thesis, I will try to answer those questions and explore whether and how the novel theory of harm in *Dow/DuPont* can be incorporated into the assessment under Article 101 and 102 TFEU. I will examine the interrelationship between merger policy and Article 101 and 102 TFEU and classify the rationale in the Dow/DuPont Decision in terms of the differences and commonalities of the three pillars of competition law.

The Dow/DuPont Decision was issued in 2017; accordingly little literature on its approach to innovation competition exists.[4] Previously, the concept of innovation markets – which treats innovation as a distinct market – had been discussed in the literature[5] and has also found its way into

4 The main legal Articles on Dow/DuPont are *Petit*, Innovation Competition and *Cary*, Festschrift für Dirk Schroeder.

5 See for example *Barth*, Innovationsmärkte in der Fusionskontrolle or *Glader*, Innovation Markets and Competition Analysis.

several competition authorities' guidelines.[6] However, as will be shown,[7] the Commission does not treat innovation as a market on its own in the Dow/DuPont Decision.

So far, there is no literature on incorporating the approach found in *Dow/DuPont* into a setting under Article 101 or 102 TFEU. However, as innovation becomes increasingly important in all industries and can also be considered a basic driver of competition law – and therefore of the completion of the internal market –[8] a consistent approach needs to be discussed, taking into account the different functions of merger control, Article 101 TFEU and 102 TFEU in the internal market.

6 See to the concept of innovation markets *Section II) F) 2).*

7 See *Section II) B) 2) (c).*

8 See *Section II) C) 4).*

II) Innovation Competition: The Dow/DuPont Decision

In March 2017, the Commission issued a merger decision based largely on innovation concerns. In the *Dow/DuPont* merger, the notifying parties were forced to divest a large part of their research and development ("R&D") organization based on concerns of harm to innovation. In the first part of this thesis, I will discuss and analyze the rationale behind the Dow/DuPont Decision and relate it to other existing approaches. After looking at the general interrelation between the internal market, innovation and competition and an explanation and classification of the Dow/DuPont Decision as well as its economic foundation, I will examine whether the Commission's approach is novel, necessary and valid.

A) Innovation, competition and the internal market

One may wonder why innovation is an important factor in the assessment of a merger. There are, in fact, provisions in the European Treaties protecting research and development, as well as specific indications in the rules on competition in the Treaties and beyond all related to the concept of the internal market.

Article 3 of the Treaty on European Union ("TEU") sets up the objectives of the European Union. According to Article 3 (1) TEU, the "*Union's aim is to promote peace, its values and the well-being of its peoples.*" Article 3 (3) TEU reads:

> "*The Union shall establish an internal market. It shall work for the sustainable development of Europe based on balanced economic growth and price stability, a highly competitive social market economy, aiming at full employment and social progress, and a high level of protection and improvement of the quality of the environment. It shall promote scientific and technological advance.*"

From this basic determination of the European Union's objectives, it can already be deduced that (i) the internal market shall be a means to promote peace, the Union's values and the well-being of European citizens[9] and (ii) that "a highly competitive social market economy" and "scientific and technological advance" form a significant part of the internal market.

It must be analyzed how the Commission's decision in the *Dow/DuPont* merger – focusing, as will be shown, for the first time on innovation beyond defined markets – relates to those objectives.

Since all the Union's institutions are bound by Article 3 TEU[10] and all Union action must ultimately be guided by the objectives set up therein,[11] the "innovation competition" approach must somehow fit into the triangle of the internal market, the competition rules and rules on innovation.

1) The internal market

(a) Definition and guiding principles

According to Article 26 (2) of the Treaty on the Functioning of the European Union ("TFEU"), the "*internal market shall comprise an area without internal frontiers in which the free movement of goods, persons, services and capital is ensured in accordance with the provisions of the Treaties.*" Article 26 TFEU concretizes Article 3 TEU[12] and emphasizes that realizing these fundamental freedoms is one of the central objectives of the Treaties.[13]

The internal market may be described as the "economic heart" of integration.[14] The position at the beginning of Title I of the Section "Union policies and internal actions" in the TFEU and as the first aim in Article 3 (3) TEU underlines its outstanding importance as a separate policy area.[15] The internal market is not just the sum of the Union's other policies but has an independent meaning of its own[16] as a starting point and driving

9 Article 3 (2) to Article 3 (6) TEU concretize the objectives in Art. 3 (1) TEU, *Geiger* in Geiger/Khan/Kotzur, EUV/AEUV, Art. 3 EUV para 4; cf. *Pechstein* in Streinz, EUV/AEUV, Art. 3 EUV para 1.

10 *Pechstein* in Streinz, EUV/AEUV, Art. 3 EUV para 4.

11 *Pechstein* in Streinz, EUV/AEUV, Art. 3 EUV para 2.

12 *Hatje* in Schwarze/Becker/Hatje/Schoo, EU-Kommentar, Art. 26 AEUV para 1; *M. Schröder* in Streinz, EUV/AEUV, Art. 26 AEUV para 6.

13 *Pechstein* in Streinz, EUV/AEUV, Art. 3 EUV para 7.

14 *Pechstein* in Streinz, EUV/AEUV, Art. 3 EUV para 7.

15 *M. Schröder* in Streinz, EUV/AEUV, Art. 26 para 7; *Khan/Eisenhut* in Vedder/Heintschel von Heinegg, Europäisches Unionsrecht, Art. 26 AEUV para 1.

16 *M. Schröder* in Streinz, EUV/AEUV, Art. 26 AEUV para 7.

force of a political movement aimed at reviving and continuing the process of European integration.[17] In other words, the process of securing the peace and well-being of the European citizens – as mentioned in Article 3 (1) TEU – requires above all an integrated internal market.

However, which factors determine a market or market features may change over time. Economic interests as mentioned above may not only be price-driven but also determined by innovative ideas. Competition serves the purpose of disempowerment and redistribution from top to bottom[18] and thus also has social consumer-oriented purposes. The European Union – and thus the internal market as its core element – is not limited to economic interests but also serves the realization of civil rights[19] and other general public interests.[20]

In this context, it cannot be ignored that the internal market has increasingly been exposed to skepticism by the European citizens. *Mario Monti* described the challenges as follows:

> "*The single market is seen by many Europeans – citizens as well as political leaders – with suspicion, fear and sometimes open hostility. Two mutually reinforcing trends are at work: an "integration fatigue", eroding the appetite for more Europe and for a single market; and more recently, a "market fatigue", with a reduced confidence in the role of the market. The single market today is less popular than ever, while Europe needs it more than ever.*"[21]

There needs to be

> "*a new strategy to safeguard the single market from the risk of economic nationalism, to extend it into new areas key for Europe's growth and to build an adequate degree of consensus around it.*"[22]

The concept of the internal market will only be accepted in the long term if it is not unilaterally geared towards free trade but also takes account of

17 *Leible* in Streinz (2003), EUV/EGV, Art. 14 EGV para 9; *M. Schröder* in Streinz, EUV/AEUV, Art. 26 AEUV para 18.

18 Cf. *Laitenberger*, NZKart 2017, 89, 90.

19 *M. Schröder* in Streinz, EUV/AEUV, Art. 26 AEUV para 36; *Reich* in Everling/Roth, Mindestharmonisierung im Europäischen Binnenmarkt 1997, p. 175.

20 *Leible* in Streinz (2003), EUV/EGV, Art. 14 EGV para 27; *M. Schröder* in Streinz, EUV/AEUV, Art. 26 AEUV para 36.

21 *Mario Monti*, A New Strategy for the Single Market, p. 6.

22 *Mario Monti*, A New Strategy for the Single Market, p. 7.

other objectives of the Treaties.[23] On the one hand, this could be achieved by giving more weight to those other objectives. On the other hand, one may wonder whether, upon closer look, many of the objectives of the Treaties – such as innovation – are part of an updated concept of the internal market. The "free movement of goods, persons, services and capital", as mentioned in Article 26 (2) TFEU, may be achieved by strengthening competition and innovation. This could also be a way of emphasizing the position of the internal market in the context of the Treaties – that is, a means to promote peace, the Union's values and the well-being of the European citizens.

(b) The notion of competition in the internal market

In fact, competition and the internal market are closely connected. The ECJ found with respect to the internal market that "*a precondition for such a market is the existence of conditions of competition which are not distorted.*"[24] This is now emphasized by the fact that the system of undistorted competition is no longer mentioned as an explicit Union objective in Article 3 TEU (Article 3 (1) lit. g) of the EC Treaty[25] included as an objective "*a system ensuring that competition in the internal market is not distorted*"), but that undistorted competition is defined in a protocol to the Lisbon Treaty as a part of the internal market.[26]

France had difficulties with the concept of free and undistorted competition in the negotiations for the referendum on the Treaty.[27] Competition should no longer be seen as an end in itself, but as a means of the internal market.[28] Finally, Protocol (No 27)[29] was attached to the TEU stating that

23 *M. Schröder* in Streinz, EUV/AEUV, Art. 26 AEUV para 47.

24 ECJ, Judgment of 11.06.1991, Case C-300/89, ECLI:EU:C.1991:244, para 14, *Commission/Council*; see also ECJ, Judgment of 13 .07.1995, Case C-350/92, ECLI:EU:C:1995:237, para 32, *Spain/Council.*

25 Treaty establishing the European Community, OJ C 325, 24.12.2002, p. 33-184.

26 *M. Schröder* in Streinz, EUV/AEUV, Art. 26 AEUV para 24; *Jacqué* in von der Groeben/Schwarze/Hatje, Europäisches Unionsrecht, Art. 3 EUV para 5; *Behrens*, EuZW 2008, 193; *Basedow*, EuZW 2008, 225.

27 *Jacqué* in von der Groeben/Schwarze/Hatje, Europäisches Unionsrecht, Art. 3 EUV para 5; *Behrens*, EuZW 2008, 193.

28 *Jacqué* in von der Groeben/Schwarze/Hatje, Europäisches Unionsrecht, Art. 3 EUV para 5; *Weitbrecht/Mühle*, EuZW 2010, 327; *Behrens*, EuZW 2008, 193; *Basedow*, EuZW 2008, 225.

29 OJ 115, 09.05.2008, p. 309.

"*the internal market as set out in Article 3 of the Treaty on European Union includes a system ensuring that competition is not distorted.*" According to Article 51 TEU, Protocol (No 27) forms an integral part of primary Union law. Outsourcing the objective of undistorted competition into a protocol is therefore legally irrelevant,[30] but shows the close connection between competition policy and the internal market. In addition, Article 3 (1) lit b) TFEU sets up the Union's exclusive competence for "*the establishing of the competition rules necessary for the functioning of the internal market*".

The internal market requires undistorted competition.[31] There is a market integration function assigned to the competition rules.[32] Already in the 1960s, the ECJ[33] made it clear that these rules are intended not only to pursue the traditional objectives of competition (namely the optimal allocation of resources), but also to ensure that barriers to the internal market are eliminated. State barriers to the internal market, which have been removed by the primarily state-directed internal market rules (the fundamental freedoms and secondary law), shall not be replaced by market foreclosure measures of private undertakings.[34] Consequently, the Commission states:

> "*The Commission's policy towards restrictive practices on the part of firms pursues two complementary objectives: in the first it must enable competition to perform its traditional role in helping to improve the allocation*

30 *Eilmansberger/Kruis* in Streinz, EUV/AEUV, Vorbemerkung zu Art. 101 bis 106 AEUV para 2; *Brinker* in Schwarze/Becker/Hatje/Schoo, EU-Kommentar, Art. 101 AEUV para 47; *Khan/Suh* in Geiger/Khan/Kotzur, EUV/AEUV, Art. 101 AEUV para 1; cf. *Behrens*, EuZW 2008, 193; *Basedow*, EuZW 2008, 225; differentiating *Lippert*, DVBl 2008, 492, 498-499.

31 *M. Schröder* in Streinz, EUV/AEUV, Art. 26 AEUV para 24; *Voet van Vormizeele* in von der Groeben/Schwarze/Hatje, Europäisches Unionsrecht, Art. 26 AEUV para 8; *Grabitz* in FS Steindorff 1990, 1229, 1240; *Hatje* in Schwarze/Becker/Hatje/Schoo, EU-Kommentar, Art. 26 AEUV para 10; *Korte* in Calliess/Ruffert, EUV/AEUV, Art. 26 AEUV para 39; *Tietje* in Grabitz/Hilf/Nettesheim, Das Recht der Europäischen Union, Art. 114 AEUV para 49; differing opinion *Everling* in FS Steindorff 1990, 1155, 1170-1171.

32 *Eilmansberger/Kruis* in Streinz, EUV/AEUV, Vorbemerkung zu Art. 101 bis 106 AEUV para 4.

33 ECJ, Judgment of 13.07.1966, Case 32/65, ECLI:EU:C:1966:42, p. 405, *Italy/Council and Commission*.

34 *Eilmansberger/Kruis* in Streinz, EUV/AEUV, Vorbemerkung zu Art. 101 bis 106 para 4; *Brinker* in Schwarze/Becker/Hatje/Schoo, EU-Kommentar, Art. 101 AEUV para 1; *Günther*, WuW 1957, 275, 276; *Khan/Suh* in Geiger/Khan/Kotzur, EUV/AEUV, Art. 101 AEUV para 2.

of resources, increase businessmen's capacities for adjustment and better satisfy the requirements of consumers; secondly, it must reinforce the unity of the Community market by eliminating obstacles to trade between Member States."[35]

In addition to the traditional (and not necessarily Union-specific) goals of undistorted competition, the competition rules in the Treaties have the purpose of ensuring equal competition conditions that are the basis for the realization of the fundamental freedoms and thus the internal market. However, aside from the equality component, there is also a welfare-promoting and freedom-securing factor of competition that goes beyond free trade. It is not only about equal conditions in all Member States but also about economic prosperity as a driver of European integration.

Competition as a means of disempowerment guarantees genuine economic exchange processes.[36] This is because private autonomy of market players may not fully be realized by a market economy alone.[37] Another important instrument is competition, which ensures that exchange processes are not distorted by the creation of economic power.[38] In fact, it seems reasonable that undistorted competition protects the individual freedom of market players, thus enhancing overall prosperity[39] in the European Union. In case of an abuse of dominance or anticompetitive agreements, resources are misallocated and economies lose momentum. It is, however, important for the acceptance of the European Union that it promotes welfare to all European citizens. Economic decline leads not only to poverty in the Member States but also in a decline in the acceptance of the European Union as such.

Just like the internal market shall lead to economic welfare and therefore success of the European project, undistorted competition is a means to secure a market without borders, resulting in greater prosperity than small national markets would. Competition not only leads to equality of market conditions in the Member States (laying the foundation for the develop-

35 Commission of the European Communities, Twelfth Report on Competition Policy, 1982, p. 12.

36 *Eilmansberger/Kruis* in Streinz, EUV/AEUV, Art. 101 AEUV para 50.

37 *Eilmansberger/Kruis* in Streinz, EUV/AEUV, Vorbemerkung zu Art. 101 bis 106 AEUV para 6.

38 *Eilmansberger/Kruis* in Streinz, EUV/AEUV, Vorbemerkung zu Art. 101 bis 106 AEUV para 6.

39 *Eilmansberger/Kruis* mention the welfare-enhancing effect of competition on the merits, *Eilmansberger/Kruis* in Streinz, EUV/AEUV, Art. 101 AEUV para 50.

ment of the fundamental freedoms) but aims at positive performance: economic welfare is a basic driver of the process of European integration,[40] and the competition rules in the Treaties secure that welfare within the internal market.

This does not mean that it is the aim of competition law and policy to create the best possible competition. It is not the object of Union policy to optimize competition. However, the abovementioned conditions for European integration may best be achieved by removing any obstacles to a free market. Thus, free competition as such may lead to the integration and international competitiveness of the European Union resulting in an optimization of welfare.

This fits in with the European Commission's statement that the "*single market is an important factor enhancing our international competitiveness.*"[41] The ECJ finds that the reference to undistorted competition in the Treaties

> "*implies the existence on the market of workable competition, that is to say the degree of competition necessary to ensure the observance of the basic requirements and the attainment of the objectives of the Treaty, in particular the creation of a single market achieving conditions similar to those of a domestic market.*"[42]

Undistorted competition is a precondition for the functioning of the internal market.

2) Innovation and the internal market

Innovation is one of the objectives of European Union policy. This includes research and development as a part of the overall innovation process.

---

40 The Commission finds that the European market creates a „de facto solidarity" between Europeans, Communication from the Commission to the European Parliament, the Council, the Economic and Social Committee and the Committee of the Regions, Towards a Single Market Act, 27.10.2010, COM(2010) 608 final, p. 3.

41 Communication from the Commission to the European Parliament, the Council, the Economic and Social Committee and the Committee of the Regions, Towards a Single Market Act, 27.10.2010, COM(2010) 608 final, p. 2.

42 ECJ, Judgment of 25.10.1977, Case 26/76, ECLI:EU:C:1977:167, para 20, *Metro/Commission*.

(a) Research and development as an objective in the EU Treaties

In connection with the internal market, Article 3 (3) TEU also states that the Union "*shall promote scientific and technological advance*". The Treaties refer at various points to "research and development" as well as "technical progress".[43]

Already in 1974, the Council adopted several resolutions on objectives and activities in the research, technology and science sector.[44] The Council explicitly found that a common policy in the field of science and technology "*is likely to contribute to social progress, to balanced economic expansion and to an improvement of the quality of life*"[45]. This reasoning mirrors the arguments in favor of the creation of an internal market as mentioned above.

The promotion of scientific and technical progress as a separate constitutional objective of European Union policy has been newly established with the Lisbon Treaty.[46] It is related to the fundamental right of freedom of the arts and sciences in Article 13 of the Charter of Fundamental Rights of the

---

43 Article 179 et seq. TFEU mention research and technological development; technical progress is mentioned with respect to specific policy areas: Article 39 (1) TFEU („*The objectives of the common agricultural policy shall be: (a) to increase agricultural productivity by promoting technical progress {...}*"); Article 189 (1) TFEU ("*To promote scientific and technical progress, industrial competitiveness and the implementation of its policies, the Union shall draw up a European space policy.*"); see also Article 42 (3) and Article 45 (d) TEU (The European Defence Agency shall contribute to implementing any measure needed to strengthen the industrial and technological base of the defence sector; it shall support defence technology research and coordinate joint research activities and the study of technical solutions meeting future operational needs). Technical development is also mentioned in the rules on competition in Article 101 et seq., as will be further elaborated upon in *Section III) A) 1)*.

44 OJ of the European Communities, 29.01.1974, C 7, p. 2-9; *Mellein/von Lepel* in Schwarze/Becker/Hatje/Schoo, EU-Kommentar, Art. 179 AEUV para 4.

45 OJ of the European Communities, 29.01.1974, C 7, p. 6.

46 *Ruffert* in Calliess/Ruffert, EUV/AEUV, Art. 3 EUV para 40; however, there have been rules on research and technological development in the EC Treaty since 1987, cf. OJ L 29.06.1987, p. 1-19; see for the historical development: *Trute/Pilniok* in Streinz, EUV/AEUV, Art. 179 AEUV para 2-8.

European Union ("CFR").[47] Furthermore, it is concretized in Title XIX of the TFEU.[48]

Title XIX of the TFEU deals with Research and Technological Development and Space. Article 179 (1) TFEU[49] reads:

> *"The Union shall have the objective of strengthening its scientific and technological bases by achieving a European research area in which researchers, scientific knowledge and technology circulate freely, and encouraging it to become more competitive, including in its industry, while promoting all the research activities deemed necessary by virtue of other Chapters of the Treaties."*

According to Article 179 (2) TFEU, the Union shall support undertakings in

> *"their efforts to cooperate with one another, aiming, notably, at permitting researchers to cooperate freely across borders and at enabling undertakings to exploit the internal market potential to the full, in particular through the opening-up of national public contracts, the definition of common standards and the removal of legal and fiscal obstacles to that cooperation."*

Research may be described as the methodically guided generation of new knowledge.[50] Technological development is a subsection of research, namely the technology-related part.[51] Accordingly, the provisions on research and technical development aim at protecting and inciting the effort to generate new solutions to existing problems.

The achievement of a European research area includes, i.e., cross-border cooperation between researchers.[52] Nevertheless, cross-border cooperation

---

47 *Ruffert* in Calliess/Ruffert, EUV/AEUV, Art. 3 EUV para 40; *Terhechte* in Grabitz/Hilf/Nettesheim, Das Recht der Europäischen Union, Art. 3 EUV para 50.

48 Cf. *Ruffert* in Calliess/Ruffert, EUV/AEUV, Art. 3 EUV para 40; ; *Terhechte* in Grabitz/Hilf/Nettesheim, Das Recht der Europäischen Union, Art. 3 EUV para 50.

49 The first two objectives of Article 179 (1) TFEU have also been revised with the Treaty of Lisbon, cf. *Mellein/von Lepel* in Schwarze/Becker/Hatje/Schoo, EU-Kommentar, Art. 179 AEUV para 9.

50 *Ruffert*, in VVDStRL 65, Kultur und Wissenschaft, 146, 157; *Ruffert* in Calliess/Ruffert, EUV/AEUV, Art. 179 AEUV para 1; *Mellein/von Lepel* in Schwarze/Becker/Hatje/Schoo, EU-Kommentar, Art. 179 AEUV para 1.

51 *Ruffert* in Calliess/Ruffert, EUV/AEUV, Art. 179 AEUV para 3.

52 *Ruffert* in Calliess/Ruffert, EUV/AEUV, Art. 179 AEUV para 20.

must be in line with competition law. Article 179 TFEU does not generally exempt research cooperation from the application of Article 101 TFEU.[53]

Article 179 (1) TFEU establishes a triad of objectives,[54] namely (i) the strengthening of the Union's scientific and technological bases through establishing a European research area; (ii) encouraging the development of its international competitiveness, including that of its industry; and (iii) supporting research activities deemed necessary by virtue of other Chapters of the Treaties. Relevant for the interrelation between the internal market, competition policy and innovation are the first two objectives. Whereas the first objective links to the internal market, the second one marks a special part of competition policy. Article 179 (1) provides for a normative extension of European research policy to all scientific fields and all stages of research.[55] Article 179 (2) TFEU emphasizes the importance of (cross-border) cooperation.

(b) European research area

According to Article 179 (1) TFEU, there shall be a European research area. According to the European Commission this area can be described as the "internal market for research"[56]. There shall be a Union-wide competition between researchers and research institutions.[57]

Research and development not only enhances welfare but also leads to integration.[58] The Union's "Horizon 2020" Framework Programme states:

> *"The Union is committed to achieving the Europe 2020 strategy which set the objectives of smart, sustainable and inclusive growth, highlighting*

---

53 *Ruffert* in Calliess/Ruffert, EUV/AEUV, Art. 179 AEUV para 21.

54 *Trute/Pilniok* in Streinz, EUV/AEUV, Art. 179 AEUV para 10.

55 *Eikenberg*, EuR 2008, 125, 126; *Trute/Pilniok* in Streinz, EUV/AEUV, Art. 179 AEUV para 12.

56 European Commission, Green Paper, The European Research Area: New Perspectives, COM(2007) 161 final, p. 2; see also *Mellein/von Lepel* in Schwarze/Becker/Hatje/Schoo, EU-Kommentar, Art. 179 AEUV para 9; *Kotzur* in Geiger/Khan/Kotzur, EUV/AEUV, Art. 179 AEUV para 9.

57 European Commission, Green Paper, The European Research Area: New Perspectives, COM(2007) 161 final, p. 12 et seq; *Trute/Pilniok* in Streinz, EUV/AEUV, Art. 179 AEUV para15.

58 Cf. *Trute/Pilniok* in Streinz, EUV/AEUV, Art. 179 AEUV para 12.

> *the role of research and innovation as key drivers of social and economic prosperity and of environmental sustainability {...}.*"[59]

In line with the objectives of the internal market, research and development shall be regarded as a means to integrate the Union and thus secure welfare. Research and development can be described as a main pillar of the internal market and increased market integration. A competitive and sustainable internal market requires research activities across borders. The potential of integration can only be fully realized if researchers from all Member States interact and search for new solutions. Limiting research activities to a national level gives away opportunities and prevents the European Union from effectively competing on the world market.

(c) Competitiveness of the Union

Consequently, Article 179 (1) TFEU also has the objective of strengthening the Union's international competitiveness. This is not just a matter of preventing the distortion of competition, but also using resources in the field of research and development to strengthen competitiveness as such.[60] The promotion of competitiveness has two dimensions: an internal and an external one.[61] The Union's industry shall on the one hand be able to compete in the domestic European market against international rivals. On the other hand, it shall be prepared for internationally competing on foreign markets – ultimately, on the world market.[62]

This dynamic implies a certain tension between research policy and competition enforcement, mainly in the fields of R&D cooperation and technology transfer.[63] Article 179 (2) TFEU explicitly provides for the sup-

---

59 Para 3 of Regulation (EU) No 1291/2013 of the European Parliament and of the Council of 11 December 2013 establishing Horizon 2020 – the Framework Programme for Research and Innovation (2014-2020) and repealing Decision No 1982/2006/EC, OJ L 347, 29.12.2013, p. 104-173.

60 *Trute/Pilniok* in Streinz, EUV/AEUV, Art. 179 AEUV para 19.

61 *Mellein/von Lepel* in Schwarze/Becker/Hatje/Schoo, EU-Kommentar, Art. 179 AEUV para 23.

62 *Mellein/von Lepel* in Schwarze/Becker/Hatje/Schoo, EU-Kommentar, Art. 179 AEUV para 23.

63 *Trute/Pilniok* in Streinz, EUV/AEUV, Art. 179 AEUV para 19; *Kotzur* in Geiger/Khan/Kotzur, EUV/AEUV, Art. 179 AEUV para 10.

port of undertakings in their efforts to cooperate.[64] However, cross-border cooperation must be in line with competition law.[65] Article 179 TFEU does not generally exempt research cooperation from the application of Article 101 TFEU.[66] The Commission explains:

> *"The right balance should be found between competition and cooperation. Researchers and research institutions should be stimulated by higher levels of competition on a European level to develop world-class excellence. At the same time, they should be engaged in stronger cooperation and partnerships across Europe and beyond to effectively address issues of common concern."*[67]

The balance between competition and cooperation is already provided for in Article 101 (3) TFEU. According to this provision, cooperation between undertakings that restricts competition may be permissible if it contributes to promoting technical or economic progress (and certain additional criteria are fulfilled). This approach is further refined in the research and development Block Exemption Regulation ("R&D BER").[68]

Article 179 (2) TFEU and Article 101 (3) TFEU generally point into the same direction: Research collaborations should be strengthened, not at the expense of competition but rather in order to strengthen competition. While Article 179 (1) and (2) TFEU emphasize the importance of cross-border cooperation as a basis for further integration of the "internal market for research", Article 101 (3) TFEU provides for the criteria that must be fulfilled for a cooperation in order to secure effective competition in the long run. Research cooperation does not take place outside the system of the free market economy but is an integrated part of it.

---

64 In addition, Article 180 TFEU provides for the promotion of cooperation between undertakings.

65 Cf. *Mellein/von Lepel* in Schwarze/Becker/Hatje/Schoo, EU-Kommentar, Art. 179 para 25.

66 *Ruffert* in Calliess/Ruffert, EUV/AEUV, Art. 179 AEUV para 21; *Mellein/von Lepel* in Schwarze/Becker/Hatje/Schoo, EU-Kommentar, Art. 179 AEUV para 25.

67 European Commission, Green Paper, The European Research Area: New Perspectives, COM(2007) 161 final, p. 9.

68 Commission Regulation (EU) No 1217/2010 of 14 December 2010 on the application of Article 101 (3) of the Treaty on the Functioning of the European Union to certain categories of research and development agreements, OJ L 335, 18.12.2010, p. 36-42.

(d) Research and development vs. innovation

Whereas "research and development" seems to describe the generation of new knowledge, meaning the process itself, the term "innovation" appears to be broader, incorporating not just the process but also the final result. Nevertheless, both expressions point in the same direction. First of all, "scientific and technological advance", as mentioned in Article 3 (3) TEU, and the term "development" in the headline of Title XIX, seem to emphasize the final outcome, because only a final result leads to advancement and constitutes a development. In addition, Article 180 (c) TFEU states that the Commission shall carry out "*dissemination and optimisation of the results of activities in Union research, technological development and demonstration*". The results of the research and development process are apparently also part of the Union's research and development policy.

In 2010, the European Commission established a so-called Innovation Union.[69] The concept is not anchored in primary law.[70] The Innovation Union is intended to be an umbrella covering the entire research and innovation chain from basic research to marketing, thus including the European Research Area as defined in Article 179 TFEU.[71] Accordingly, research and development can be understood as part of innovation. However, the reasoning behind the establishment of a European Research Area and the strengthening of research and development is without a doubt the achievement of innovation understood as new findings and results that enable European firms and citizens to solve problems or create new products. This is emphasized by the second goal of Article 179 TFEU, the promotion of competitiveness of the European Union. Research and technical development is not an end in itself, but shall lead to results that enhance competition in markets. Accordingly, innovation must be one of the overarching objectives of Title XIX TFEU.[72]

---

69 Communication from the Commission to the European Parliament, the Council, the European Economic and Social Committee and the Committee of the Regions: Europe 2020 Flagship Initiative – Innovation Union, SEC(2010) 1161, 6.10.2010, COM(2010) 546 final.

70 *Eikenberg* in Grabitz/Hilf/Nettesheim, Das Recht der Europäischen Union, Art. 179 AEUV para 94; *Eikenberg*, EuR 2015, 802, 805.

71 *Eikenberg* in Grabitz/Hilf/Nettesheim, Das Recht der Europäischen Union, Art. 179 AEUV para 95; *Mellein/von Lepel* in Schwarze/Becker/Hatje/Schoo, EU-Kommentar, Art. 179 AEUV para 20; *Eikenberg*, EuR 2015, 802, 805-806.

72 Cf. *Mellein/von Lepel* in Schwarze/Becker/Hatje/Schoo, EU-Kommentar, Art. 179 AEUV para 1; *Eikenberg* in EuR 2015, 802, 806; in this sense probably also

It should also be taken into account that the term "innovation"/"innovative approaches" is mentioned in the TFEU in connection with industry policy,[73] social policy[74] and employment.[75] As such, the TFEU may generally be considered as being innovation-friendly. The importance of innovation is also emphasized in connection with economic policy in the Declaration[76] on Article 126 TFEU.[77]

Furthermore, research and development on the one hand and innovation on the other are inseparably linked: whereas research and development as a stochastic process does not causally lead to a marketable innova-

---

Kotzur who finds that the European research area is about the exchange of scientific knowledge and technical innovation, *Kotzur* in Geiger/Khan/Kotzur, EUV/AEUV, Art. 179 AEUV para 3.

73 Article 173 (1) TFEU: „*The Union and the Member States shall ensure that the conditions necessary for the competitiveness of the Union's industry exist. For that purpose, in accordance with a system of open and competitive markets, their action shall be aimed at: {...} – fostering better exploitation of the industrial potential of policies of innovation, research and technological development.*"

74 Article 153 (2) TFEU: "*To this end, the European Parliament and the Council: (a) may adopt measures designed to encourage cooperation between Member States through initiatives aimed at improving knowledge, developing exchanges of information and best practices, promoting innovative approaches and evaluating experiences, excluding any harmonisation of the laws and regulations of the Member States*".

75 Article 149 TFEU: "*The European Parliament and the Council, acting in accordance with the ordinary legislative procedure and after consulting the Economic and Social Committee and the Committee of the Regions, may adopt incentive measures designed to encourage cooperation between Member States and to support their action in the field of employment through initiatives aimed at developing exchanges of information and best practices, providing comparative analysis and advice as well as promoting innovative approaches and evaluating experiences, in particular by recourse to pilot projects. {...}*".

76 Declarations are not part of the Treaties and do not have primary law quality; however, they can be used for the interpretation of the Treaties and Protocols, *Kokott* in Streinz, EUV/AEUV, Art. 51 EUV para 5; cf. ECJ, Judgment of 18.12.2007, Case C-77/05, ECLI:EU:C:2007:803, para 67, *United Kingdom/Council*; ECJ, Judgment of 02.03.2010, Case C-135/08, ECLI:EU:C:2010:104, para 40, *Rottmann*.

77 Declaration on Article 126 TFEU: "*{...} The Union aims at achieving balanced economic growth and price stability. Economic and budgetary policies thus need to set the right priorities towards economic reforms, innovation, competitiveness and strengthening of private investment and consumption in phases of weak economic growth. This should be reflected in the orientations of budgetary decisions at the national and Union level in particular through restructuring of public revenue and expenditure while respecting budgetary discipline in accordance with the Treaties and the Stability and Growth Pact.*"

tion, there is usually no innovation without the performance of research and development activities.[78] In other words, without research there will not be new products. The achievement of product innovation by mere coincidence is rather rare and almost impossible in highly developed and complex sectors such as the pharmaceutical or chemical industry. Even though research and development may not lead to the desired outcome but rather to a different new product, methodical and targeted efforts are still prerequisites for any innovative result.[79]

In conclusion, the protection of research and development in European Union primary law serves the purpose of enhancing innovation. However, this finding must be distinguished from the possibility of directing and inciting research and development as opposed to innovation. As will be further explained in *Section II) C) 3)*, it is not possible to directly influence innovation in the meaning of the result of research and development. Policy can set incentives for increased research and development activities, but it cannot predict the success of the stochastic scientific process.

The Commission is bound to the aims and foundations of the Treaties and, accordingly, must take innovation into account as an aspect of its decision-making process. Ignoring innovation concerns would counteract the objectives mentioned above. In fact, the Commission has increasingly focused on innovation since the establishment of the Innovation Union. [80]

The abovementioned concept of innovation has to be distinguished from the European Union's approach to legal innovation. *Terhechte* points out that the European Union can be characterized as an "innovation network" designed to continuously generate legal innovations.[81] *Terhechte* mainly relies on the Preamble of the TEU in which it is written that the Member states are "*resolved to mark a new stage in the process of European integration*" (Recital 1 to the TEU), "*resolved to continue the process of creating an ever closer union among the peoples of Europe*" (Recital 13 to TEU) and

---

78 In connection with the Innovation Market Approach (see *Section II) F) 2)*), *Rapp* finds: „*Since innovation is hard to measure, the innovation market approach focuses on research and development, the primary innovation-creating activity of modern firms.* " *Rapp*, 64 Antitrust Law Journal (1995) 19, 20.

79 The off-label use of pharmaceuticals may serve as an example. Some drugs are finally used to a large extent for other purposes than those they have originally been designed (and approved) for. Nevertheless, targeted research efforts had been required to develop the drug in the first step.

80 *Mellein/von Lepel* in Schwarze/Becker/Hatje/Schoo, EU-Kommentar, Art. 179 AEUV para 19.

81 *Terhechte*, EuR 2017, 3.

that there are "*further steps to be taken in order to advance the European integration*" (Recital 14 to TEU). In addition, Article 1 TEU mentions the "*process of creating an ever closer union among the peoples of Europe*".[82] Consequently, the European Union is dependent on legal innovation in order to fulfill the objectives and tasks assigned by the Treaties.[83] Legal innovation can be described as an overarching concept and requirement of European Union policy.

While the notion of legal innovation generally speaks in favor of introducing new provisions and concepts such as the innovation competition approach, it is different from the Union's policy objective – as for example underlying Article 179 et seq TFEU – to foster scientific and technological innovations. The latter may be a result of legal innovations as well as require innovative approaches.[84] However, while innovation in the context of research and development is an objective in the European Treaties and – as will be shown – an important parameter of competition both aiming at a further integration of the internal market, it is not a *per se* objective of the Treaties.

With view to Article 3 (3) TEU and Article 179 (1) TFEU, technical and scientific innovation is part of the internal market. However, the internal market is not the only objective of the Treaties. Other objectives must be taken into account even where this is not explicitly legally required.[85] Actions aiming at realizing the internal market may not disregard other objective of the Treaties.[86] Collisions between individual objectives must be resolved by establishing practical concordance,[87] that is, that the various objectives must be put into perspective and appropriately balanced. There is no general abstract hierarchy of Union objectives but collisions have to be solved on a case-by-case basis.[88]

Even within the concept of the internal market, there is no general priority of innovation considerations. Article 3 (3) TEU mentions "scientific and technological advance" on par with other factors impacting the inter-

82 *Terhechte*, EuR 2017, 3, 6 and fn. 18.
83 *Terhechte*, EuR 2017, 3, 29.
84 Cf. *Terhechte*, EuR 2017, 3, 11, 18, 28.
85 *M. Schröder* in Streinz, EUV/AEUV, Art. 26 para 35.
86 *M. Schröder* in Streinz, EUV/AEUV, Art. 26 AEUV para 35.
87 *M. Schröder* in Streinz, EUV/AEUV, Art. 26 AEUV para 36; *Korte* in Calliess/Ruffert, EUV/AEUV, Art. 26 AEUV para 15; *Ruffert* in Calliess/Ruffert, EUV/AEUV, Art. 3 AEUV para 11.
88 *M. Schröder* in Streinz, EUV/AEUV, Art. 26 AEUV para 36; Cf. *Ruffert* in Calliess/Ruffert, EUV/AEUV, Art. 3 para 11.

nal market. Article 179 (1) TFEU establishes the concept of a "European research area" but does not set up any general hierarchy with view to other policy objectives impacting the internal market.

Technical and scientific innovation – being at the core of the Euroean Commission's innovation competition concept – cannot be considered a *per se* objective of the Treaties but must be put into relation to other European Union objectives within and beyond the internal market.

3) The Position of Competition Law: Innovation as a Driving Force

As mentioned above, competition law is not a self-contained system but serves the completion of the internal market.[89] However, this connection has been questioned in recent years.[90] The European Commission's "more economic approach" – focusing on the effect of an undertaking's behavior on the consumer – no longer just protects the internal market but rather the general welfare of consumers.[91]

These approaches are not mutually exclusive.[92] In fact, as already mentioned, the internal market itself has the objective of promoting the welfare of European citizens. The European Commission's "more economic approach" can thus be understood as an adjustment of competition policy to the evolution of the objectives of the internal market. In addition to their economic and socio-political function, the competition rules also serve to realize the basic freedoms[93] which build the basis of the internal market.[94]

Article 3 (3) TEU mentions scientific and technological advance in connection with the internal market. Article 179 TFEU further mentions research and development as a means of promoting the competitiveness of the European Union. The interrelationship between innovation and competition law indicated in these two Articles is further elaborated in the context of EU competition law. As it is clear that innovation is important

89 Cf. *Brinker* in Schwarze/Becker/Hatje/Schoo, EU-Kommentar, Art. 101 AEUV para 11; *Khan/Suh* in Geiger/Khan/Kotzur, EUV/AEUV, Art. 101 AEUV para 3.

90 *Brinker* in Schwarze/Becker/Hatje/Schoo, EU-Kommentar, Art. 101 AEUV para 11.

91 *Brinker* in Schwarze/Becker/Hatje/Schoo, EU-Kommentar, Art. 101 AEIV para 12.

92 *Laitenberger*, NZKart 2017, 89, 90; *Brinker* in Schwarze/Becker/Hatje/Schoo, EU-Kommentar, Art. 101 AEUV para 12.

93 *Khan/Suh* in Geiger/Khan/Kotzur, EUV/AEUV, Art. 101 AEUV para 1.

94 See Article 26 (2) TFEU.

for society and consumers, in many industries it is also a key parameter of competition.[95]

(a) Background: The process of creative destruction

The idea of innovation as a major driver of competition can be traced back to *Joseph A. Schumpeter*. *Schumpeter* developed the concept of "*creative destruction*".[96] He found that capitalism could be described as an "*evolutionary process*".[97] According to *Schumpeter*, the

> "*fundamental impulse that sets and keeps the capitalist engine in motion comes from the new consumers' goods, the new methods of production or transportation, the new markets, the new forms of industrial organization that capitalist enterprise creates.*"[98]

In his opinion, the latter are much more important parameters of competition than price.[99] In his words, "*the competition from the new commodity, the new technology, the new source of supply, the new type or organization*"[100] is intended to be "*the powerful lever that in the long run expands output and brings down prices*"[101].

In addition, *Friedrich Hayek* introduced the theory of competition as a "*process of discovery*"[102]. Individuals have only limited, subjective knowledge. They do not know the preferences of the consumers and with which products to satisfy them.[103] Accordingly, competition can be described as an experimental process, in which market participants have to try out different solutions in order to find the relatively best.[104] It must therefore

---

95 *Esteva Mosso*, Innovation in EU Merger Control, p. 2; see also *Wirtz/Schulz*, NZKart 2019, 20, 22; Horizontal Merger Guidelines (fn. 152), para 8; Non-Horizontal Merger Guidelines (fn. 168), para 10.

96 *Schumpeter*, Capitalism, Socialism and Democracy, p. 81 et seq.

97 *Schumpeter*, Capitalism, Socialism and Democracy, p. 82.

98 *Schumpeter*, Capitalism, Socialism and Democracy, p. 82-83.

99 *Schumpeter*, Capitalism, Socialism and Democracy, p. 84.

100 *Schumpeter*, Capitalism, Socialism and Democracy, p. 84.

101 *Schumpeter*, Capitalism, Socialism and Democracy, p. 85.

102 *Hayek*, Recht, Gesetz und Freiheit, p. 373 et seq; *Kerber/Schwalbe* in MüKo, B. Die ökonomischen Grundlagen des Wettbewerbsrechts, para 107.

103 *Hayek*, Recht, Gesetz und Freiheit, p. 374, 375; *Kerber/Schwalbe* in MüKo, B. Die ökonomischen Grundlagen des Wettbewerbsrechts, para 107.

104 *Hayek*, Recht, Gesetz und Freiheit, p. 374; *Kerber/Schwalbe* in MüKo, B. Die ökonomischen Grundlagen des Wettbewerbsrechts, para 107.

be the aim of competition policy to secure the ability and incentives for innovation.

Innovation and competition are, therefore, not incoherent or even generally conflicting parameters of EU policy, but rather intrinsically connected. Innovation is one of the main drivers of competition. As a result, when protecting competition in the common market, it is compelling to take into account innovation incentives. This outcome is mirrored in the legal provisions on EU competition law.

(b) Competition Rules in the Treaties

The abovementioned thoughts of *Schumpeter* and *Hayek* have found their way in the European competition rules. The finding that innovation is a means of competition is reflected in Article 101 and Article 102 TFEU. Article 101 (1) (b) TFEU explicitly mentions "technical development" as a protective purpose. According to Article 101 (1) TFEU, agreements and other concerted practices that restrict competition are prohibited, "*and in particular those which: {…} (b) limit or control production, markets, technical development, or investment; {…}*".

Furthermore, in order for a behavior to be exempted according to Article 101 (3) TFEU, it has to contribute to "*improving the production or distribution of goods*" or promote "*technical or economical progress*".

Also, Article 102 (2) (b) TFEU refers to innovation in the form of technical development. According to that article, the abuse of a dominant position "*may, in particular, consist in {…} limiting production, markets or technical development to the prejudice of consumers*".

It becomes clear that the rules on competition within the internal market also emphasize the importance of technological development with the aim of creating innovation. What's more, the specific wording of Article 101 (1) TFEU and Article 102 TFEU implies that competition and the protection of innovation may point in the same direction. Article 101 (1) (b) TFEU and Article 102 (2) (b) TFEU, for example, state that the limitation of technical development in particular restricts competition or constitutes an anticompetitive abuse of a dominant position. As will be discussed in *Section II) H) 1)*, this link between competition and innovation is not undisputed.

In contrast, Article 101 (3) TFEU may resolve potential conflicts between competition and innovation. A restriction of competition may exceptionally be permissible if the restriction is indispensable for promoting innovation.[105]

Article 101 (3) TFEU is based on the recognition that while unrestricted competition generally leads to beneficial outcomes, in some cases competition alone may not be sufficient for optimal results.[106] Restrictive agreements are therefore exempted if they achieve the same effects as the market, namely by promoting the production and distribution of goods or technical and economic progress leading to the most favorable supply of the market.[107] Basis of the exemption is accordingly a competitive function of the agreements referred to.[108]

Like Art. 101 TFEU as a whole and the other competition rules in the Treaties, Article 101 (3) TFEU must be seen as part of the overall system of the protection of competition.[109] The positive conditions of Article 101 (3) TFEU – such as the promotion of technical progress – express traditional economic efficiency gains.[110] The systematic position of Article 101 (3) TFEU as part of the Rules on Competition in Chapter 1 of Title VII (Common Rules on Competition, Taxation and Approximation of Laws) and within the overall context of Article 101 TFEU suggests that the exemption must be seen in the context of protecting competition from restrictions, in the foreground being the protection of the freedom of action of market participants, economic efficiency in the allocation of resources and overall market integration.[111]

It is not the purpose of Article 101 (3) TFEU to suspend competition but rather to supplement the prohibition in Article 101 (1) TFEU in cases in

---

105 Cf. *Eilmansberger/Kruis* in Streinz, EUV/AEUV, Vorbemerkung zu Art. 101 bis 106 AEUV para 7.

106 Cf. European Commission, Decision of 15.12.1975, IV/27.073, OJ L 30, 05.02.1976, p. 13-22, III) B) 1), *Bayer/Gist-Brocades*; European Commission, Decision of 29.04.1994, IV/34.456, OJ L 131, 26.05.1994, p. 15-22, para 18 et seq, *Stichting Baksteen*; *Schuhmacher* in Grabitz/Hilf/Nettesheim, Das Recht der Europäischen Union, Art. 101 AEUV para 267; *Weiß* in Calliess/Ruffert, EUV/AEUV, Art. 101 AEUV para 157; *Eilmansberger/Kruis* in Streinz, EUV/AEUV, Art. 101 AEUV para 155; *Hengst* in Bunte, Kartellrecht, Art. 101 AEUV para 401.

107 *Weiß* in Calliess/Ruffert, EUV/AEUV, Art. 101 AEUV para 157.

108 *Weiß* in Calliess/Ruffert, EUV/AEUV, Art. 101 AEUV para 157.

109 *Schuhmacher* in Grabitz/Hilf/Nettesheim, Das Recht der Europäischen Union, Art. 101 para 268.

110 *Schuhmacher* in Grabitz/Hilf/Nettesheim, Das Recht der Europäischen Union, Art. 101 para 268.

111 Cf. *Schuhmacher* in Grabitz/Hilf/Nettesheim, Das Recht der Europäischen Union, Art. 101 para 268.

which more flexibility is needed to provide for commercial efficiency.[112] The exemption is part of the overall system of protecting a competitive allocation of market resources.

The promotion of technical progress – and consequently innovation – must be seen in this context. Article 101 (3) TFEU legally mirrors *Schumpeter's* and *Hayek's* finding that innovation is not necessarily different from but rather inherent to competition. A short-term restriction of the freedom of action of independent undertakings can lead to more innovation and in turn to increased competitive pressure. This, however, requires that competition as such in a market is not fully eliminated since otherwise the competitive effect of innovation would not be captured. For this reason, the exemption in Article 101 (3) TFEU is linked to the existence of certain conditions which are intended to ensure the preservation of competition as a general principle of the market economy.[113]

On the other hand, Article 101 (1) lit b) TFEU and Article 102 lit b) TFEU draw a direct link between competition and the existence of technical development. As opposed to Article 101 (3) TFEU that allows for a certain restriction of competition, the aforementioned Articles state that a limitation of technical development is as such a restriction of competition.

The interplay of Article 101 (3) TFEU, Article 101 (1) TFEU and Article 102 TFEU suggests that innovation and competition in the long run point in the same direction. Both parameters are related to each other. Only in the short term can a restriction of the competitive freedom of action of market participants lead to a privileged promotion of innovation. This short-term restriction must be accepted in view of the long-term goal of securing the free market economy through innovation.

Wolf finds that the application of Article 101 (3) TFEU is characterized by a short-term, market-oriented approach, whereas Article 101 (1) TFEU allows for a process-oriented, open-ended approach.[114] Article 101 (3) TFEU sets the legal framework for how to deal with the prospect of a

---

112 Cf. *Ellger* in Immenga/Mestmäcker, Wettbewerbsrecht EU, Art. 101 Abs. 3 AEUV para 7, 10; *Schuhmacher* points out that there needs to be a balancing exercise of the function of economic efficiency with the freedom of competition as protected under Article 101 (1) TFEU, *Schuhmacher* in Grabitz/Hilf/Nettesheim, Das Recht der Europäischen Union, Art. 101 para 268.

113 *Ellger* in Immenga/Mestmäcker, Wettbewerbsrecht EU, Art. 101 Abs. 3 AEUV para 10; *Nordemann* in Loewenheim/Meessen/Riesenkampff/Kersting/Meyer-Lindemann, Kartellrecht, Art. 101 Abs. 3 AEUV para 4.

114 *Wolf* in MüKo, Art. 101 AEUV para 1008.

very specific market outcome.[115] But Wolf misses that the protective goal of Article 101 (3) TFEU is not the specific product or service but rather an allocation of market resources or an innovative process allowing for increased competition in the future.[116] If that were not the case, Article 101 (3) TFEU would establish a system off the free market economy which – with view to the systematics and teleology mentioned above – is contrary to the purpose of the provision.

Unlike *Wolf* states,[117] Article 101 (3) TFEU does not break with the concept of the protection of the competitive process and especially does not take a market outcome approach. The process of competition is at the core of Article 101 (3) TFEU as it is of Article 101 (1) TFEU regarding the market as a whole as well as a specific cooperation. Article 101 (3) TFEU merely helps in situations in which a restriction of competition in the short term leads to a more efficient allocation of resources. This in fact secures the free competitive process in the long run.

While Article 101 (3) TFEU sets up criteria for solving a possible antagonism of competition and innovation in the short run, it does not say when such antagonism actually exists. As will be further explained, increased as well as reduced competition may lead to more innovation, depending on the specific market features. The innovation competition concept has to be assessed against this background. In *Dow/DuPont*, the Commission sets up criteria – in the context of the EC Merger Regulation – as to when an antagonism actually exists focusing on the conditions on a specific market.

(c) Secondary Competition Law: EC Merger Regulation

When technical development and improved production are protective purposes in the scope of agreements and other forms of cooperation as well as within the scope of abuse of a dominant position, the same must apply with respect to merger policy. Merger control rules are not part of primary Union law. But merger policy and enforcement are part of the establishment of a competitive market economy and thus fall within Article 3 (3) TEU. There are differences between the three main pillars of competition

---

115 *Wolf* in MüKo, Art. 101 AEUV para 1007.

116 In this sense also *Hengst* in Bunte, Kartellrecht, Art. 101 AEUV para 402 who finds that in the context of Article 101 (3) TFEU, the focus should not be on superficial and short-term improvements.

117 *Wolf* in MüKo, Art. 101 AEUV para 1006.

law (mergers, restrictive agreements and abuse of a dominant position).[118] However, the protective purposes remain the same, and if innovation is an important factor with respect to cooperation and unilateral conduct, it should be included in the merger assessment as well.

In this regard, it is worth looking at the historical development of merger control rules. Traditionally, mergers have been assessed under Article 102 TFEU. In *Continental Can*, the European Court of Justice acknowledged that Article 102 TFEU was applicable in case of a transaction involving a dominant undertaking.[119] Upon the adoption of the first EC Merger Regulation[120] in 1989, the Commission and the Council communicated that the Commission would not intend to apply Article 101 TFEU or 102 TFEU to mergers within the scope of the EC Merger Regulation anymore.[121] In legal terms, however, the application of Article 101 TFEU and 102 TFEU in parallel to the EC Merger Regulation remains possible.[122] Accordingly, there is a close interrelation between primary competition law and the EC Merger Regulation.

Innovation aspects are incorporated in Article 2 (1) EC Merger Regulation:

> *"Concentrations within the scope of this Regulation shall be appraised in accordance with the objectives of this Regulation and the following provisions with a view to establishing whether or not they are compatible with the common market.*
> *In making this appraisal, the Commission shall take into account:*
> *(a) the need to maintain and develop effective competition within the common market in view of, among other things, the structure of all the markets concerned and the actual or potential competition from undertakings located either within or outwith the Community;*
> *(b) the market position of the undertakings concerned and their economic and financial power, the alternatives available to suppliers and users, their access to supplies or markets, any legal or other barriers to entry, supply*

---

118 See, for example, *Section III) A) 2)* and *Section III) B) 2) (c) and (d)* as well as *Section III) C)*.

119 ECJ, Judgment of 21.02.1973, Case 6/72, ECLI:EU:C:1973:22, para 18 et seq, *Continental Can*.

120 Council Regulation (EC) No 139/2004 of 20 January 2004 on the control of concentrations between undertakings, OJ L 24, 29.1.2004, p. 1-22 (hereinafter „**EC Merger Regulation**").

121 *Mestmäcker/Schweitzer*, Europäisches Wettbewerbsrecht, § 24 para 16 et seq.

122 *Fuchs* in Immenga/Mestmäcker, Wettbewerbsrecht EU, Art. 102 AEUV para 395, 396.

and demand trends for the relevant goods and services, the interests of the intermediate and ultimate consumers, and the development of technical and economic progress provided that it is to consumers' advantage and does not form an obstacle to competition."

Accordingly, innovation in the form of technical and economic progress is also one of the objectives laid out in the EC Merger Regulation. It is important to note that the EC Merger Regulation distinguishes between actual and, in particular, potential competition on the one hand and the development of technical and economic progress on the other. The concept of potential competition is mentioned in connection with market structure and market definition. The development of technical and economic progress, in contrast, is contextualized by the market position of the undertakings concerned. From the mere reading of the EC Merger Regulation, technical and economic progress (and thus innovation) seems to be a means of measuring market power rather than being considered in the scope of structural market definition.

When looking at innovation concerns in merger control, Article 2 (1) (b) and (3) EC Merger Regulation may serve as a starting point. Aspects of the development of technical and economic progress must be incorporated into the assessment of a possible significant impediment to effective competition. A market-share-based assessment can be supplemented with additional criteria such as the impact of a transaction on innovation competition.

The wording of Article 2 (1) EC Merger Regulation ("the Commission shall take into account {...} the development of technical and economic progress") indicates that innovation is an important parameter of competition. The provision, however, does not make a statement as to whether "technical and economic progress" and free competition are always in line or whether there may be situations in which they are conflicting. In view of the overall purpose of the EC Merger Regulation to ensure free competition in the long term[123] and its historical development on the basis of Article 101 and Article 102 TFEU, one can certainly conclude that the principles developed with regard to primary law can also apply to merger policy: While there may be an antagonism of competition and innovation in the short run, both parameters are aligned in the long term.

---

123 Cf. Recital 5 of the EC Merger Regulation according to which it should be ensured that the process of reorganization does not result in a lasting damage to competition.

In *Dow/DuPont*, the Commission analyses the short-term relationship between competition and innovation and provides for criteria when reduced competitive pressure leads to immediately decreased innovation incentives.

(d) Guidelines and approaches from other jurisdictions and areas of law

There are further references to innovation in many of the European Commission's Guidelines. Those Guidelines are not binding for the Union Courts or authorities or courts in the Member States.[124] However, in practice most decision marking bodies adhere to the Guidelines.[125] Furthermore, they bind the Commission itself to a certain extent comparable to the principle of protection of legitimate expectations. The ECJ states:

> "*It should be noted in that regard that, whilst rules of conduct designed to produce external effects, as is the case of the Guidelines, which are aimed at traders, may not be regarded as rules of law which the administration is always bound to observe, they nevertheless form rules of practice from which the administration may not depart in an individual case without giving reasons that are compatible with the principle of equal treatment {…}.*"[126]

Even though concepts from other jurisdictions or antitrust areas may not serve as a formal legal basis, they may give guidance on how to address specific questions. Antitrust policy is to a great extent based on economic principles that claim global validity. Despite the fact that there are differences in the appraisal of certain behavior between various national competition law frameworks and authority practices, the underlying basis remains the same. The incorporation of innovation concerns in U.S. law as well as in the EU with respect to licensing and technology transfer can be used as an argument and a starting point for the assessment of innovation competition in merger control cases.

---

124 *Körber/Schweitzer/Zimmer* in Immenga/Mestmäcker, Wettbewerbsrecht EU, I. Abschnitt. Einleitung. C. Ökonomische Grundlagen und die Leitlinienpolitik der Kommission, para 10.

125 Cf. *Körber/Schweitzer/Zimmer* in Immenga/Mestmäcker, Wettbewerbsrecht EU, I. Abschnitt. Einleitung. C. Ökonomische Grundlagen und die Leitlinienpolitik der Kommission, para 10.

126 ECJ, Judgment of 18.05.2006, Case C-397/03 P, ECLI:EU:C:2006:328, para 91, *Archer Daniels Midland*.

The incorporation of innovation concerns in the Commission's Guidelines, as well as innovation concepts from other jurisdictions, will be discussed in the further course of this thesis.[127]

4) Intermediate result

The internal market is a means to promote peace, the Union's values and the well-being of the European citizens. However, the concept of the internal market has been subject to skepticism of the European citizens. Therefore, there needs to be an updated concept of the internal market that focuses on welfare and well-being of the Europeans. Such concept could be achieved by emphasizing the importance of innovation and competition as freedom-protecting and welfare-enhancing concepts. In fact, Article 3 (3) TEU already states that a highly competitive social market economy and scientific and technological advance form a significant part of the internal market.

Competition and innovation may be considered as two important pillars of the internal market. Article 101 and Article 102 TFEU show that both pillars are related to each other. Article 101 (3) TFEU provides for conditions to solve a short-term antagonism between the emergence of innovation and the freedom of action of the market participants. However, Article 101 (3) TFEU is part if the overall system of the protection of free competition. Technical progress – as fostered by Article 101 (3) TFEU – in the long run protects a competitive environment by realizing efficient market features and a competitive allocation of research and development resources.

The law does not make a statement as to when a short-term antagonism between innovation and competition may exist. In fact, it is not clear from the Treaties when competition and innovation correspond and when they are contradictory.

The Dow/DuPont Decision must assessed against this background. With respect to merger policy it sets up rules for when there is a short-term antagonism between competition and innovation and provides for a comprehensive approach to innovation as part of an updated concept of the internal market. It will further be discussed whether those rules can be used in the scope of Article 101 TFEU and Article 102 TFEU as well.

---

127 See *Section II) B) 2) (b) and (c)*, *Section III) A) 1) (b) and (c)* and *Section III) B) 1) (a)*.

B) The Dow/DuPont Decision

1) Overview of the Decision

In *Dow/DuPont*, the Commission assesses a merger of equals in the crop protection sector.[128] As a first step, the Commission takes into account actual and potential competition on existing product[129] and technology[130] markets in the crop protection business. Generally, crop protection products can be divided into four sectors: Herbicides[131], insecticides[132], fungicides[133] and nematicides[134]. The relevant markets are defined on the basis of demand side substitutability[135] as crop/pest combinations.[136] As a second step, the Commission focuses on innovation competition[137]. Apart from existing markets and partly even from existing or observable research activities, the Commission finds that the merger would lead to a reduction of the incentives to innovate in certain innovation spaces as well as on industry level.[138]

On the one hand, according to the Commission, in certain "innovation spaces" important lines of research and early pipeline products are likely to be discontinued, deferred or redirected due to the transaction.[139] On the other hand, since the parties are two out of only a few global R&D-integrated crop protection organizations, the merger is likely to significantly

128 Both companies are also active in the development and manufacture of seeds and traits as well as plastics and other chemicals; since the innovation concerns were only expressed with view to crop protection, the other activities of the parties are not part of this thesis.

129 Dow/DuPont Decision, para 306, 403 et seq.

130 Dow/DuPont Decision, para 333, 1937 et seq.

131 Dow/DuPont Decision, para 256.

132 Dow/DuPont Decision, para 261.

133 Dow/DuPont Decision, para 266.

134 Dow/DuPont Decision, para 270.

135 Demand side substitutability is the main criteria for the definition of the relevant market according to the Commission notice on the definition of the relevant market for the purposes of Community competition law, OJ C 372, 9.12.1997, p. 5-13 (hereinafter "Market Definition Notice"). According to para 15 of the Market Definition Notice, demand side substitutability is defined as "*the range of products which are viewed as substitutes by the consumer*".

136 Dow/DuPont Decision, para 319.

137 Dow/DuPont Decision, para 342 et seq, 1955 et seq.

138 Dow/DuPont Decision, para 1955, 1956.

139 Dow/DuPont Decision, para 1955.

reduce the overall level of innovation competition and therefore product innovation in the industry as a whole.[140]

According to the Commission,

> "*the assessment of innovation competition requires the identification of those companies which, at an industry level, do have the assets and capabilities to discover and develop new products which, as a result of the R&D effort, can be brought to market.*"[141]

The Commission points to the research and development capability of the respective undertakings rather than actual research and development activities.[142] Furthermore, "*it is also relevant to identify and analyse those spaces in which innovation competition occurs {…}.*"[143]

With regard to innovation spaces, the Commission analyzes overlaps between the parties' lines of research and early pipeline products.[144] A "line of research" is defined as a "*set of scientists, patents, assets, equipment and chemical classes dedicated to a given discovery target*".[145] The assets and personnel do not have to be exclusively dedicated to only one discovery target. Nevertheless, according to the Commission, it is important that the costs of changing from one line of research to another would be very high due to expertise involved and investment required at each stage of R&D.[146] Innovation spaces can be described as targeted innovation efforts towards a goal broader than a specific product.

At industry level, the decision focuses on overlaps between the parties' global R&D organizations, such as resources; personnel; facilities and other tangible and intangible assets dedicated to research, development and registration, including field testing facilities and registration capabilities.[147]

The Commission divides the process of innovation into the discovery stage, development stage and registration and marketing.[148] The process of launching a new product takes approximately 11 years; 3-4 years for discov-

---

140 Dow/DuPont Decision, para 1955.
141 Dow/DuPont Decision, para 349.
142 *Panhans*, DG COMP, at the 2. Kölner Kartellrechtsgespräche, see *Hasselhorn*, NZKart 2019, 546.
143 Dow/DuPont Decision, para 350.
144 Dow/DuPont Decision, para 1957.
145 Dow/DuPont Decision, para 1958.
146 Dow/DuPont Decision, para 1959.
147 Dow/DuPont Decision, para 1957.
148 Dow/DuPont Decision, para 295.

ery and 5-6 years for development.[149] The rest will likely be attributable to production and marketing.[150] Products in the development stage have a success rate of 80-90 % for entering the market.[151] Those products are therefore included in the product market analysis as potentially[152] competing products.[153] In the innovation competition assessment, the Commission includes activities at the discovery and pre-development stage, namely "early pipeline products".[154] The Commission focuses on companies active in all stages of the innovation process (R&D-integrated companies).[155]

The Commission used a similar approach as in *Dow/DuPont* in the subsequent *Bayer/Monsanto*[156] merger, a transaction also covering the crop protection sector.

2) The Commission's legal basis for innovation concerns in merger control

(a) Legal basis in EC Merger Regulation

Legal basis for the assessment of a merger is the EC Merger Regulation. According to Article 2 (3) EC Merger Regulation,

> "*a concentration which would significantly impede effective competition, in the common market or in a substantial part of it, in particular as a result of the creation or strengthening of a dominant position, shall be declared incompatible with the common market*".

149 Dow/DuPont Decision, para 161, 168.

150 The Commission does not comment on the difference between the sum of discovery and development time and the total duration of the launching process, cf. Dow/DuPont Decision, para 161 et seq.

151 Dow/DuPont Decision, para 295, 297.

152 The concept of potential competition is, for example, mentioned in the Guidelines on the assessment of horizontal mergers under the Council Regulation on the control of the concentration between undertakings, OJ C 031, 05.02.2004, p. 5-18 (hereinafter „Horizontal Merger Guidelines"). According to para 68 of the Horizontal Merger Guidelines, for potential entrants to constrain the behavior of incumbents post-merger, the entry has to be likely, timely and sufficient; see also Dow/DuPont Decision, para 287.

153 Dow/DuPont Decision, para 302.

154 Dow/DuPont Decision, para 1960.

155 See Dow/DuPont Decision, para 1960.

156 Commission Decision of 21.03.2018, C(2018) 1709 final, OJ C 459, 20.12.2018, p. 10-23, Case M.8084, *Bayer/Monsanto*.

As the Commission bases its innovation competition assessment in *Dow/ DuPont* on the significant impediment to effective competition[157] (instead of the presumptive example of the creation or strengthening of a dominant position), it is important to understand the reasoning behind the so-called "SIEC test" (SIEC = **S**ignificant **I**mpediment to **E**ffective **C**ompetition).

The first version of the EC Merger Regulation[158] established the principle that concentrations creating or strengthening a dominant position, as a result of which effective competition would be significantly impeded, should be declared incompatible with the common market. In order to extend the scope of the EC Merger Regulation to non-coordinated effects in oligopolies, the wording of Article 2 (3) EC Merger Regulation was changed. Recital 25 to the current EC Merger Regulation states:

> *"In view of the consequences that concentrations in oligopolistic market structures may have, it is all the more necessary to maintain effective competition in such markets. Many oligopolistic markets exhibit a healthy degree of competition. However, under certain circumstances, concentrations involving the elimination of important competitive constraints that the merging parties had exerted upon each other, as well as a reduction of competitive pressure on the remaining competitors, may, even in the absence of a likelihood of coordination between the members of the oligopoly, result in a significant impediment to effective competition. The Community courts have, however, not to date expressly interpreted Regulation (EEC) No 4064/89 as requiring concentrations giving rise to such non-coordinated effects to be declared incompatible with the common market. Therefore, in the interests of legal certainty, it should be made clear that this Regulation permits effective control of all such concentrations by providing that any concentration which would significantly impede effective competition, in the common market or in a substantial part of it, should be declared incompatible with the common market. The notion of "significant impediment to effective competition" in Article 2(2) and (3) should be interpreted as extending, beyond the concept of dominance, only to the anti-competitive effects of a concentration resulting from the non-coordinated behaviour of undertakings which would not have a dominant position on the market concerned."*

157 See for example Dow/DuPont Decision, para 1988, 2006, 2007.

158 Council Regulation (EEC) No 4064/89 of 21 December 1989 on the control of concentrations between undertakings, OJ L 395, 30.12.1989, p. 1-12; Council Regulation (EC) No 1310/97 of 30 June 1997 amending Regulation (EEC) No 4064/89 on the control of concentrations between undertakings, OJ L 180, 09.07.1997, p. 1-6.

Accordingly, the creation or strengthening of a dominant position is now only an example of a significant impediment to effective competition. The assessment framework is broader and extends beyond the traditional market share based approach. However, it is still about competition on a market, namely an oligopolistic market. The SIEC test does not refrain from market definition and market structure. It does not set up a somehow detached assessment of abstract competitive pressure.

The legal concept of "significant impediment to effective competition" is also one of the main differences from the standard of review in the scope of Article 102 TFEU which, according to its wording, requires "*a dominant position within the internal market or in a substantial part of it*". This will further be discussed in *Section III) B) 2) (c)*.

(b) The Commission's Horizontal Merger Guidelines and innovation

According to Recital 28 of the EC Merger Regulation, the Commission shall publish guidance on the criteria for assessing a concentration. Accordingly, the Commission has published the Horizontal Merger Guidelines. Those guidelines are not legally binding for the Union Courts, but the Commission may not deviate from them without plausible reason.[159] The Horizontal Merger Guidelines concretize Article 2 (3) of the EC Merger Regulation.

The Horizontal Merger Guidelines incorporate innovation concerns at various positions. Recital 8 defines "increased market power" as the ability of a firm to, *inter alia*, diminish innovation and clarifies that the term "increased prices" in the Guidelines is shorthand for all forms of competitive harm including reduced innovation activities:

> "*Effective competition brings benefits to consumers, such as low prices, high quality products, a wide selection of goods and services, and innovation. Through its control of mergers, the Commission prevents mergers that would be likely to deprive customers of these benefits by significantly increasing the market power of firms. By "increased market power" is meant the ability of one or more firms to profitably increase prices, reduce output, choice or quality of goods and services, diminish innovation, or otherwise influence parameters of competition. In this notice, the expression "increased prices" is*

159 See *Section II) A) 3) (d)*.

often used as shorthand for these various ways in which a merger may result in competitive harm. {…}."

Note that in the Guidelines, innovation is on par with price or output reduction.[160] This reflects the importance of innovation concerns in merger assessment and is in line with the general highlighting of innovation concerns in EU competition law.[161]

In order to measure concentration levels, the Commission uses economic metrics – for example the Herfindahl-Hirschman-Index (HHI).[162] In Recital 20 of the Horizontal Merger Guidelines, the Commission explains certain HHI levels that usually do not raise competitive concerns unless "*one or more of the merging parties are important innovators in ways not reflected in market shares*"[163]. At this point, the Commission clearly acknowledges the fact that for the assessment of a significant impediment to competition, market shares on existing markets may be amended or counterbalanced by other factors such as innovation capacity. This outcome is confirmed by Recital 15 of the Horizontal Merger Guidelines, according to which

"*the Commission interprets market shares in the light of likely market conditions, for instance, if the market is highly dynamic in character and if the market structure is unstable due to innovation or growth.*"

Most important for the assessment of innovation incentives in merger control are Recitals 37 and 38 of the Horizontal Merger Guidelines. The competitive influence of a firm may not only be due to market shares but also involve other factors. According to Recital 37:

"*Some firms have the more of an influence on the competitive process than their market shares or similar measures would suggest. A merger involving such a firm may change the competitive dynamics in a significant, anticompetitive way, in particular when the market is already concentrated.*"

When dealing with non-coordinated effects, Recital 38 states that innovation may be taken into account as a parameter for competitive pressure:

"*In markets where innovation is an important competitive force, a merger may increase the firms' ability and incentive to bring new innovations to the*

160 Cf. *Haucap*, Merger Effects on Innovation, p. 4.
161 See *Section II) A) 3)*.
162 Horizontal Merger Guidelines, para 16.
163 Horizontal Merger Guidelines, para 20 lit b).

> *market and, thereby, the competitive pressure on rivals to innovate in that market. Alternatively, effective competition may be significantly impeded by a merger between two important innovators, for instance between two companies with "pipeline" products related to a specific product market. Similarly, a firm with a relatively small market share may nevertheless be an important competitive force if it has promising pipeline products.*"

Even though the first part of Recital 38 mentions the general ability and incentive to innovate, the second part is more about product-related innovation activities. In *Dow/DuPont*, the Commission used an approach that mainly moves away from pipeline products or research and development activities directed towards a specific market.[164] Yet, the wording of Recital 38 ("for instance") shows that pipeline products serve as an example and that other forms of harm to innovation are conceivable.[165]

According to Recital 71 lit. b) of the Horizontal Merger Guidelines, innovation and R&D may create barriers to entry. On the other hand, efficiency gains in the sphere of R&D and innovation can result in benefits for consumers and thus counteract negative effects of the merger on competition.[166]

In conclusion, the Horizontal Merger Guidelines address innovation as an important parameter for merger control assessment aside from the traditional market share based approach. Even though the Horizontal Merger Guidelines are not a formal law, they have a binding effect on Commission decisions and have been confirmed by Union Courts.[167] They may therefore serve as a basis for the assessment of innovation in merger control. With respect to non-horizontal mergers, Recital 10 and 26 of the Non-Horizontal Merger Guidelines[168], set up a similar framework.

There are additional indications that innovation matters in merger assessment. Mergers that would combine two important innovators are less likely to be accepted under the Commission's simplified merger review

---

164 See *Section II) C) 5)*. Even though the Commission includes an assessment of early pipeline products, that assessment rather serves as an example for capabilities in specific innovation spaces.

165 Cf. Dow/DuPont Decision, para 1997.

166 Horizontal Merger Guidelines, para 81.

167 See *Section II) A) 3) (d)*.

168 Guidelines on the assessment of non-horizontal mergers under the Council Regulation on the control of concentrations between undertakings, OJ C 265, 18.10.2008, p. 6-25 (hereinafter "Non-Horizontal Merger Guidelines").

procedure[169] and the parties to a proposed concentration need to provide information on the intensity of research and development, recent innovations, IP rights and pipeline products as well as the technological development of relevant markets in the standard merger notification forms[170]. Those procedural issues underline the importance of innovation for the Commission's merger assessment.[171]

All in all, there are provisions showing that innovation must be taken into account when assessing the effects of a merger. Nevertheless, there are no criteria on how to analyze specific innovation concerns. There is no guidance on how to "measure" innovation capacity or innovation competition.[172]

(c) The Commission refers to US Guidelines and EU Technology Transfer Guidelines

When introducing the concept of innovation spaces, the Commission refers to the U.S. concept of innovation markets.[173] The U.S. Intellectual Property Guidelines incorporate that concept and distinguish between goods markets, technology markets and research and development markets.[174] According to Section 3.2.3 of the Guidelines, research and development markets

> *"consist of the assets comprising research and development related to the identification of a commercializable product, or directed to particular new or*

---

169 See Commission Notice on a simplified procedure for the treatment of certain concentrations under Council Regulation (EC) No 139/2004, OJ C 366, 14.12.2013, p. 5-9, para 11.

170 See Section 8.7 and 8.9 of the Form CO relating to the Notification of a Concentration pursuant to Regulation (EC) No 139/2004 and Section 7.2.3. of the Short Form CO for the Notification of a Concentration pursuant to Regulation (EC) No 139/2004.

171 *Esteva Mosso*, Innovation in EU Merger Control, p. 3.

172 *Petit* finds that the Horizontal Merger Guidelines *„provide no guidance on specific theories of harm that are potentially applicable to mergers."*, *Petit*, Innovation Competition, p. 7.

173 Dow/DuPont Decision, para 343; to the concept of innovation markets see *Section II) F) 2)*.

174 Dow/DuPont Decision para 343 refers to DoJ and FTC, Proposed Update of Antitrust Guidelines for the Licensing of Intellectual Property, 12 August 2016; the Guidelines have been issued on January 12, 2017 without changes in respect to the concept of innovation markets.

improved goods or processes, and the close substitutes for that research and development."[175]

Furthermore, the Commission also mentions the U.S. Horizontal Merger Guidelines.[176] Chapter 6.4 deals with Innovation and Product Variety:

"Competition often spurs firms to innovate. The Agencies may consider whether a merger is likely to diminish innovation competition by encouraging the merged firm to curtail its innovative efforts below the level that would prevail in the absence of the merger. That curtailment of innovation could take the form of reduced incentive to continue with an existing product-development effort or reduced incentive to initiate development of new products.

The first of these effects is most likely to occur if at least one of the merging firms is engaging in efforts to introduce new products that would capture substantial revenues from the other merging firm. The second, longer-run effect is most likely to occur if at least one of the merging firms has capabilities that are likely to lead it to develop new products in the future that would capture substantial revenues from the other merging firm. The Agencies therefore also consider whether a merger will diminish innovation competition by combining two of a very small number of firms with the strongest capabilities to successfully innovate in a specific direction.

The Agencies evaluate the extent to which successful innovation by one merging firm is likely to take sales from the other, and the extent to which post-merger incentives for future innovation will be lower than those that would prevail in the absence of the merger. The Agencies also consider whether the merger is likely to enable innovation that would not otherwise take place, by bringing together complementary capabilities that cannot be otherwise combined or for some other merger-specific reason."

As will be seen in the further course of this thesis, the Commission very much relied upon the U.S. approach. The Commission focuses on assets enabling the companies concerned to perform research and development. The basic theory of harm is about reduced incentives to initiate and continue innovation activities. The cannibalization concern ("*products that would capture substantial revenues from the other merging firm*") is also

175 DOJ and FTC, Antitrust Guidelines for the Licensing of Intellectual Property, 12 January 2017 (hereinafter "U.S. Intellectual Property Guidelines"), p. 11.

176 Dow/DuPont Decision, para 1999 refers to DOJ and FTC, Horizontal Merger Guidelines, 19 August 2010 (hereinafter "U.S. Horizontal Merger Guidelines").

already expressed in the U.S. Horizontal Merger Guidelines. Finally, the U.S. Guidelines deal with efficiencies.

The innovation market concept has also found its way into the EU Technology Transfer Guidelines.[177] According to para 26 of these Guidelines,

> *"innovation is a source of potential competition which must be taken into account when assessing the impact of the agreement on product markets and technology markets. In a limited number of cases, however, it may be useful and necessary to also analyse the effects on competition in innovation separately. This is particularly the case where the agreement affects innovation aiming at creating new products and where it is possible at an early stage to identify research and development poles. In such cases it can be analysed whether after the agreement there will be a sufficient number of competing research and development poles left for effective competition in innovation to be maintained."*

In *Dow/DuPont*, the Commission refers to that concept in the Technology Transfer Guidelines and concludes that there is no separate innovation market, but that innovation should rather be treated as an input activity for upstream technology and downstream product markets.[178] Even though the Commission specifies that it does not define separate innovation markets, the assessment shall take place at the upstream level of innovation efforts: "*This however does not prevent the Commission to assess the impact of the Transaction at the level of innovation efforts by the Parties and its competitors.*"[179]

The assessment of innovation as input activity to upstream and downstream markets is different from the traditional innovation market concept in U.S. literature and law, as will be explained in the further course of this thesis.[180]

---

177 Communication from the Commission - Guidelines on the application of Article 101 of the Treaty on the Functioning of the European Union to technology transfer agreements, OJ C 89, 28.03.2014, p. 3-50 (hereinafter "Technology Transfer Guidelines").

178 Dow/DuPont Decision, para 348.

179 Dow/DuPont Decision, para 348.

180 See *Section II) F) 2) (b)*.

3) Theory of harm in *Dow/DuPont*

In *Dow/DuPont*, the Commission assesses the transaction with a focus on early pipeline products and lines of research not yet directed towards a specific product market, as well as innovation incentives in the industry as a whole.

The Dow/DuPont Decision is formally based on Article 2 EC Merger Regulation and Recital 8 of the Horizontal Merger Guidelines. The Commission refers to Recital 22 of the Horizontal Merger Guidelines, stating that for innovation as well as for price competition a merger may be "*eliminating important competitive constraints on one or more firms, which consequently would have increased market power, without resorting to coordinated behaviour*".[181] In line with Recital 25 EC Merger Regulation, reflected in Recital 24 and 25 of the Horizontal Merger Guidelines, the Commission considers both the loss of competition between the merging firms and the reduction of competitive pressure on other non-merging firms.[182]

The Commission bases its analysis on the assumption that the market features of the specific industry suggest that rivalry is an important factor driving innovation and that a merger between Dow and DuPont as two important rival innovators will likely lead to a reduction in innovation.[183] According to the Commission, the reasons for that assumption are the following:[184]

1) The individual markets in the specific industry "*are contestable on the basis of innovation*", meaning that innovation rather than price is the driving factor to gain market shares.
2) There are strong Intellectual Property Rights ("IPRs") that lead to high appropriability. Appropriability means that "*the original innovator can be expected to reap the benefits from its innovation, by preventing rivals from imitating the successful innovation*" (for example, by patents or other exclusive rights).
3) Innovation in crop protection mainly takes the form of product innovation instead of process innovation. There are hints in economic liter-

181 Dow/DuPont Decision, para 2004 referring to Recital 22 of the Horizontal Merger Guidelines; the Commission adopts that reasoning in para 1994.
182 Dow/DuPont Decision, para 1998.
183 Dow/DuPont Decision, para 2000.
184 Dow/DuPont Decision, para 2001.

ature that process innovation may benefit from increased economies of scale resulting from a merger, whereas product innovation may not.[185]

4) Under the specific circumstances of the case, consolidation between rivals is unlikely to lead to efficiencies.
5) The "*fear of cannibalization of own existing products is a disincentive to innovate*". This disincentive is "*likely to be reinforced by a merger between rival innovators*".

The Commission therefore develops a theory of harm that is "*based on the fact that a merger between competing innovators by reducing rivalry in the industry and increasing cannibalization of existing and future sales is likely to result in a decrease in the incentives to innovate by the merging parties.*"[186] The effect is supposed to be similar to that of price competition.[187] The Commission explains that this theory of harm may also explain why past concentration in the industry led to a decrease in innovation and concludes that innovation is an important competition parameter in the crop protection industry.[188]

The Commission points out in para 2007 of the Dow/DuPont Decision that the crop protection industry is characterized by oligopolistic innovation competition. After successive waves of consolidation, there remain five global R&D-integrated players that cover the entire innovation process, from discovery to development, registration and marketing. Also, the barriers to entry and expansion are very high, so that new players are not likely to enter the market within reasonable time. Other smaller players on the market do not have the same capabilities and incentives to perform innovation activities.[189]

The Commission further concludes that at each level of the identified innovation spaces, the number of players with similar capabilities and incentives to innovate is even lower than the five global R&D-integrated companies due to differentiated assets, capabilities and strengths, limited capacity and differentiated incentives.[190] Thus, the parties of the transaction may be more important competitors with regard to innovation than their downstream market shares and their R&D expenditure would suggest.[191] Furthermore, the parties are not only important innovators in

185 See further to that point *Section II) D) 1) (c)*.
186 Dow/DuPont Decision, para 2002.
187 Dow/DuPont Decision, para 2004.
188 Dow/DuPont Decision, para 2003.
189 On the aforementioned Dow/DuPont Decision, para 2007.
190 Dow/DuPont Decision, para 2008.
191 Dow/DuPont Decision, para 2010.

general but are also closely competing in innovation with respect to a number of identified innovation spaces.[192] They also compete on existing markets where they currently take away revenue from each other.[193] In conclusion, the Commission assesses the stand-alone importance of each of the parties as innovators in each innovation space, but also the closeness of their innovation efforts in those spaces.

Two effects may arise as a result of the transaction: the Commission fears that the merged entity might curtail its innovation efforts resulting in the

> "*immediate reduction of incentives to continue with some existing innovation efforts (either by discontinuing, redirecting or deferring early pipeline products or lines of research) in the case of overlapping lines of research and early pipeline products between the parties*".[194] Furthermore, there may be "*reduced incentives to develop in the longer term the same number of new products as the combined targets of the parties before the Transaction.*"[195]

The starting point of the Commission's assessment are the features of the specific industry with respect to innovation.[196] Past developments can be an indication of interrelations between concentration and innovation activities.[197] Subsequently, the Commission identifies the important players in the industry and comes to the conclusion that there is a narrow industry oligopoly.[198] The Commission also assesses the specific features and players in certain innovation spaces (thus narrowing down the broader industry innovation concept).[199] After looking at the general structure and the individual players, the Commission focuses on the merging parties, again with respect to the whole industry[200] as well as specific innovation spaces[201]. The Commission completes its assessment by addressing countervailing reactions of competitors[202] and efficiency claims[203] by the parties.

---

192 Cf. Dow/DuPont Decision, para 2012.
193 Dow/DuPont Decision, para 2012.
194 Dow/DuPont Decision, para 2014.
195 Dow/DuPont Decision, para 2014.
196 Dow/DuPont Decision, para 2039 et seq.
197 Dow/DuPont Decision, para 2124 et seq.
198 Dow/DuPont Decision, para 2192 et seq.
199 Dow/DuPont Decision, para 2353 et seq.
200 Dow/DuPont Decision, para 2396 et seq.
201 Dow/DuPont Decision, para 2600 et seq.
202 Dow/DuPont Decision, para 3225 et seq.
203 Dow/DuPont Decision, para 3265 et seq.

Three things are important to note: First, the Commission argues that certain factors which, according to the parties,[204] are important innovation drivers – such as generic entry, regulation and resistance – are not altered by the transaction and are therefore not important in the innovation assessment of the transaction.[205] The Commission draws a causal link between rivalry and innovation and concludes that by reducing rivalry, a merger is likely to reduce innovation incentives, regardless of other innovation drivers that remain unchanged.[206] Second, the Commission recurs to the immediate effect of the transaction on the parties' incentives to innovate.[207] The requisite standard "*does not differ from assessing typical price effects that flow directly from structural changes in the market.*"[208] According to the Commission, "*it is not about behaviour in the long term but shortly after the transaction.*"[209] Third, the Commission rejects the efficiency claims brought forward by the parties because they are likely to happen in the long term, based on a long chain of events[210] and the parties dod not provide any concrete evidence[211] for the efficiences. The Commission concludes that "*{i}n the absence of any substantiated submission and proof, the Commission cannot assess whether the claimed efficiencies are likely, verifiable, merger-specific and beneficial to consumers.*"[212]

4) Underlying rationale

The Commission's assessment is based on the following assumption:

> "*Economic principles indicate that a merger between two out of a limited number of significant innovators is likely to reduce product innovation when appropriability is high (that is, when IPRs are effective), and when there are no merger-specific efficiencies associated with the merger.*"[213]

---

204 Dow/DuPont Decision, para 2025.
205 Dow/DuPont Decision, para 2030.
206 Dow/DuPont Decision, para 2030.
207 Dow/DuPont Decision, para 2034.
208 Dow/DuPont Decision, para 2036.
209 Dow/DuPont Decision, para 2036.
210 Dow/DuPont Decision, para 3280.
211 Dow/DuPont Decision, para 3280.
212 Dow/DuPont Decision, para 3284.
213 Dow/DuPont Decision, para 2042.

This assumption underlies the whole decision and can be described as the basic rationale in *Dow/DuPont*.

The Commission argues in para 2043 of the Dow/DuPont Decision that pre-merger, the parties would have incentives to capture current and future sales from each other when introducing new and improved products. Post-merger, these incentives would be reduced as innovation of one party would then cannibalize profits of the partner firm preventing an overall increase in sales captured from third parties. The cannibalization effect is internalized with the merger and adds to the opportunity cost of innovation, thus depressing innovation incentives.[214]

Furthermore, incentives to innovate may be affected by changes in current and future product market competition.[215] The merged entity is likely to be able to increase prices through increased market power. This may raise incentives to innovate because the expected revenues for an innovative product will be higher post-merger. However, the effect of less intense product market competition is seen as ambiguous, as it can increase the net revenues earned by a product line both when firms are innovating to improve the product and when they are not.[216] Beyond that ambiguity , the Commission concludes that the potentially countervailing effects of less intense competition on a specific product market may not outweigh the direct loss of innovation competition between rivals.[217]

Thus, the economic rationale behind the Commission's assessment is based on two separate effects: with respect to innovation competition, the Commission finds that a reduction in rivalry reduces incentives to innovate; with respect to product market competition, a reduction of competition may have effects that increase as well as decrease innovation incentives, depending on the specific innovation activity. But the ambiguous effect of a reduction in product market competition may not counteract the negative effect of a reduction in innovation competition. In sum, a reduction in innovation competition results in reduced incentives to innovate (under certain conditions).

The Commission mentions two other factors possibly countervailing the loss of competition between rivals: the ability to apply process innovations over a larger scale post-merger and the lower risk of imitation.[218] If a

---

214 On the aforementioned Dow/DuPont Decision, para 2043.
215 Dow/DuPont Decision, para 2044.
216 Dow/DuPont Decision, para 2044; see to that effect *Section II) D) 1) (b)*.
217 Dow/DuPont Decision, para 2045.
218 Dow/DuPont Decision, para 2046.

merger leads to fewer competitors on a market without IPRs, the risk of copying is reduced and this may enhance innovation.[219] However, in the case at hand, the Commission finds that both factors are not important because there are mainly product innovations in the industry and IPRs are strong.

In conclusion, the Commission's assessment is based on the assumption that, under specific circumstances, there is a causal link between market concentration and incentives to innovate and that an increase in concentration will result in a decrease in innovation.

C) Classification and appraisal

In order to find out whether the Commission's approach in *Dow/DuPont* is new, necessary and valid, its underlying rationale, purpose and structure must be assessed. This is also important for its possible application in the scope of other competition law fields, such as Article 101 and 102 TFEU.

1) Theory of harm and underlying rationale

The Commission's theory of harm consists of two lines of reasoning:[220]

- As a result of the transaction, lines of research or early pipeline products in certain innovation spaces are likely to be discontinued, deferred or redirected.
- The transaction is likely to significantly reduce innovation competition and thus ultimately product innovation in the whole industry.

As underlying rationale, the Commission refers to the following assertion:

> "*Economic principles indicate that a merger between two out of a limited number of significant innovators is likely to reduce product innovation when appropriability is high (that is, when IPRs are effective), and when there are no merger-specific efficiencies associated with the merger.*"[221]

Accordingly, there are four conditions that must be fulfilled for a merger to lead to the abovementioned harm to product innovation:

219 Cf. Dow/DuPont Decision, para 2064.
220 Dow/DuPont Decision, paras 2014, 3056, 3057.
221 Dow/DuPont Decision, para 2042.

1. Significant and close innovators: The acting parties must be close and significant innovators. Generally, for innovators to be important with respect to competition, the respective markets need to be contestable on the basis of innovation. Thus, as a preliminary point it is decisive whether innovation is an important parameter on a market in order to gain market shares. Only if this question can be answered in the affirmative is the Commission's theory of harm applicable.
   To be considered a significant innovator, the respective undertaking must be able to market the innovation. Basic research is not important for competition policy. The innovator must therefore be vertically integrated and have at its disposal the necessary financial resources to successfully pass the regulatory process (if there is one) and perform marketing and distribution.[222] Vertical integration is particularly important in markets that are characterized by economies of scale. In that case, the necessary financial resources to market a product can only be achieved by a large return of revenues.[223] Furthermore, in order to discover and develop a product that is marketable, an undertaking needs to possess knowledge of the market conditions. That knowledge is usually acquired through marketing experience. There is an interaction between the discovery, development and marketing process that can be optimized in case of a vertically integrated undertaking.[224]
   In addition, the two merging undertakings must be close innovators, meaning they target the same research goals. This precondition partly interacts with the question if there are efficiencies arising from a merger. If two undertakings are not closely targeting the same research areas, they are likely to have complementary assets and approaches that lead to innovation efficiencies. In contrast, if two undertakings are close competitors with respect to their research activities, they are

222 Cf. Dow/DuPont Decision, para 2193, 2201.

223 Cf. Dow/DuPont Decision, para 2202, 2204.

224 Cf. Dow/DuPont Decision, para 2203; *Cary* states: *„The Decision justifies its requirement to limit „R&D players" based on global downstream market success because otherwise an innovator could not successfully „compete" in Europe. But, the Decision misses the point – the issue of this part of the analysis is not whether a firm can compete in Europe as marketer, but whether a firm will continue to contribute to ongoing innovation in the industry."* *Cary*, Festschrift für Dirk Schroeder, p. 191. A firm will, however, only be able to perform research and development in the crop protection industry if it is a successful marketer, because otherwise, it would not have at its disposal the necessary financial resources and knowledge for innovation activities.

more likely to cannibalize each other's current and future sales and may therefore reduce innovation efforts.

2. Limited number: The Commission's theory requires that there is only a limited number of important innovators in an industry. This implies that there is an oligopolistic market structure with high barriers to entry. If there are numerous players performing research and development in an industry, a merger between two of them may not significantly affect the overall level of innovation in that industry. Furthermore, if there are no high barriers to entry, a reduction of the level of innovation following a merger may be compensated by new players which enter the industry.
3. High Appropriability: Appropriability may be described as the ability of an undertaking to appropriate the value of an innovation. In other words, appropriability is high if a firm can generate revenues with a new product without other firms free-riding on the innovation. Strong IP rights usually indicate a high level of appropriability. However, the level does not depend on the legal enforceability of rights but rather on the factual circumstance in an industry. Appropriability can also be high if there are effective marketing strategies or know-how protection preventing competitors from copying the invention. As will be discussed in the further course of this thesis, one of the main arguments in the dispute about the interrelation between market concentration and innovation incentives is that a monopolist can prevent competitors from free-riding on its invention, thereby increasing incentives for that monopolist to innovate. If, however, free-riding is difficult in the first place, due to high appropriability, this argument loses its momentum.
4. No merger-specific efficiencies: There may be efficiencies specifically related to innovation incentives due to a merger. Those efficiencies may outweigh the negative effects of a merger between two out of a limited number of close and important innovators. In case of, for example, the combination of complementary R&D assets, the establishment of greater scale economies in process innovation or the facilitation of cost efficiencies in R&D,[225] the innovation benefits may predominate the negative effects of a concentration, ultimately resulting in pro-competitive effects of the transaction.

225 Cf. *Esteva Mosso*, Innovation in EU Merger Control, p. 4.

The economic rationale underlying the Commission's assessment can be summarized as "rivalry drives innovation".[226] In that regard, the Commission focuses on cannibalization concerns. An undertaking is likely to invest in research and development if it can gain (that is, "cannibalize") market shares from competitors. The undertaking is more likely to invest if the amount of market shares cannibalized from competitors is higher than the amount of market shares cannibalized from its own existing products. Post-merger, the product range of the merged entity is usually higher than that of each separate undertaking. The entity is thus more likely to cannibalize own sales. This is at least true, if the product portfolio of the two merging parties is homogenous. The Commission expands that approach from existing to future products. With innovative products the merged entity may divert sales from both existing and future products if both undertakings are pre-merger performing research activities in the same areas. The Commission finds that this extension of the cannibalization concept leads to the so-called innovation competition.[227]

In conclusion, the assessment of innovation competition takes place along the following scheme:

Table 1: Overview of the Commission's theory in Dow/DuPont

Parties are close and important innovators	– Market is contestable on the basis of innovation. – Parties are able to successfully market an innovation (vertical integration, financial resources). – Parties are close innovation competitors, targeting the same research goals.
Limited Number of innovators in the industry	– Oligopolistic market structure. – High barriers to entry.
Appropriability is high	– IP rights are effective. – Other strategies enable the innovator to capture the value of an innovation.
No merger-specific efficiencies	– Combination of complementary R&D assets, economies of scale, cost efficiencies may outweigh negative effects on innovation.

226 *Podszun* finds that the Dow/DuPont Decision *„assumes that innovation only comes into play when there is rivalry.“*, *Podszun*, IIC 2019, 720, 740.

227 See Annex 4 (fn. 293), para 167.

2) Unilateral Effects Analysis

The basis of the Commission's innovation competition assessment in *Dow/DuPont* is the concept of non-coordinated effects (also called standard unilateral effects) in the Horizontal Merger Guidelines in para 24 et seqq.[228] The Commission basically uses the same assessment as with regard to price competition in existing product markets and transfers it to innovation. On the basis of the closeness of the parties as competitors, as mentioned in paras 28 et seqq. of the Horizontal Merger Guidelines, the Commission assesses whether the merger is likely to eliminate an important competitive force (paras 37 et seq. of the Horizontal Merger Guidelines) and whether competitors are likely to offset the reduced innovation incentives of the merging parties (in line with the test in the Horizontal Merger Guidelines whether competitors are likely to increase supply if prices increase in paras 32 et seqq.). Instead of large market shares as mentioned in para 27 of the Horizontal Merger Guidelines, the Commission assesses the importance of the merging parties as innovators (comparable to "innovation capacity shares").

3) Protective purpose and time horizon

It is not entirely clear from the Dow/DuPont Decision what the Commission is trying to protect with its innovation competition approach.[229] Innovation incentives, innovation activities or innovation results (that is, the final products and competition on future markets) can be considered. On the one hand,

> "*{t}he Commission considers that the reduced innovation incentives and capabilities are likely to manifest themselves in the form of:*
> (1) *immediate reduction of incentives to continue with some existing innovation efforts (either by discontinuing, redirecting or deferring early pipeline products or lines of research) in the case of overlapping lines of research and early pipeline products between the parties, and*

228 Dow/DuPont Decision, para 2043 states that the depression of innovation incentives *„is a standard unilateral effect from a merger"*; see also: *Petit*, Innovation Competition, p. 17; *Jung/Sinclair*, 40 E.C.L.R. (2019) 266, 271; *Chernenko*, 40 E.C.L.R. (2019) 9, 10; *Cary*, Festschrift für Dirk Schroeder, p. 188.

229 Cf. *Wirtz/Schulz*, NZKart 2019, 20, 21; *Thiede/Müller*, EuZW 2019, 628, 633.

(2) *reduces incentives to develop in the longer term the same number of new products as the combined targets of the Parties before the Transaction.*"[230]

In this regard, the reduction of innovation incentives in existing innovation spaces as well as on industry level as a whole seems to be the significant point. The innovation effort and activity may as well be the protective purpose of the Commission's intervention.[231]

On the other hand, the Commission finds that "*{c}onsumers would be harmed by both the loss of product variety, and the reduced intensity of future product market competition in the markets where the discontinued, deferred or redirected products would have been introduced but for the Transaction.*"[232]

In this sentence, the Commission clearly focuses on the final product and competition on future markets as protective purposes. The situation becomes even more confusing when looking at the time horizon the Commission takes into account:

> "*In the case of the Transaction, the Commission considers that a first form of harm to innovation competition would likely be the discontinuation of overlapping lines of research and early pipeline products which target the same innovation spaces. This effect would likely be a short-term effect of the Transaction for those overlapping lines of research and early pipeline products that would likely be discontinued, deferred or redirected very soon after the merger is implemented as a result of the integration efforts following the Transaction. {…}*"[233]
>
> "*The Commission finds that a second form of harm would result from the lower overall incentives of the merged entity to innovate as compared to the merging parties separately before the transaction. This is likely to be a medium and long term structural effect of the transaction going beyond the mere discontinuation of current innovation projects. The concern here is that in the medium and long-term, because of the lack of rivalry incentives to innovate, the merged entity would pursue less discovery work, less lines of research, less development and registration work and ultimately bring less*

---

230 Dow/DuPont Decision, para 2014.

231 In that regard: *Wirtz/Schulz*, NZKart 2019, 20, 21; *Petit* finds that the competitive harm „*is an exit by one of the merging parties from an innovation space.*" *Petit*, Innovation Competition, p. 21; this, however, does not relate to the decrease of innovation at industry level.

232 Dow/DuPont Decision, para 2016.

233 Dow/DuPont Decision, para 3056.

> *innovative AIs*[234] *to the market than the merging parties would have done absent the transaction."*[235]

With respect to overlapping lines of research and early pipeline products, the Commission seems to focus on the innovation incentive (because the innovation result itself is at the stage of an early pipeline product up to 10 years away from marketing[236]), whereas the concern that there is a reduction in innovation at industry level tends to focus on the innovation activity as well as the final product.

To make things more complicated, the Commission itself finds that (in contrast to its findings with respect to the medium to long term effect mentioned above), the harm would occur immediately after the merger:

> *"In addition, the Commission's theory of harm innovation implies an immediate effect of the Transaction on the Parties' behaviour, and not only in a timeframe of 10 to 15 years. In fact, although the reduction on innovation competition would harm consumers directly in the long-term, it would result in effects in the innovation spaces that would take place shortly after the Transaction, namely the immediate discontinuity, redirection or deferment of early pipeline products or lines of research by the merged entity."*[237]

The reduction of activity in innovation spaces seems to be only an example of short-term harm, and the harm to consumers is obviously not the direct target of Commission action. From the Dow/DuPont Decision itself it is, as a result, not possible to infer the protective purpose of the innovation competition assessment. The Commission does not clearly point to either the innovation incentive, the innovation effort/activity, the final product or competition on future markets (or a combination).

This leaves three possible objectives for competition policy:

1. The innovation incentive, meaning the impulse to start or continue research and development, including the general ability to perform such activities.

---

234 Active ingredient („AI").

235 Dow/DuPont Decision, para 3057.

236 See for example Dow/DuPont Decision, para 2032.

237 Dow/DuPont Decision, para 2034; *Esteva Mosso* states: "*The adverse effect on innovation activities may take place almost immediately after the merger is implemented and, in the long term, consumers would be harmed by a loss of product variety.*", *Esteva Mosso*, Innovation in EU Merger Control, p. 7.

2. The innovation effort or the innovation activity; that is the actual process of performing research and development in the sense of specific discovery and development actions.
3. The final product or competition on a future market; this approach requires research and development success and, with respect to competition on future markets, several undertakings successfully introducing new products.

There are the best arguments for innovation incentives as a protective purpose of Commission action. Since research and development is a stochastic process, policy cannot set incentives to raise the likelihood of successful result, meaning the innovative product. It is impossible to predict the result of innovation efforts. There is a likeliness that more R&D will lead to more innovation, but that is not necessarily so. Furthermore, even if that were the case, the only starting point for policy intervention would again be the research and development incentive and not the final outcome. The uncertain interrelation between research and development and the innovative product is not at all affected by competition policy. The success of innovation activities is by no means changed through an increase in rivalry. It may be that undertakings set up more effective and precise research and development programs because of competitive pressure. However, it is then still the incentive to set up valuable programs that is increased by competition and not the likelihood of success itself. There is no possible interrelation between competition policy and innovation success. The stochastic research and development process does not become deterministic in a less concentrated and more competitive surrounding. In other words, it does not become more likely that research is successful if market features change.

This finding does not counteract the objectives of the European Treaties as mentioned in *Section II) A) 2) (d)*. The Treaties' focus on research and development expresses the hope that a protection and promotion of research and development will lead to innovation. In fact, as mentioned above, there is an argument in favor of more innovative products in case of more targeted research and development. However, there is a difference between the desired result and the possible starting point for policy intervention. Whereas there is the hope that ultimately there will be innovation, competition policy can only increase or decrease the incentives to perform R&D.[238]

---

238 Beyond the Dow/DuPont Decision, *Drexl* finds that "*the challenge consists in addressing the artificial reduction of the pro-competitive incentives for innovation*",

The same is true with respect to innovation activities: The activities themselves are not influenced by changes in market concentration. They would be in case of regulatory intervention or other actions that would directly terminate the respective innovation activity. However, even in the case of a more concentrated market, undertakings would be free to continue their research and development activities. They also could terminate R&D activities freely. The question is rather if they would do so, meaning if their incentives to perform R&D would be changed through changes in the market features. The only intervention approach of competition policy are the incentives to perform research and development activities. According to the Commission's assessment in *Dow/DuPont*, those incentives may be changed with a view to cannibalization (or broader innovation competition) concerns. If an undertaking fears that it will cannibalize more of its own sales (as is the case post-merger), its incentive to perform R&D will decrease, not the possibility to continue the R&D activity. In conclusion, the protective purpose of Commission action regarding competition policy must be to maintain innovation incentives.

Those incentives may be decreased immediately after the implementation of the transaction as a result of reduced innovation competition, both with respect to innovation spaces as well as concerning innovation at industry level.[239] It is not important at what time future products may have been introduced, as after the initial incentive to start research, the actual success of that research does not depend on competition policy or market structure.

Drexl, Anti-Competitive Stumbling Stones, p. 19, see also p. 1; *Dreher* assumes that it is critical if mergers reduce "*innovation pressure*" on the market, *Dreher*, ZWeR 2009, 149, 173; *Federico/Scott Morton/Shapiro* argue that a merger between firms with overlapping R&D capabilities "*can lead to a reduction in the incentives to initiate new R&D efforts in the overlapping R&D areas*", *Federico/Scott Morton/Shapiro*, Antitrust and Innovation, p. 18.

239 In that regard also *Panhans*, DG COMP, at the 2. Kölner Kartellrechtsgespräche, see *Hasselhorn*, NZKart 2019, 546. *Panhans* finds that the expected harm does not occur in the distant future, but rather immediately after the implementation of the merger as a result of a loss of innovation competition (resulting, for example, in a cut down of research expenditure); *Petit* finds that the Dow/DuPont assessment "*is essentially based on the R&D conduct of the merged entity in the short-term.*", *Petit*, Innovation Competition, p. 5.

Commentators have claimed that the Commission finally takes into account dynamic effects in merger control in *Dow/DuPont*.[240] Even the Commission itself seems not to be fully aware of the time frame of its assessment. A Commission official stated that

> „*(o)verall, the legal framework of EU merger control is well geared to capture not only short-term static effects of mergers on price but also their longer-term dynamic effects on competition, including effects on choice, quality and innovation.*"[241]

But unlike with choice and quality, it is not about the final innovation outcome but, as explained above, rather about the preservation of the innovation incentive as a short-term effect.

It may well be that the marketing of product innovations takes place in the distant future and therefore may be considered as a dynamic effect in merger control. Dynamic competition focuses on the new product, the new technology, the new source of supply or the new form of organization.[242]

The theory of harm in *Dow/DuPont*, however, does not point to the product innovation itself but to the innovation incentive. Effects on the incentive happen in the short term in the very moment of the completion of a transaction as a result of decreased competitive pressure from a reduced number of industry participants. The incentive of the undertakings to start (!) R&D is diminished.

The assessment of innovation competition in *Dow/DuPont* is not about long-time dynamic effects, but adopts a static view of the competitive pressure leading to innovation incentives at the time of the Transaction. This approach is most comparable to the concept of allocative efficiencies. Allocative efficiency describes the optimal distribution of production fac-

---

240 *Podszun*, IIC 2019, 720, 741; *Chernenko* finds that „*the economic concern is a medium-to-long-term structural effect*", *Chernenko*, 40 E.C.L.R. (2019) 9, 18; *Denicolò/Polo*, The innovation theory of harm, p. 1.

241 *Esteva Mosso*, Innovation in EU Merger Control, p. 4; in contrast, *Esteva Mosso* states on p. 10: „*However, one should not confuse the uncertain outcome of innovation in relation to any specific project with the likelihood of negative effects on innovation.*"

242 *Schumpeter*, Capitalism, Socialism and Democracy, p. 82-83; *Mestmäcker/Schweitzer*, Europäisches Wettbewerbsrecht, § 32 para 1; for an overview on dynamic efficiencies see *Leber*, Dynamische Effizienzen in der EU-Fusionskontrolle, p. 87 et seq.

tors.[243] The theory of harm in *Dow/DuPont* (partly) focuses on the optimal distribution of innovation assets.

The Commission's approach can be illustrated as follows:

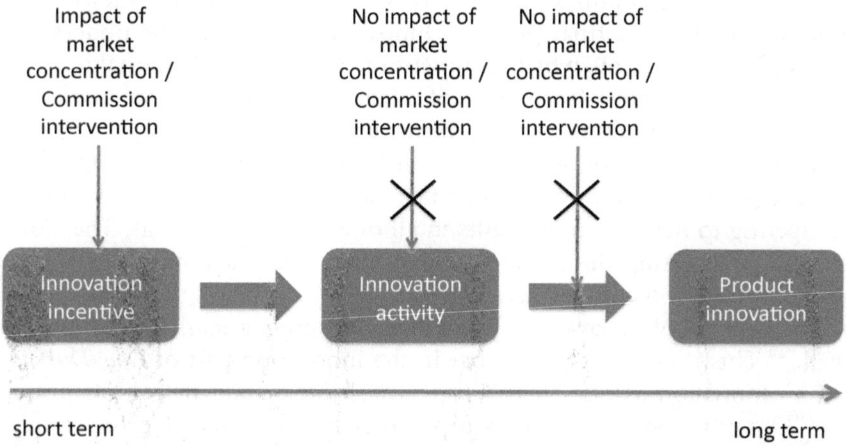

4) Innovation markets, innovation spaces and innovation competition

In line with the assessment by means of the standard unilateral effects model in the Horizontal Merger Guidelines,[244] the Commission treats innovation as a parameter of competition rather than a market on its own.[245] Consequently, the Commission states:

> "*When considering both the downstream product markets and the upstream technology markets, innovation should not be understood as a market on its own right, but as an input activity for both the upstream technology*

243 *Schwalbe/Zimmer*, Kartellrecht und Ökonomie, p. 4; *Leber*, Dynamische Effizienzen in der EU-Fusionskontrolle, p. 86.

244 In line with the unilateral effects analysis „*then innovation would have to be considered as a parameter of competition which would be negatively affected by the increased market power of Dow and DuPont.*", *Chernenko*, 40 E.C.L.R. (2019) 9, 15.

245 „*The theory of harm dispenses with the delineation of current or future product markets.*" *Petit*, Innovation Competition, p. 19; beyond the Dow/DuPont Decision, *Drexl* finds that "*from an economic perspective, R&D is to be considered as an input to the goods and services sold in the downstream product market.*", *Drexl*, Anti-Competitive Stumbling Stones, p. 9.

> *markets and the downstream […] markets. This however does not prevent the Commission to assess the impact of the Transaction at the level of innovation efforts by the Parties and its competitors.*"[246]

The notion of an input factor is not entirely correct since, as mentioned above, there is no definite causality between innovation activities in general and the specific final product. Innovation can rather be understood as a different level on which competition takes place. Undertakings are competing on various levels, first of all of course the product market(s), but also in personnel, marketing, distribution, accounting, financing and as well research and development.[247] All those factors influence the final market position of the respective firm. Accordingly, all undertakings are competing to have the best results in all of their business areas. The Commission is assessing the research and development capability as the core area of innovation competition.[248]

The concept of innovation spaces does not imply a market definition as well.[249] This is despite the fact that in the innovation part of *Dow/DuPont*, the Commission assesses the "Crop protection market definition principles"[250] with a division into "Crop protection formulated product markets"[251], "Technology markets"[252] and "Innovation spaces"[253]. However, in addition to the fact that the Commission explicitly states that it does not assess innovation as a market,[254] the concept of innovation spaces does not fulfill the criteria for market definition. According to the Commission's Market Definition Notice, "*{a} relevant product market comprises all those*

246 Dow/DuPont Decision, para 348.

247 In Germany, several factors beyond the market level have been recognized as influencing the market position of an undertaking in § 18 (3) and (3a) of the Act against Restraints of Competition. The paragraph mentions, for example, financial strength, access to supply markets, links with other undertakings and innovation-driven competitive pressure.

248 *Panhans*, DG COMP, at the 2. Kölner Kartellrechtsgespräche, see *Hasselhorn*, NZKart 2019, 546.

249 In that sense not entirely clear *Wirtz/Schulz*: „*Linking the competitive analysis to innovation spaces replaces the defined market as analytical framework.*" *Wirtz/Schulz*, NZKart 2019, 20, 23.

250 Dow/DuPont Decision, headline on page 38.

251 Dow/DuPont Decision, headline on page 39.

252 Dow/DuPont Decision, headline on page 42.

253 Dow/DuPont Decision, headline on page 43.

254 In the scope of the „Innovation spaces" assessment starting on page 43 of the Dow/DuPont Decision, the Commission mentions in para 348 that it does not assess a market.

products and/or services which are regarded as interchangeable or substitutable by the consumer, by reason of the products' characteristics, their prices and their intended use."[255]

With regard to innovation spaces, the activities within those spaces cannot be interchangeable for the consumer. First of all, there is no direct relation to consumer markets as mentioned above. Thus, the activities in innovation spaces cannot be analyzed from the consumer's perspective. Furthermore, activities in innovation spaces do not have specific characteristics, prices or an intended use. In innovation spaces, there are no products or services yet.[256] There is nothing that could be interchanged or substituted from the perspective of a consumer. The innovation activities themselves in innovation spaces are far from being interchangeable, as their likeliness to success as well as their "quality" or maturity is entirely unclear and impossible to assess.

The Market Definition Notice further sets up basic principles for market definition: "*Firms are subject to three main sources {of} competitive constraints: demand substitutability, supply substitutability and potential competition.*"[257] All of those constraints are related to specific products. But in innovation spaces, there are no products, and the activities in those spaces also do not yet target specific products. As the Commission points out in

> *Dow/DuPont*: "*A given discovery target is based on lead crops and lead pests and may thus comprise AIs that can be used in several downstream formulated product markets (for example chewing Lepidopteran insecticides, broadleaf herbicides). The spaces where innovation competition takes place are thus broader than an individual downstream crop protection market, but are nonetheless small.*"[258]

In conclusion, the concept of innovation spaces is a means to concretize innovation activities in the industry.[259] As pointed out in *Dow/DuPont*, at innovation spaces level, "*the Commission findings are that concentration is even higher as not all the R&D-integrated players are present in each innovation space.*"[260] Accordingly, the Commission supplements its assessment of

255 Market Definition Notice, para 7.

256 For a further discussion of the concept of innovation markets and critique see *Section II) F) 2)*.

257 Market Definition Notice, para 13.

258 Dow/DuPont Decision, para 351.

259 *Esteva Mosso* defines innovation spaces as the place „*where innovation competition actually took place.*“, *Esteva Mosso*, Innovation in EU Merger Control, p. 10.

260 Dow/DuPont Decision, para 2353.

innovation competition in the industry with a "deep-dive" into specific areas of innovation in order to capture the full picture. Innovation spaces can be understood as a link between innovation activities on industry level and the final product market, showing the direction of research and development.

Furthermore, the Commission concludes that:

> *"[...], the Commission considers that for the innovation spaces where the Parties have overlapping lines of research and early pipeline products, the merged entity would have fewer incentives to put the same level of effort on innovation as the Parties would independently put, but for the Transaction. This would be likely to result in several of the Parties' early pipeline products (and eventually lines of research) being discontinued, deferred, or simply redirect.*
>
> *The Commission may not be able to identify precisely which early pipeline products or lines of research the Parties would likely discontinue, defer or re-direct. However, the Commission finds it probably that the early pipeline products and lines of research described in Sections V.8.9.2 to V.8.9.4 are the candidates for a likely reduction of innovation effort given the closeness of innovation competition between the Parties on the targeted innovation spaces. In fact, discontinuation of an early pipeline product or line of research is more likely to occur the higher the expected sales which that early pipeline product from the merged entity would capture (if launched) from another existing or future product of the merged entity."*[261]

Those paragraphs show that it is about the general innovation activity in certain narrower spaces instead of specific product markets targeted with the research and development. Otherwise, the Commission would have to name the specific innovation spaces relating to specific products where activities would likely be discontinued, deferred or redirected. If the Commission would use innovation spaces as markets, it could not leave open the respective innovation spaces if it concludes that there is actual competitive harm leading to Commission intervention. Whereas the Commission can leave open the precise market definition in case a transaction does not raise competitive concerns on whatever market, it is part of the principle of legal certainty (and the party's right of defense) to define the markets where the Commission intervenes. Since in *Dow/DuPont* the Commission only uses innovation spaces to show general innovation activities that are

261 Dow/DuPont Decision, para 3024, 3025.

not market-based, the definition of the innovation spaces in which harm is likely to occur can accordingly be left open.

Taken together, these points suggest that innovation is not a market on its own, but rather a factor that influences the market position of an undertaking on a different level. Innovation spaces concretize the activities on that level, completing the picture of the respective innovation conditions.

5) No product/pipeline analysis

In connection with the innovation competition analysis beyond specific markets, it is important to understand that the Commission does not assess specific products[262] or pipelines.[263] Numerous commentators[264] argue that the time horizon in *Dow/DuPont* exceeds two to three years[265] and the assessment of the Commission is therefore rather speculative.[266] This is by no means the case. The relevant time horizon does not exceed two to three

---

262 *Todino/van de Walle/Stoican* find that the Commission "adopts a general assessment of harm to innovation, unrelated to a specific product market {…}.", *Todino/van de Walle/Stoican*, 64 The Antitrust Bulletin (2019), 11, 12.

263 *Federico/Scott Morton/Shapiro* distinguish between "*mergers involving competing firms with identifiable products or projects in the development pipeline*" and "*mergers involving established firms with competing innovation capabilities*" and put the *Dow/DuPont* merger in the second category, *Federico/Scott Morton/Shapiro*, Antitrust and Innovation, p. 11, 48-49.

264 *Hasselhorn*, NZKart 2019, 546, 547: „*Götz also critically assessed the 10-year time horizon used in recent Commission decisions to examine the impact on research and development. Despite the uncertainties (e.g. with regard to technological and regulatory risks), using such long time horizons as a basis would be tantamount to assuming knowledge.*" {authors translation}; *Haucap* finds with respect to Dow/DuPont that "*the Commission has even investigated overlaps of research at very early stages (phase I), the success of which is very difficult to predict.*", *Haucap*, Merger Effects on Innovation, p. 3; *Petit* finds that the Commission "*expands the scope of merger review to early R&D, where products are several years away from reaching the market.*" *Petit*, Innovation Competition, p. 20; *Jung/Sinclair*: "*not only specific potential future products, but also early stage R&D efforts in relation to ideas or products which are undefined and/or are years away from reaching the market.*" *Jung/Sinclair*, 40 E.C.L.R. (2019) 266, 271.

265 Two years would be the timeframe usually taken into account with respect to potential competition (a competitor may already exert a significant constraining influence if its market entry is likely, timely and sufficient), see for example Horizontal Merger Guidelines, paras 60, 64, 74.

266 *RBB Economics*, RBB Brief 54, p. 1.

years. Since the Commission's theory of harm in *Dow/DuPont* is about the innovation incentives, the respective harm will occur in the short run right after the closing of the transaction. It is not about specific products or specific future developments the Commission is trying to secure,[267] but rather about the competitive pressure with respect to research and development activities in general.[268] In that regard, the Commission's theory is also not speculative since it does not deal with the (stochastic) success of innovation activities. This is even the case with respect to the innovation spaces, as they only serve as an example for the levels of competitive constraints the parties exert on each other. The assessment beyond specific current or future products is one of the main novelties in *Dow/DuPont*, as will be discussed in *Section II) F)*.

6) Importance of specific industry features

The Commission sets up a theory stating that in innovation-driven industries, a merger between two important innovators is likely to reduce innovation incentives if there is an oligopolistic market structure with high barriers to entry and high appropriability (absent efficiencies).[269] Industry specific features are thus key to the applicability of the Commission's theory. It has been argued that the Commission's approach may prevent the emergence of start-ups, because the investors would fear that their exit (sale to big market players) would be made impossible due to the innovation competition concept.[270] But this argument ignores the fact that start-ups are not important innovators according to the Commission's definition in *Dow/DuPont* as they will very likely not be vertically integrated

267 *Chernenko* mentions that *„the Commission is able to identity a relevant industry but not the precise targets of a likely R&D reduction."*, *Chernenko*, 40 E.C.L.R. (2019) 9, 18.

268 *Wirtz/Schulz*: *„With this approach, the Commission is moving away from its competition law view of defined product markets and focuses more on the consequences of the merger for innovation as such."* {authors translation}, *Wirtz/Schulz*, NZKart 2019, 20, 20.

269 See *Section II) C) 1)*; *Federico* explicitly mentions the specific factors necessary to draw conclusions from the relationship between horizontal mergers and innovation, *Federico*, Horizontal Mergers, Innovation and the Competitive Process, p. 19-22; see also *Federico/Scott Morton/Shapiro*, Antitrust and Innovation, p. 20.

270 *Jung/Sinclair*, 40 E.C.L.R. (2019) 266, 268, 275.

and have the financial strength to market their inventions on a great scale (that is usually the reason why start-ups are sold to big players).

Furthermore, there are not many innovation-driven industries with oligopolistic market structures and high barriers to entry.[271] For example, one may question whether platforms, search engines and social networks are innovation-driven industries. It rather seems as if they are using network effects and extensive data access to extend existing ideas. However, even if the Big Tech companies[272] were seen as being innovative, one would have to assess the market structure and the barriers to entry in order to apply the Commission's theory in *Dow/DuPont* to that sector.

The industry specifics are, according to the Commission's assessment, fulfilled in the crop protection sector. One may also think of the pharmaceutical industry.[273] The main difference between agrochemicals and pharmaceuticals is that the latter are much more expensive leading to a significantly higher stream of revenues that can refinance innovation efforts within a shorter time period. While the Blockbuster agrochemical Coragen starts at about 120 Euro per 500 ml (still to be attenuated to around 18 ml/hl),[274] innovative pharmaceuticals may have prices starting at six-digit or seven-digit Euro amounts per treatment.[275] This implies two things: First, agrochemicals need to be manufactured on a much larger scale to pay back the research and development costs. Second, even if produced on a great scale, it will take much more time to refund the financial resources used for discovery and development. Accordingly, whereas in crop protection it is absolutely necessary for performing research and development to be a big vertically integrated player with a huge amount of financial resources gained through manufacturing on a large scale, those requirements do not necessarily have to be fulfilled with respect to pharmaceuticals. In the latter case, small research and development companies can join forces with service providers for the regulatory process and the manufacturing and marketing. If including these kinds of partnership in the assessment,

---

271 *Petit* finds that the Commission's approach could possibly be used in the pharmaceutical, defense and digital communications industry, *Petit*, Innovation competition, p. 6.

272 Such as Google, Facebook, Amazon; Apple may in contrast be considered innovative.

273 Cf. *Panhans*, DG COMP, at the 2. Kölner Kartellrechtsgespräche, see *Hasselhorn*, NZKart 2019, 546.

274 See for example *shopping.agrimag.it/en/products/702/coragen*.

275 See for the most expensive medication: *medicalxpress.com/news/2019-05-fda-2m-medicine-expensive.html*.

the pharmaceutical industry most likely does not constitute an oligopoly. Furthermore, barriers to entry are much lower if smaller undertakings also have a chance of financing their innovation activities. However, it does not seem unlikely that in some parts of the pharmaceutical sector, there may be conditions where the Commission's innovation competition approach must be applied – namely if there is a need to produce cheaper, innovative drugs on a large scale.

In addition, one may think of the defense and aircraft sectors. In both industries, innovation matters, barriers to entry are high and there are usually only a few vertically-integrated players.

All in all, attention must be paid to the peculiarities of a specific transaction. What the Commission explicitly does not do is set up a rule that mergers always reduce innovation.[276] The Commission's approach in *Dow/ DuPont* can only be applied in full.

7) Written evidence of reducing innovation efforts

One peculiarity in *Dow/DuPont* is that the Commission was in the possession of written evidence of the parties that indicated a planned reduction of innovation efforts. *Carles Esteva Mosso*, Deputy Director General for Mergers in the Directorate General for Competition of the European Commission, said in a speech:

> „*The second effect of this particular merger regarding the likely reduction in the incentive to invest in R&D effort in relation to new products in the future was specifically confirmed by concrete evidence regarding the significant planned cut backs in the parties' innovation efforts (e.g. in terms of planned R&D inputs, such as R&D spend, FTEs number, etc., and output targets), compared to their pre-merger plans.*"[277]

---

276 In that sense it is at least incomplete when *Thiede/Müller* find that the Commission has taken a stand in the Schumpeter/Arrow controversy, *Thiede/Müller*, EuZW 2019, 628, 632. This is only true with respect to very specific market conditions; under those specific circumstances there does not seem to be a controversy between Schumpeter and Arrow anyway, see *Section II) H) 1)*. *Esteva Mosso* explains that Annex 4 of the Dow/DuPont Decision (fn. 293) does not seek "*to establish a general conclusion that horizontal mergers generally harm consumers through adverse effects on innovation.*" *Esteva Mosso*, Innovation in EU Merger Control, p. 12.

277 *Esteva Mosso*, Innovation in EU Merger Control, p. 11.

Even though most of its text is deleted from the non-confidential version of the Dow/DuPont Decision, the written evidence nevertheless seems to be an important factor in the Commission's assessment. That does not mean that the Commission's theory is invalid without further evidence of concrete plans to reduce innovation efforts. However, concrete evidence may be outweighing an otherwise not-so-clearly-verifiable decrease in innovation incentives.

The written evidence is particularly important when looking at economic theory finding that a 3-to-2 merger is much more problematic than a 5-to-4 merger:

> *„Overall, and in stark contrast to price effects of mergers, the case for a general presumption that an increase in concentration leads to (unilateral) reductions in R&D expenditures and innovation incentives is not warranted. {...} Having said this, however, both economic theory and empirical evidence suggests that 3-to-2 mergers tend to be more problematic than 5-to-4 mergers, not only in terms of price effects, but also due to their potentially adverse effects on innovation, at least in research intensive industries. In fact, with respect to 5-to-4 mergers there is no reliable general presumption on a merger's innovation effects."*[278]

It seems as if in case of a merger from 5 to 4 innovation players, additional evidence of reduced innovation activities is required. At this point, however, one must keep in mind that the abovementioned economic theory deals with a presumption of increased concentration leading to reductions in R&D incentives. As will be explained further in *Section II) H) 1)*, such a general presumption is not valid anyway. When taking into account the specific features of the Commission's approach, especially with respect to innovation spaces, a reliable result can be established even without written evidence.

8) Integration of the Commission's approach into the existing legal framework

In summary, there are two main novelties of the innovation competition concept developed by the Commission in *Dow/DuPont*.

First of all – and maybe most important – innovation is not considered to constitute a market on its own. As will be further explained, there

278 *Haucap*, Merger Effects on Innovation, p. 7.

has been the so-called Innovation Market Analysis which defines a separate "innovation market". In contrast, the Commission in *Dow/DuPont* explicitly refers to innovation as a means of competition that affects the market position of the merging parties. Market definition according to the demand-side oriented market concept remains unchanged.[279] The relevant product and geographic market is still defined as traditionally.[280] What changes is the assessment of the competitive strength of the merging undertakings on a pre-defined market. In brief, market shares can be substituted or at least supplemented by the innovation capacity of an undertaking.

This notion of innovation is without apparent alternative. A "market" requires buy/sell transactions.[281] Without an opposite market side, there are no indications for any possible market definition. There cannot be competition on a "market" without third-party interactions.

Second, innovation is treated as an indirect means of competition. Innovation does not take place on market level but rather upstream of any pre-defined market. There is a novel "theory" in the meaning of a definition and explanation of innovation concerns beyond specific product markets or observable research activities. The innovation capacity of an undertaking cannot directly be linked to specific product markets but rather creates a certain level of competitive strength across several defined separate markets. While there have been other cross-market factors such as financial strength or links with other undertakings,[282] the Commission

---

279 For this concept see the Commission's Market Definition Notice and in particular para 15 et seq.

280 For the traditional market definition see the Commission's Market Definition Notice.

281 See *Section II) F) 2) (c)*.

282 For the criterion of financial strength see CFI, Judgment of 31.01.2001, T-156/98, ECLI:EU:T:2001:29, para 125, *RJB Mining*; Commission Decision of 28.04.1992, OJ L 204, 21.07.1992, p. 1-12, Case IV/M.126, para 25, *ACCOR/Wagons-Lits*; Commission Decision of 30.04.1992, OJ C 165, 02.07.1992, p. 26, Case IV/M.197, Rn. 33, *Solvay-Laporte/Interox*; Commission Decision of 30.07.1997, OJ L 336, 08.12.1997, p. 16-47, Case IV/M.877, para 72 et seq, *Boeing/McDonnell Douglas*; Horizontal Merger Guidelines, para 36; *Körber* in Immenga/Mestmäcker, Wettbewerbsrecht EU, Art. 2 FKVO para 265-267; for the criterion of links with other undertakings see Commission Decision of 23.10.2003, C(2003)4002, Case COMP/M.3248, para 33, *BAT/ETI*; Commission Decision of 09.04.2002, SG (2002) D/229298, OJ C 153, 27.06.2002, Case COMP/M.2690, para 52, *Solvay/Montedison-Ausimont*; Horizontal Merger Guidelines, para 48;
Körber in Immenga/Mestmäcker, Wettbewerbsrecht EU, Art. 2 FKVO para 263.

in *Dow/DuPont* for the first time treats innovation as an indirect factor of competition.

In order to prevent the innovation competition approach from becoming to broad, the Commission uses the concept of innovation spaces to link innovation capacity to certain traditionally defined markets. Innovation spaces are the sectors in which innovation activities of the undertaking in question usually take place or have occurred in the past and therefore could relate to in the future. Innovation competition affects all markets that fall within the innovation spaces. There is no competition beyond markets but rather a different approach to the notion of competition that takes place in markets defined with view to the demand-side oriented market concept.

As mentioned above,[283] the legal framework in Article 101 and 102 TFEU and the EC Merger Regulation do not set up criteria for the assessment of the interrelation of competition and innovation in the short run and in a specific case. For the full protection of innovation as a basic driver of competition not only specific products or observable research and development activities must be taken into account. The innovation capacity of an undertaking can be a crucial factor for competition in several markets in the long run. The Commission is bound to securing effective competition in the internal market by the Treaties and must therefore take into account factors that may impede such effective competition. In *Dow/DuPont*, the Commission uses the existing legal framework to expand the scope of "competition" or a "market position" to important innovators – that is, undertakings with a high "innovation power" or innovation capacity.

The Commission's novel approach in *Dow/DuPont* helps to consider innovation more comprehensively. As already mentioned, innovation is an object of the Treaties and an important pillar of the internal market. Innovation competition fits into the existing framework and helps to fully realize market integration.

With respect to the EC Merger Regulation, the novel approach can be incorporated as follows:

Article 2 (3) EC Merger Regulation stipulates that a merger shall be prohibited if it "*would significantly impede effective competition, in the common*

283 See *Section II) A) 3)*.

market or in a substantial part of it, in particular as a result of the creation or strengthening of a dominant position."[284]

The assessment consists of two steps:[285] first of all, there needs to be a market (the common market or a substantial part of it). Second, the authority must analyze whether the merger significantly impedes effective competition in particular by creating or strengthening a dominant position.

As mentioned above, the Commission uses the innovation competition approach to determine the parameters of competition rather than to define a market on its own.[286] In fact, "innovation" or "research and development" does not meet the requirements of a market. Innovation as such cannot be sold or acquired. The lack of market features was one of the main lines of critique with respect to the Innovation Market Analysis – that treats innovation as a market – developed and used in the U.S.[287]

The Commission's innovation competition approach is used when determining the market position of undertakings. It could be a means of establishing the "creation or strengthening of a dominant position".[288] The European Court of Justice defines a dominant position as:

> "*{…} a position of economic strength enjoyed by an undertaking which enables it to prevent effective competition being maintained on the relevant market by affording it the power to behave to an appreciable extent independently of its competitors, its customers and ultimately of the consumers {…}.*"[289]

A high share in an existing product market is not the only parameter allowing an undertaking to prevent competition and behave independently. In fact, market shares are constantly only the starting point for the assess-

284 Article 2 (2) EC Merger Regulation uses a similar standard as a basis for declaring a merger to be compatible with the common market.

285 *Körber* in Immenga/Mestmäcker, Wettbewerbsrecht Fusionskontrolle, Art. 2 FKVO para 16; *Riesenkampff/Steinbarth* in Loewenheim/Meessen/Riesenkampff/Kersting/Meyer-Lindemann, Kartellrecht, Art. 2 FKVO para 9.

286 See *Section II) C) 4).*

287 For a more elaborated assessment see *Section II) F) 2).*

288 For a more detailed analysis see *Section III) B) 1) and 2) (c).*

289 ECJ, Judgment of 13.02.1979, Case 85/76, ECLI:EU:C:1979:36, Summary 4, para 38-39, *Hoffmann-La Roche*; settled case law since ECJ, Judgment of 14.02.1978, Case 27/76, ECLI:EU:C:1978:22, Summary 2, para 65-66, *United Brands*; recently in ECJ, Judgment of 06.12.2012, Case C-457/10 P, ECLI:EU:C:2012:770, para 175, *AstraZeneca.*

ment of a market dominant position.[290] They are supplemented by other factors such as financial strength, access to supply or sales markets, or links with other undertakings.[291] In its Dow/DuPont Decision, the Commission establishes innovation capacity as another factor for determining market power.

The creation or strengthening of a dominant position is an example of a significant impediment to effective competition (see wording of Article 2 (3) EC Merger Regulation "in particular…"). The assessment is similar in both cases: the first step is defining a market; the second step is determining the conditions in that market. It is either about a dominant position in a market or about any other way of impeding effective competition in a market.

With respect to the criterion of a "significant impediment to effective competition", Recital 25 of the EC Merger Regulation explains:

> *"In view of the consequences that concentrations in oligopolistic market structures may have, it is all the more necessary to maintain effective competition in such markets. Many oligopolistic markets exhibit a healthy degree of competition. However, under certain circumstances, concentrations involving the elimination of important competitive constraints that the merging parties had exerted upon each other, as well as a reduction of competitive pressure on the remaining competitors, may, even in the absence of a likelihood of coordination between the members of the oligopoly, result in a significant impediment to effective competition. {…} The notion of "significant impediment to effective competition" in Article 2(2) and (3) should be interpreted as extending, beyond the concept of dominance, only to the anti-competitive effects of a concentration resulting from the non-coordinated behaviour of undertakings which would not have a dominant position on the market concerned."*

290 ECJ, Judgment of 14.02.1978, Case 27/76, ECLI:EU:C:1978:22, para 66, *United Brands*; *Körber* in Immenga/Mestmäcker, Wettbewerbsrecht Fusionskontrolle, Art. 2 FKVO para 222; *Riesenkampff/Steinbarth* in Loewenheim/Meessen/Riesenkampff/Kersting/Meyer-Lindemann, Kartellrecht, Art. 2 FKVO para 72; see also *Section III) B) 1) (b)*.

291 For an overview of possible factors see Section 18 (3) and (3a) of the German Act against Restraints of Competition („**ARC**"); *Körber* in Immenga/Mestmäcker, Wettbewerbsrecht Fusionskontrolle, Art. 2 FKVO, para 263, 264 et seq, 275 et seq; *Riesenkampff/Steinbarth* in Loewenheim/Meessen/Riesenkampff/Kersting/Meyer-Lindemann, Kartellrecht, Art. 2 FKVO para 90 et seq, 94-96.

This shows that while the abovementioned two-step assessment remains the same, the concept of „significant impediment to effective competition“ covers non-coordinated effects in an oligopoly below the level of market dominance[292] as well as the traditional creation or strengthening of a dominant position.

The innovation competition approach could be of use in either setting. Even though the Commission's approach requires an oligopolistic market structure, there may also be market dominance of undertakings in an oligopoly. However, even if there is no dominant position of the parties to a merger, innovation competition can be used for establishing non-coordinated effects in an oligopoly, resulting in a significant impediment to effective competition.

Innovation is not a market on its own but a means of determining the conditions of competition in a market. The Commission's approach in *Dow/DuPont* does not constitute an unwritten element in Article 2 (3) EC Merger Regulation but is a means for determining a „dominant position“ or a „significant impediment to effective competition“.

D) Economic foundation

1) Annex 4 of the Dow/DuPont Decision

In order to better understand the logic behind the Commission's concept in *Dow/DuPont*, it is worth looking at the economic assessment included in Annex 4[293] of the Decision. Even though the Commission claims not to have relied on specific economic models in the innovation competition assessment of *Dow/DuPont*,[294] the Annex may give important indications of how the Commission generally approaches innovation concerns.[295]

---

292 *Körber* in Immenga/Mestmäcker, Wettbewerbsrecht Fusionskontrolle, Art. 2 FK-VO para 3, 4, 9; *Riesenkampff/Steinbarth* in Loewenheim/Meessen/Riesenkampff/Kersting/Meyer-Lindemann, Kartellrecht, Art. 2 FKVO para 57, 64, 65.

293 Case M.7932, *Dow/DuPont*, Annex 4 to the Commission Decision, Implications of the economic theory on mergers, competition and innovation in light of the features of the Transaction (hereinafter: „Annex 4“).

294 *Esteva Mosso*, Innovation in EU Merger Control, p. 5.

295 Petit finds that the *„dispositive value of Annex 4 is difficult to assess since it is not entirely clear to what extent the selected models influenced the Commission decision to intervene in the merger.“* Petit, Innovation Competition, page 37.

Like the legal assessment in *Dow/DuPont*, the Annex is also based on the general finding that

> "*the economic principles laid out in economic literature indicate that a merger between two out of a limited number of significant innovators is likely to reduce product innovation when appropriability is high (that is, when Intellectual Property Rights (IPR) are effective) and when there are no merger-specific efficiencies.*"[296]

Generally,

> "*the incentives to innovate are driven by the difference in the expected innovator's profits earned if an innovation takes place and the profits earned if an innovation does not occur. A merger can affect this difference for each of the firms in the industry (including both the merging and the non-merging parties), and with that the overall rate of innovation.*"[297]

The Commission refers to three different mechanisms through which a merger can reduce innovation (which means affect the difference in the abovementioned profits with and without innovation)[298]:

First, a merger can affect innovation competition. This refers to the effect of cannibalization of profits of the other party through the introduction of a new product or, broader speaking, the "negative externality"[299] that an innovator imposes on its competitors. The cannibalization effect is internalized post-merger, "*adding to the opportunity cost of innovation and thus depressing the innovation incentive.*"[300] Post-merger, one party no longer gains profits from a competing firm but from the merging partner when introducing a new product. According to the Commission, this is a standard unilateral effect from a merger.[301]

Second, innovation incentives may also be affected by changes in current and future product market competition that typically occur with a merger.[302] The Commission finds that "*the effect of a less intense product market competition on innovation is potentially ambiguous.*"[303] Nevertheless, even though less intense product market competition may, under certain

296 Annex 4, para 5.
297 Annex 4, para 15.
298 Annex, para 16.
299 Annex 4, para 17.
300 Annex 4, para 6.
301 Annex 4, para 6, 17.
302 Annex 4, para 7.
303 Annex 4, para 7.

circumstances, incentivize innovation, this effect is unlikely to outweigh the loss of innovation competition mentioned above.[304] This holds at least true for concentrated markets.[305]

Third, the Commission identifies two important efficiencies increasing innovation incentives that may come along with a merger: a possible lower risk of imitation by other market players (increasing the innovator's possibility to appropriate the value of the innovation) and the ability for process innovations to be applied over a larger scale.[306] Since the last points are distinct from the loss of competition brought about by a merger,[307] they should, according to the Commission, be treated as efficiencies for which the parties of a transaction bear the burden of proof.[308] This does not hold true for the investigation of the general level of appropriability on a market but rather for its increase due to a merger.

(a) Competition in innovation

According to the Commission, the economic literature suggests that in innovative industries, a merger may generate standard unilateral effects in innovation.

> "*In circumstances where by innovating a firm captures significant sales from rivals while a firm that does not risks losing its current sales to rivals that do (thus increasing the profit gain from innovating), competition in innovation will be an important parameter of competition between firms, just like price and quality are.*"[309]

The Commission refers to economic literature emphasizing that rivalry is an important driver in the process of introducing innovations.[310] The Commission also points to the importance of R&D diversity for the success of innovation efforts: "*Parallel research paths can accelerate innovation if there is uncertainty about the correct solution to a specific technological {must*

304 Annex 4, para 8.
305 Annex 4, para 8.
306 Annex 4, para 9.
307 Annex 4, para 29.
308 Annex 4, para 9.
309 Annex 4, para 37.
310 In Annex 4, para 38, the Commission refers to *Baker*, 74 Antitrust Law Journal (2007), 575, 579; *Shapiro*, Competition and innovation, p. 364.

read: problem}."[311] The Commission brings further reference to the finding that "*{a} merger between two out of a limited number of innovators is likely to reduce competition in innovation, and thus limit the overall rate of innovation.*"[312]

At this point, the Commission refers to the U.S. Horizontal Merger Guidelines, according to which the diversion of future sales between the merging parties is one main reason why a merger can lead to less innovation.[313] The lost expected profit of one of the merging parties when the respective other party introduces an innovative product becomes an opportunity cost that was not present before the merger.[314]

The Commission concludes that the effect is even more pronounced if the market is concentrated and there are high barriers to entry.[315] Also, there are stronger effects for close competitors that have similar innovation trajectories or target the same product markets with innovation.[316]

---

311 Annex 4, para 39; the Commission further refers to *Comanor/Scherer*, 32 Journal of Health Economics, 106, 110; *Shapiro*, Competition and innovation, p. 382, *Gilbert*, Competition and innovation, p. 9.

312 Annex 4, para 40; the Commission refers, *inter alia*, to *Gilbert/Greene*, 83 The George Washington Law Review (2015), 1919, 1938: „*An increase in the market power from a merger can dull the incentives to invent in at least two ways. By increasing the flow of profits from existing products and services, the merger can reduce the merged firm's incentive to create new products and services. Alternatively, the merger can combine two firms, each of which would have taken significant sales from the other if they had been successful innovators. The merger internalizes this externality, thereby reducing incentives for invention.*"; see also *Whinston*, Comment, p. 409.

313 In Annex 4, para 41, the Commission refers to section 6.4 („Innovation and Product Variety") of the U.S. Horizontal Merger Guidelines: „*Competition often spurs firms to innovate. The Agencies may consider whether a merger is likely to diminish innovation competition by encouraging the merged firm to curtail its innovative effort below the level that would prevail in the absence of the merger. The curtailment of innovation could take the form of reduced incentive to continue with an existing product-development effort or reduced incentive to initiate development of new products. The first of these effects is most likely to occur if at least one of the merging firms is engaging in efforts to introduce products that would capture substantial revenues from the other merging firm. The second, longer-run effect is most likely to occur if a least one of the merging firms has capabilities that are likely to lead it to develop new products in the future that would capture substantial revenues from the other merging firm. The Agencies therefore also consider whether a merger will diminish innovation competition by combining two of a very small number of firms with the strongest capabilities to successfully innovate in a specific direction.*"

314 Annex 4, para 41.

315 Annex 4, para 42.

316 Annex 4, para 42.

> *"{A}dverse effects on innovation increase when the "innovation diversion ratio" between the merging parties increases (that is, the higher is the fraction of additional profits earned by one of the merging parties when it invests more in innovation which come at the expense of the other merging party)."*[317]

The innovation diversion ratio is thus usually higher for close competitors. Finally, the Commission finds that the effect on innovation is similar to that in price competition:

> *"{...}, the existence of significant adverse unilateral effects in competition is not predicated on the merger strengthening or leading to a dominant position, and it can also hold in a concentrated oligopolistic market {...}."*[318]

The Commission makes clear that even though the merging parties may not have overlaps in existing product markets, there may still be negative externalities if one party is an important innovator on a market where the other party is an existing or potential supplier.[319] Reduced incentives to innovate can lead to lower research efforts as well as lower development efforts for products that have already been discovered.[320] The latter depends also on the level of development and commercialization costs and the amount of sales the new product would capture from sales of the merging party.[321]

The Commission finds that reduced innovation activities by the merging parties may lead to a counter-reaction by other market participants and finally to higher innovation efforts of those players.[322] Nevertheless, this reaction is usually of lower magnitude than the reduction of innovation efforts by the merging parties (at least in a concentrated market).[323] Overall, there will be a lower innovation level.[324]

As an important point, the Commission refers to the economic literature on patent races. A patent race can be defined as "*a competition between two or more investors {...} to discover an invention first in order to obtain patent*

317 Annex 4, para 42; the Commission refers to *Farell/Shapiro*, 10 The B.E. Journal of Theoretical Economics (2010), Article 9, p. 33-34.

318 Annex 4, para 42.

319 Annex 4, para 43.

320 Annex 4, para 44.

321 Annex 4, para 44.

322 Annex 4, para 44.

323 Annex 4, para 45.

324 Annex 4, para 45; the Commission refers to *Whinston*, Comment, p. 409; *Motta/Tarantino*, The Effect of a Merger on Investments, see for example p. 27.

protection for the invention and exclude competitors."[325] As patent race models do not deal with a reduction in the number of independent firms, they are not directly applicable with regard to mergers.[326] Nonetheless, those models are informative with a view to the general interrelation between rivalry and innovation that also has to hold true in case of a merger. The Commission finds that,

> "*{e}conomic models of uncertain patent races indicate that a reduction in the number of firms racing to be the first to patent a new product leads to a delay in the expected arrival date of a new invention.*"[327]

An innovation effort is uncertain if firms are not certain of the commercial value of their discovery at the time of starting innovation efforts.[328] Even though the reduction of competitors may, under certain circumstances, increase the level of innovation investments per firm, the overall innovation rate is slowed down.[329]

Finally, the Commission refers to two papers dealing with deterministic process innovation. The Commission finds that the results of those papers are likely to claim validity in the scope of product innovation as well.[330] The paper of *Lopez* and *Vives* is concerned with structural changes in coordination between undertakings (for example, by reaching a higher level of common ownership or cross shareholding).[331] The paper finds that less intense competition leads to a decline in process innovation, absent spillovers. Furthermore, the authors claim that the effects of reduced innovation competition are not outweighed by possible innovation-enhancing effects from reduced product market competition.[332] The paper of *Motta* and *Tarantino* shows that, in the absence of efficiencies, a merger typically reduces total process innovation while increasing the merged entities' prof-

325 Definition from „The Innovation Policy Platform", www.innovationpolicyplatform.org/content/patent-races.

326 Annex 4, para 47.

327 Annex 4, para 49.

328 Annex 4, para 48.

329 Annex 4, para 49.

330 Annex 4, para 52.

331 Annex 4, para 53; the Commission refers to *Lopez/Vives*, Cross-ownership, R&D Spillovers, and Antitrust Policy.

332 Annex 4, para 53; the Commission refers to *Lopez/Vives*, Cross-ownership, R&D Spillovers, and Antitrust Policy, see especially p. 3-4, 40 et seq.

its.[333] The Commission concludes that, even though the results of the two papers

> *"do not apply directly to uncertain product innovation, overall these papers indicate that the intensity of competition between rival innovators is positively associated with market-wide innovation, absent specific forms of efficiencies."*[334]

(b) Product market competition

Generally, the degree of product market competition may affect the difference between profits earned if innovation takes place and profits earned if innovation does not take place and therefore affect innovation incentives.[335]

The Commission deals with different effects taking place with respect to product market competition potentially influencing innovation incentives. The "escape competition" effect with respect to innovation takes place if *"{b}y innovating, a firm "escapes" the pre-innovation competitive pressure and gets a degree of post-innovation market power and associated profits."*[336] The Commission refers to a paper by *Aghion et al.* that studies the "escape competition" effect with respect to uncertain innovation effort.[337] The paper, according to the Commission, supports *"the proposition that more product market competition (modelled as less product differentiation) leads to more innovation, by enhancing the "escape competition" effect."*[338]

The Commission dismantles the famous inverted-U relationship, which *Aghion et al.*[339] had observed in a paper in 2005. The inverted-U has been

333 Annex 4, para 55; the Commission refers to *Motta/Tarantino*, The Effect of a Merger on Investments., see for example p. 27.

334 Annex 4, para 59.

335 Annex 4, para 61.

336 Annex 4, para 66.

337 Annex 4, para 69; the Commission refers to *Aghion et al.*, 68 Review of Economic Studies (2001), 467.

338 Annex 4, para 70; *Aghion et al.* find that *„{w}ith respect to PMC {Product Market Competition}, we find that at least a little competition is always growth-enhancing. {...} Thus it seems that the usual Schumpeterian effect of more intense competition is almost always outweighed by the increased incentive for firms to innovation in order to escape competition.*", *Aghion et al.*, 68 Review of Economic Studies (2001), 467, 470.

339 *Aghion et al.*, 120 Quarterly Journal of Economics (2005), 701.

referred to in quite some literature on innovation and competition.[340] The result of the paper can be summarized as follows: with increasing intensity of competition, innovation also increases until, from a certain level of intensity of competition onwards, innovation activities start to decrease. The curve describing innovation activities with increasing intensity of competition has the shape of an inverted U. The Commission in its economic assessment shows why that finding of *Aghion et al.* is not suitable for merger assessment.[341] *Aghion et al.* use a model where two firms compete on a product market; a market leader with superior technology and a laggard with inferior technology. Only the laggard can innovate in a way that innovation takes place with one step up to the leader (meaning that after the innovation both companies offer a homogenous product). In that setting, the firms can only earn profits if they collude in the product market. The Commission finds that the model is based on "*specific and not very realistic assumptions on the nature of innovation {…}.*"[342] First of all, the fact that only the laggard can innovate and only one step up to the leader (not leapfrogging the leader) seems unrealistic.[343] Further, since the laggard after the innovation effort only offers the same product as the leader, there is not really a product innovation in the sense of a new or improved product.[344] Finally, the model is not fit for the assessment of mergers between innovators, "*as it only allows for a consideration of the changes in the degree of collusion between firms in the product market (but*

340 Cf. for example Director General for Competition *Italianer*, Level-playing field and innovation in technology markets, page 4 Fn. 2; *Federico*, Horizontal Mergers, Innovation and the Competitive Process, p. 13; *Federico/Scott Morton/Shapiro*, Antitrust and Innovation, p. 10; FCO, Innovationen – Herausforderungen für die Kartellrechtspraxis, p. 11: „*This suggests that at least in already concentrated markets, there is a positive correlation between existing competitive intensity and innovation incentives.*" (authors translation of the German text: „Dies spricht dafür, dass jedenfalls in bereits konzentrierten Märkten ein positiver Zusammenhang zwischen bestehender Wettbewerbsintensität und Innovationsanreizen vorliegt."); Monopolkommission, XXII. Hauptgutachten, para 716.

341 Cf. conclusion in Annex 4, para 74.

342 Annex 4, para 73.

343 Annex 4, para 73.

344 Annex 4, para 73.

not in innovation)."[345] In a different model by *Aghion et al.*[346] with both firms being able to innovate and innovation taking place step-by-step, the inverted U-shape does not appear.[347]

The Commission closes its assessment of the interrelation between competition in product markets and innovation citing the inventors of the Innovation Market Analysis, *Gilbert* and *Sunshine*:

> "*Individual circumstances weigh heavily on the likely relation between industry structure an R&D. There is nonetheless broad support for the Areeda and Turner admonishment that "{N}either theory nor evidence suggests that substantial market power is so generally conducive to technological progress that toleration or encouragement would be desirable", and there is additional evidence to support the stronger conclusion that protection from competition is inimical to technological progress.*"[348]

(c) Efficiencies: Focus on Appropriability

Appropriability is, according to the Commission, defined as "*the ability by an innovator to prevent rivals (including generic suppliers) from imitating successful innovation and/or the ability to monetize inventions through licensing.*"[349] A merger may lead to greater appropriability by eliminating a potential imitator or, absent licensing opportunities (or in case of limited licensing opportunities), by enabling the application of process innovations over a larger scale.[350] The Commission finds that, "*{i}ncreased appropriability is a possible merger efficiency which may at least partially offset the reduction in innovation incentives due to the elimination of innovation competition between the merging parties.*"[351]

---

345 Annex 4, para 73; *Shapiro* points out that "*{m}eaningful product innovation involves the development of new products that are superior to, or at least significantly distinct from, existing products. {…} These static models of oligopoly do not involve anything I recognize or credit as innovation.*", *Shapiro*, Competition and innovation, p. 371.

346 *Aghion et al.*, 68 Review of Economic Studies (2001), 467, 470.

347 Annex 4, para 73.

348 Annex 4, para 89, citing *Gilbert/Sunshine*, 63 Antitrust Law Journal (1995), 569, 581.

349 Annex 4, para 19.

350 Cf. Annex 4, para 9, 19.

351 Annex 4, para 91.

The Commission identifies two factors that show that there is already a high level of appropriability on a market: First, there are already limited spillovers or imitation from innovation; and second, innovation takes place largely in the form of product rather than process innovation.[352] The Commission refers to economic literature suggesting that concentration may imply a lower risk of imitation and thus increase innovation incentives unless there are already effective IPRs.[353] IPRs in that sense include patent rights but also other exclusive rights (for example, supplementary data protection certificates) and strategies to protect off-patent innovation against imitation (for example, introduction of mixtures of patent and off-patent products).[354]

The Commission finds that *"{i}n case of process innovation, the literature has posited that a reduction in product market competition may result in greater sales by an innovator and may therefore enhance the incentives to engage in process innovation."*[355] This is especially the case if there are imperfect licensing opportunities. In case licensing opportunities are limited, a merger can lead to the application of a process innovation over a greater scale provided that the innovation can technically be applied to the other merging parties' products.[356] The Commission explicitly mentions that these findings do not hold for product innovation.[357] This is partly because intellectual property protection is generally stronger for product innovation than for process innovation, and therefore imperfect licensing issues are typically connected with process innovations.[358] The Commission concludes: *"in general a reduction of competition is more likely to reduce product innovation under conditions of high appropriability."*[359]

---

352 Annex 4, para 92.

353 Annex 4, para 94; the Commission refers, *inter alia*, to *Gilbert*, Competition and innovation.

354 Annex 4, para 95, 96.

355 Annex 4, para 98; the Commission refers to *Gilbert*, Competition and innovation.

356 Annex 4, para 99; the Commission refers to *Gilbert/Greene*, 83 The George Washington Law Review (2015), 1919, 1938-1939.

357 Annex 4, para 101.

358 Cf. Annex 4, para 101; the Commission refers, *inter alia*, to *Gilbert*, Competition and innovation.

359 Annex 4, para 104; the Commission refers, *inter alia*, to *Gilbert*, Competition and innovation, p. 23: *„Although empirical evidence on the relationship of competition and innovation is mixed, several careful studies suggest that competition promotes innovation if inventors gain exclusive rights to their inventions."*; *Gilbert/Greene*, 83 The George Washington Law Review (2015), 1919, 1926: *„In contrast, if firms*

The Commission also mentions two more possible efficiencies that relate to product complementarities and cost synergies. "*{M}ore efficient coordination of pricing of complementary products post-merger may lead to stronger innovation incentives by increasing the profits that can be captured by innovators.*"[360] Furthermore, economies of scale or scope may in principle reduce R&D cost and in this way at least partially compensate for the loss of innovation competition due to the merger.[361] In any case, the Commission finds that the parties to the merger bear the burden of proof for efficiencies.[362]

(d) Dynamic market features

Finally, the Commission points to the dynamic setting in which the merger takes place. The market players in the crop protection industry continuously innovate and

> "*an innovative chemical that is in the initial stages of its development now will in the future be diverting sales from related chemicals that may be further advanced in the development pipeline but have not yet been commercialized.*"[363]

For that reason, other factors – such as regulatory pressure, biological resistance or generics – are supposed have limited impact on innovation and product market competition:

> "*{I}n a dynamic setting competing firms would be selling chemicals targeting same pests that have not had been rendered obsolete by biological resistance or regulation by the time any innovative chemical is ready for commercialization.*"[364]

The dynamic market features may not be confused with a possible dynamic approach. As argued above, the competitive harm occurs at the time of the implementation of the transaction due to reduced competitive inno-

---

can appropriate the benefits from their innovations, Arrow's conclusion applies, as profits from existing operations reduce the net returns to innovation and the incentive to invest in R&D."

360 Annex 4, para 107.
361 Annex 4, para 108.
362 Annex 4, para 109.
363 Annex 4, para 171.
364 Annex 4, para 171.

vation pressure, immediately resulting in reduced innovation incentives. Therefore, it is not necessary to assess the dynamic effects of a merger. That does not mean, however, that the Commission cannot take into account dynamic aspects when assessing the market features and possible factors outweighing the loss of (static) competitive pressure on innovation.

2) The Federico / Langus / Valletti papers

Shortly after the completion of the *Dow/DuPont* merger review in March 2017, three members of the Commission's Chief Economist Team published two papers on the interrelation between market concentration and innovation.[365] It is not clear to what extent the Commission relied on the findings expressed in those papers in its assessment of the *Dow/DuPont* merger. However, it seems likely that the Commission's case handlers deciding on *Dow/DuPont* were at least informed about the findings of their economist colleagues.[366]

In their paper from February 2018, *Federico*, *Langus* and *Valletti* examine the effect of horizontal mergers on product innovation.[367] They set up an oligopoly model to analyze a merger's impact "*on innovation incentives and on consumer surplus.*"[368] The authors identify two possible effects of a merger on innovation: the price coordination effect and the internalization of an "*innovation externality*".[369] While price coordination may have positive as well as negative effects on innovation incentives, the internalization of the innovation externality depresses innovation incentives.[370] The authors conclude that

> "*the latter effect is stronger in our simulations and, as a result, the merger leads to lower innovation incentives for the merged entity, absent cost effi-*

---

365 *Federico/Langus/Valletti*, A Simple Model of Mergers and Innovation, June 2017; *Federico/Langus/Valletti*, Horizontal Mergers and Product Innovation, February 2018.

366 The papers were not published at the time of the Dow/DuPont Decision, but the Chief Economist Team (CET) routinely is involved in the 2nd phase assessment of mergers, and therefore is likely to have expressed its view on the respective case, see *Amelio et al.*, 53 Review of industrial Organization (2018), 653, 657.

367 *Federico/Langus/Valletti*, Horizontal Mergers and Product Innovation.

368 *Federico/Langus/Valletti*, Horizontal Mergers and Product Innovation, p. 1.

369 *Federico/Langus/Valletti*, Horizontal Mergers and Product Innovation, p. 1, 14.

370 *Federico/Langus/Valletti*, Horizontal Mergers and Product Innovation, p. 1.

ciencies and knowledge spillovers. In our numerical analysis both overall innovation and consumer welfare fall after a merger."[371]

Considering factors that determine the strength of the abovementioned effects, the paper finds:

"*Similar to the standard unilateral price effect, the internalization of the innovation externality and the associated loss of innovation competition are more likely to be significant when (1) the merger brings together two out of a limited number of significant innovators and (2) the merging firms, absent the merger, would have been likely to divert to a significant extent future sales from each other when introducing innovative products.*"[372]

The latter refers to the closeness of the merging parties with respect to innovation as well as product competition. Even though non-merging firms may increase their innovation efforts post-merger, this increase does not compensate for the loss of innovation competition between the merging parties.[373]

With respect to possible countervailing efficiencies, the authors find:

"*We also consider innovation-related efficiencies that a merger may release, including reductions in R&D costs and merger-specific enhancements in the effectiveness of innovation. {…} Both the results on innovation incentives and on consumer welfare can be overturned if there are sufficiently large R&D efficiencies.*"[374]

Possible efficiencies may be the increase of appropriability ("*internalizing positive knowledge spillovers between the merging parties*"), the combination of complementary R&D assets or the increase in R&D productivity through cost efficiencies.[375]

The paper also looks at the likelihood of innovations being developed pre- and post-merger. The authors use the concept of stochastic dominance[376] and conclude that "*before the merger the probability that at least*

371 *Federico/Langus/Valletti*, Horizontal Mergers and Product Innovation, p. 1.
372 *Federico/Langus/Valletti*, Horizontal Mergers and Product Innovation, p. 2.
373 Federico/Langus/Valletti, Horizontal Mergers and Product Innovation, p. 2.
374 *Federico/Langus/Valletti*, Horizontal Mergers and Product Innovation, p. 2.
375 *Federico/Langus/Valletti*, Horizontal Mergers and Product Innovation, p. 14.
376 „*A probability distribution over possible outcomes first-order stochastically dominates another such distribution if for each number of successful innovations {…} the former has at least as high probability of at least as many innovations.*“, *Federico/Langus/Valletti*, Horizontal Mergers and Product Innovation, p. 10.

t[377] *innovations will successfully arrive to the market is higher than after the merger.*"[378]

Before publishing the abovementioned paper, *Federico*, *Langus* and *Valletti* already issued a simpler approach in June 2017.[379] With respect to the date of publication, the underlying models must have been developed in the scope of the *Dow/DuPont* assessment.[380] The authors summarize their findings:

> "*We analyze the impact of a merger on firms' incentives to innovate. We show that the merging parties always decrease their innovation efforts post-merger while outsiders to the merger respond by increasing their effort. A merger tends to reduce overall innovation. Consumers are always words off after a merger. Our model calls into question the applicability of the "inverted-U" relationship between innovation and competition to a merger setting.*"[381]

The paper anticipates most of the findings of the 2018 paper using a highly stylized model.[382] It further concludes that

> "*a merger harms consumers welfare even when, {…}, it has no effect on innovation effort. If owned independently, whenever the two labs are successful in discovery, they produce competing products – this is not the case after the merger as firm M will fully internalize its pricing decisions in product market competition. We stress that, after a merger, there is always a discontinuous change in the probability of bad states for consumers because of this effect.*"[383]

3) Intermediate result

Annex 4 of the Dow/DuPont Decision offers an explanation for the Commission's legal assessment. The Commission puts forward economic models supporting its theory of harm and deals with possible models or

377 Number of successful innovations.
378 *Federico/Langus/Valletti*, Horizontal Mergers and Product Innovation, p. 10.
379 *Federico/Langus/Valletti*, A Simple Model of Mergers and Innovation.
380 The Dow/DuPont Decision has been published in March 2017.
381 *Federico/Langus/Valletti*, A Simple Model of Mergers and Innovation, p. 1.
382 The authors assume that without innovation firms do not make any profits and there are no efficiencies taken into account.
383 *Federico/Langus/Valletti*, A Simple Model of Mergers and Innovation, p. 7-8.

findings opposing its approach. All in all, the Annex seems reasonably founded and addresses the parties' claims.

In addition, both of the *Federico / Langus / Valletti* papers support the Commission's findings in *Dow/DuPont*. They claim that a horizontal merger between two out of a limited number of innovators reduces innovation incentives when appropriability is high and there are no merger-specific efficiencies.

One of the papers[384] also concludes that the probability of innovations reaching the market is higher pre-merger than post-merger. First of all, it is not entirely clear how the authors come to that conclusion. They state: "*In all our reported simulations we assume that innovation effort translates into a probability of innovation according to the following function {....}*"[385] However, there is no explanation how to reach that function. In fact, it seems unlikely that there can be an established link between innovation effort and its success aside from empirical studies. Even the assumption under stochastic dominance that if four firms innovate there may be four innovations whereas when three firms innovate there may be even three is incorrect. An innovation effort can result in more than one innovation. It may well be that two firms engage in research and development, resulting in four innovative products (there may be several applications for one innovation or there may be two or three different research results all being useful)[386] but four firms innovate without any success at all.

But most importantly, the authors' conclusion at this point does not have anything to do with market concentration and therefore competition policy. This is also true for the finding in the other paper[387] where the authors state that the merger always has a negative effect on consumers even if it has no effects on innovation efforts. In both cases, there is the assumption that mergers always have negative effects on innovation, future competition and therefore consumers. But this does not take into account the competitive conditions in specific industries.

The authors' finding that there is a higher probability of innovations successfully reaching the market (resulting in increased future competition) if there are more firms performing R&D can be associated with

384 *Federico/Langus/Valletti*, Horizontal Mergers and Product Innovation.

385 *Federico/Langus/Valletti*, Horizontal Mergers and Product Innovation, p. 9.

386 With respect to the crop protection industry, *Cary* finds: „*Candidate AIs for one initial use are often found to be better at a different use; and many AIs work across multiple „innovation spaces"*." *Cary*, Festschrift für Dirk Schroeder, p. 194.

387 *Federico/Langus/Valletti*, A Simple Model of Mergers and Innovation.

the concept of the "resource-based view of the firm", a concept used in management literature.[388] It is based on the assumption that the more heterogeneous the staff, experience, patents or business culture of the different firms, the more likely it is that innovation activities of at least one of the firms will be successful. The original thought behind this finding can be traced back to F.A. Hayek.[389] Hayek found:

> *"The peculiar character of the problem of a rational economic order is determined precisely by the fact that the knowledge of the circumstances of which we must make use never exists in concentrated or integrated form, but solely as the dispersed bits of incomplete and frequently contradictory knowledge which all the separate individuals possess."*[390]

As a result of this incomplete knowledge, it can never be foreseen which processes and practices lead to a successful outcome.[391] Accordingly, heterogeneity of approaches seems to bear the highest probability of success. However, this so-called concept of evolutionary economics[392] does not have reference to market conditions.

Imagine the following example: In an industry, there are six innovation players, one with a market share of 30 %, one with a market share of 25 %, one with a market share of 20 %, one with a market share of 15 % and two with a market share of 5 %. If the 15 % player decided to merge with one of the 5 % firms, this would at first sight be positive for competition, because the merger would create a credible competitor in the market (assuming that it is easier for an undertaking to exert competitive pressure with 20 % market share than it is with 15 % market share). In that setting, however, one credible innovator would be removed. The same would even be true for a merger of the two 5 % firms. In fact, as a final consequence, every merger in innovation sensitive industries would remove an independent source of innovation and therefore, in the opinion of the authors of the two papers, harm consumer welfare. But even though it is the Commission's mandate to protect innovation incentives, it is also necessary for

388 *Kern*, Innovation Markets, Future Markets, or Potential Competition, p. 29; *Barney*, 17 Journal of Management (1991), 99; *Montgomery*, Resource-Based and Evolutionary Theories of the Firm.

389 *Kern*, Innovation Markets, Future Markets, or Potential Competition, p. 28.

390 *Hayek*, The Use of Knowledge in Society, 35 The American Economic Review (1945), 519.

391 *Kern*, Innovation Markets, Future Markets, or Potential Competition, p. 28.

392 See *Kern*, Innovation Markets, Future Markets, or Potential Competition, p. 28.

the functioning of the internal market to protect competition, including the possibility for firm transactions creating credible competitive forces.

Considering the abovementioned example, it is furthermore remarkable that there is no weighing of rivalry aspects versus heterogeneity aspects in the two papers. In case the 15 % and 5 % transaction would happen, the merged entity would exert higher competitive pressure, also with respect to innovation competition, on the other market participants. The merger would therefore increase innovation incentives of the other players. Those players would have to fear cannibalization of their own products from the merged entity that now has a greater market (and innovation) power. Even though there may in fact be the loss of an independent source of innovation, it is by no means clear which of the two effects prevails. The two papers, as well as Annex 4 of the Dow/DuPont Decision,[393] do not cover that aspect.

In contrast, even though the models on patent races referred to in Annex 4[394] also rely on a reduction in the number of market players, this reduction results in an increase or decrease of R&D investment per firm. In that setting the higher innovation investment of remaining firms does not compensate for the loss of an independent firm resulting in a decrease of innovation. This is because the possible increase in innovation investment is due to higher incremental returns from innovation, which is associated with an overall reduction in innovation (because otherwise the returns per innovation would remain the same).[395] Consequently, the models on patent races draw a line between the number of market players, intensity of competition and the innovation rate.

It is important to note that even though the economic background points towards some kind of general interrelation between innovation incentives and market concentration, the Commission does not draw such a general causal link in its legal assessment. The Commission's approach is based on an oligopolistic market setting with high barriers to entry and high appropriability. Only in that setting does the economic foundation seem reasonably assured to use as a basis for remedies.[396]

---

393 Annex 4, para 39 refers to economic literature on R&D diversity.

394 Annex 4, para 46-50.

395 Cf. Annex 4, para 49, fn. 27.

396 See for the difference between economic and legal proof *Section II) H) 1) (a)*.

E) Remedies: Divestment of R&D organization

The *Dow/DuPont* merger was finally cleared subject to conditions. With respect to the Commission's concerns on innovation competition, DuPont had to divest almost its entire global R&D organization to a single purchaser. The divestment included nearly all pipeline products, the global technology organization and the regional development organization with personnel, assets, IP and facilities.[397]

Remedies are based on Article 8 (2) EC Merger Regulation, which is concretized by the Remedies Notice[398]. According to Article 8 (2) EC Merger Regulation, the Commission may attach to its decision conditions and obligations intended to ensure that the undertakings concerned comply with the commitments they have entered into vis-à-vis the Commission with a view to rendering the concentration compatible with the common market. In *Dow/DuPont*, the Commission applies the Remedies Notice without further adjustment to innovation competition.[399] The Commission explains:

> "*Where a proposed concentration threatens to significantly impede effective competition, the most effective way to maintain effective competition, apart form prohibition of the concentration, is to create conditions for the emergence of a new competitive entity or for the strengthening of existing competitors via divestitures by the merging parties.*"[400]

It is especially important for the Commission that the R&D division is divested together with parts of the downstream product market business. Since it is characteristic for the competitive interaction between the merg

397 Case M.7932 – Dow/DuPont, Annex 7 to the Commission Decision, Commitments to the European Commission (hereinafter "Annex 7"), para 13; para 2 of Annex 7 reads: "*DuPont commits to divest a Divestment Business consisting of {…} DuPont's R&D organisation, consisting of all tangible and intangible assets, including but not limited to pipeline, IP rights, personnel, facilities used by DuPont worldwide for its R&D activities {…}.*"

398 Commission's Notice on Remedies acceptable under Council Regulation (EC) No 139/2004 and under Commission Regulation (EC) No 802/2004, OJ C 267, 22.10.2008, p. 1-27 (hereinafter „**Remedies Notice**").

399 In para 3902 et seq. of the Dow/DuPont Decision, the Commission lays down general principles for the assessment of remedies without even mentioning innovation concerns.

400 Dow/DuPont Decision, para 3907, referring to Remedies Notice, para 22.

ing parties that the downstream product portfolio is constantly maintained and renewed, it is important for a purchaser to be able to perform R&D.[401]

Furthermore, competition concerns may only be dispelled if all divested assets including the R&D organization are transferred to one existing integrated player rather than combining assets from different firms and creating a business that is not yet operating on a market.[402] In this way, "*the complementarities between the R&D and lines of research and downstream product portfolios are preserved.*"[403]

Also, the divested business has to have a robust financial performance (especially with respect to the divested product segments), ensuring the purchaser's capability to finance research.[404]

The Commission establishes certain criteria the purchaser will have to fulfill in order to eliminate competition concerns. The purchaser shall be independent; have financial resources, expertise and incentive to maintain and develop the divested business; the divestment to the purchaser may not create any competition concerns and, most importantly, the purchaser "*shall be a company already active in the crop protection industry, {…}.*"[405]

Part of DuPont's crop protection business was finally divested to FMC.[406] FMC was considered in the innovation competition assessment of the *Dow/DuPont* merger as not being vertically integrated.[407] At the time of the transaction, the Commission found that FMC was not active in the discovery of new active ingredients.[408] The company mainly performed the development of molecules in the crop protection sector.[409]

---

401 Dow/DuPont Decision, para 4030.

402 Dow/DuPont Decision, para 4031; 4041.

403 Dow/DuPont Decision, para 4031.

404 Dow/DuPont Decision, para 4040.

405 Annex 7, para 24.

406 European Commission, Decision of 27 July 2017, C(2017) 5441 final, OJ C 327, 7.9.2018, p. 2, Case M.8435, *FMC/DuPont Divestment Business*; the Decision included commitments offered by FMC to address concerns with respect to certain products to control broadleaf weeds.

407 Dow/DuPont Decision, para 2243 et seq, 2258.

408 Dow/DuPont Decision, para 2246; European Commission, Decision of 27 July 2017, C(2017) 5441 final, OJ C 327, 7.9.2018, p. 2, Case M.8435, para 21, *FMC/DuPont Divestment Business*.

409 Dow/DuPont Decision, para 2248, 2249, 2257.

F) What is new in Dow/DuPont?

There has been a debate on whether there is a "novel" theory of harm in *Dow/DuPont*. The Commission itself claims that it used traditional analysis tools that were not novel but rather already used in other cases and also based on "*well-established and sound law and economics.*"[410] Most commentators,[411] however, found that the Commission had established a new theory of harm based on a novel underlying rationale. In a way, both opinions claim validity. On the one hand, innovation and its interrelation with competition have been addressed in numerous Commission decisions since the 1990s.[412] Furthermore, there has been the concept of an "Innovation Market Analysis" in the United States that also incorporated innovation concerns beyond specific and identifiable product markets.[413] However, there has not been an assessment of the interrelation of market structure and incentives to innovate on such a broad basis as in *Dow/DuPont* and with a theoretical underlying rationale that a merger of two important innovators in an oligopolistic market with high appropriability will diminish innovation incentives. Most decisions before *Dow/DuPont* rather referred to identifiable product markets, observable research and development activities or at least one very narrowly defined "innovation space" with activities towards specific products. The conclusion in *Dow/DuPont*, namely that a reduction in market players would reduce innovation incentives in the whole industry, has never been spelled out in detail before.

1) Preceding Innovation Cases

There have been several cases in which the Commission assessed innovation competition in merger control on the basis of competing R&D activities. In the following, Commission decisions incorporating the idea of

410 European Commission, Competition Merger Brief, Article 1, Issue 2/2017- July, p. 8, available at: *ec.europa.eu/competition/publications/cmb/2017/kdal17002enn.pdf*.

411 See for example, *Todino/van de Walle/Stoican*, 64 The Antitrust Bulletin (2019), 11; *Petit*, Innovation Competition, p. 23-24.

412 See for an overview: *Glader*, Innovation Markets and Competition Analysis, p. 90 et seq and in particular p. 150 et seq; *Petit*, Innovation Competition, p. 7; *Jung/Sinclair*, 40 E.C.L.R. (2019) 266, 267.

413 See *Section II) F) 2)*.

competitive pressure as a means to put forward research and development will be summarized. Decisions with respect to potential competition[414] or specific research programs are not included, as they are based on a different reasoning. The cases are reported in chronologic order.

(a) Cases incorporating innovation competition aspects

Glaxo/Wellcome:[415] Starting with the *Glaxo/Wellcome* merger in 1995, the Commission analyzed overlapping R&D activities. The Commission found:

> "*In the pharmaceutical sector, in order to be complete a competition assessment will require scrutiny of products which are not yet on the market but which are at an advanced stage of development (normally after a very considerable investment of resources of time and money). The potential of such products to compete with other products, either in development or already on the market, can only be assessed by reference to their characteristics and intended use. In some areas, any such attempt at product market definition may be problematical (in the HIV/Aids area, for example).*"[416]

With respect to the geographical dimension, the Commission also identified specific circumstances for research and development:

> "*If from a pricing point of view markets in the EU remain essentially national, the situation is different with respect to R&D. From the point of view of medical Research and Development of new medicines, pharmaceutical firms compete on a wider basis and generally have world-wide R&D strategies. For the above reasons the impact of this concentration has to be assessed in relation to national markets and, in the area of R&D, to European Union or even World-wide markets.*"[417]

---

414 An undertaking may be considered a potential competitor if its market entry is timely, likely and sufficient, Horizontal Merger Guidelines, para 58 et seq, 68, Priority Guidance (fn. 793), para 16 et seq; a potential competitor does, thus, exert competitive pressure with respect to an existing product market and not with respect to the innovation process itself; for the concept of potential competition see also *Section II) G) 1)*.

415 European Commission, Decision of 28.02.1995, OJ C 65, 16.03.1995, p. 3, Case No IV/M.555, *Glaxo/Wellcome* (hereinafter: "Glaxo/Wellcome Decision").

416 Glaxo/Wellcome Decision, para 9.

417 Glaxo/Wellcome Decision, para 17, 18.

The Decision already featured the combination of R&D assets and of R&D overlaps with respect to the specific treatment of HIV/AIDS:

> *"The proposed concentration will combine the R&D resources and expertise of two leading firms in this area. Nevertheless, in the absence of a definitive treatment for HIV/AIDS, the combination Glaxo/Wellcome is not likely to inhibit to a significant extent the research for effective compounds for the treatment of HIV infections, being undertaken by other pharmaceutical companies. There are no other fields of overlap in R&D raising competition concerns."*[418]

The Decision mentioned R&D overlaps as a separate criterion in merger assessment. However, in this case, the Commission's concerns were directed towards a specific treatment and observable research activities.

Glaxo Wellcome/SmithKline Beecham:[419] In this Decision, the Commission mentioned a possible impact on R&D markets – without, however, further clarifying its concern. The Decision reads:

> *"While it is indeed true that the operation does not lead to any addition of market share, the correct assessment of the case needs to take into account SB's pipeline products in the respiratory tract. More particularly, it needs to be assessed what the impact of the transaction on existing markets and on R&D markets is."*[420]

Furthermore, the Commission analyzed a possible reduction of the general potential to conduct R&D:

> *"Therefore, while the market investigation has confirmed the parties' submission that SB's new compound is likely to be classified in a new ATC 3 category and no direct horizontal overlap occurs, it needs to be assessed whether SB's compound is likely to affect the overall market position of the new entity in the respiratory field and whether the overall R&D potential is likely to be reduced."*[421]

---

418 Glaxo/Wellcome Decision, para 33.

419 European Commission, Decision of 08.05.2000, Case No COMP/M.1846, *Glaxo Wellcome/SmithKline Beecham* (hereinafter: "Glaxo Wellcome/SK Beecham Decision").

420 Glaxo Wellcome/SK Beecham Decision, para 174.

421 Glaxo Wellcome/SK Beecham Decision, para 179.

However, the Commission moves on:

> *"Given the attractiveness of the market and the fact that GW and SB pursue different lines of research and development in COPD, the Commission considers that the operation is unlikely to lead to an elimination of the existing R&D currently being conducted by the merging parties. While it is feasible to believe that the parties will streamline their R&D efforts in the future, given the large number of current pipeline products and resourceful competitors on the market, the Commission does not consider that this would lead to the diminution of the overall R&D potential either."*[422]

Even though the Commission uses the terms "R&D markets" and "R&D potential", it becomes clear from the context of the decision that it is about R&D with respect to the specific COPD market. This is underlined in the Commission's case introduction, where it states:

> *"The Commission has to look at R&D potential in terms of its importance for existing markets, but also for future market situations."*[423]

AstraZeneca/Novartis:[424] In that merger, the Commission set up a first frame for the assessment of a concentration and its potential to decrease innovation incentives by eliminating competitive pressure. However, it is still about existing and immediate pipeline products and about defined product markets. The Commission finds:

> *"Without the merger, competition would have developed between the three companies on the basis of their innovative products. As a consequence of the merger, one of these innovators is removed from the market which may reduce the incentives to further innovate. In any event, the merger will bring together two out of only three strobilurin producers and will reduce the competition that would otherwise have developed with the existing and immediate pipeline products."*[425]

---

422 Glaxo Wellcome/SK Beecham Decision, para 188.

423 Glaxo Wellcome/SK Beecham Decision, para 71.

424 European Commission, Decision of 26.07.2000, OJ L 110, 16.04.2004, p. 1-72, Case No COMP/M.1806, *AstraZeneca/Novartis* (hereinafter: "AstraZeneca/Novartis Decision").

425 AstraZeneca/Novartis Decision, para 219.

Bayer/Aventis Crop Science:[426] The Commission takes into account R&D capabilities and incentives with respect to certain current and future product markets as well as R&D competition and the overall R&D potential:

> *"In the past the Commission has often seen reasons for concern in the grouping of companies with strengths in R&D and innovation. For the purpose of the present decision, the Commission considers that the parties R&D capabilities and incentives have to be taken into account as regards the potential elimination of future competition in current product markets and future markets. Moreover, where appropriate, the Commission considers it may be necessary to concentrate on the effects of the concentration on R&D competition between the parties and in the overall R&D potential."*[427]

The merger is particularly interesting because it also took place in the crop protection industry at a point in time when there were already tendencies towards a market concentration.[428] Even though the Commission already focuses on R&D competition,[429] it assesses R&D as a measure directly affecting the market position on a defined market.[430]

Syngenta/Monsanto's Sunflower Seed Business:[431] The competitive constraint on other innovators was also part of this decision. The Commission found:

> *"The transaction is therefore likely to have a negative impact on innovation by eliminating the competitive constraint that the breeding programme and the germplasm of Monsanto exerted on Syngenta and on other competitors to regularly bring new improved varieties into the market."*[432]

The Commission even noted that Monsanto was a strong innovator, but again concluded that this would lead to a strengthening of its position on existing markets:

---

426 European Commission, Decision of 17.04.2002, C(2002) 1462 final, OJ L 107, 15.04.2004, p. 1-136, Case No COMP/M.2547, *Bayer/Aventis Crop Science* (hereinafter: "Bayer/Aventis Decision").

427 Bayer/Aventis Decision, para 18.

428 Bayer/Aventis Decision, para 12.

429 Bayer/Aventis Decision, para 148 et seq.

430 Bayer/Aventis Decision, paras 257, 304, 805, 1036 et seq.

431 European Commission, Decision of 17.11.2010, C(2010) 7929 final, Case No COMP/M.5675, *Syngenta/Monsanto's Sunflower Seed Business* (hereinafter: "Syngenta/Monsanto Decision").

432 Syngenta/Monsanto Decision, para 321.

"Given that the sunflower seed industry is particularly R&D oriented, analysing the Target Business' position and potential was one of the main focuses of the market investigation. As will be outlined below, the investigation revealed that the Target Business was a particularly strong innovator and thus had a strong potential to enhance its market presence."[433]

Deutsche Börse/NYSE Euronext:[434] This case is the one that comes closest to *Dow/DuPont*. The term "innovation space" was first mentioned here (however, without any further definition or explanation and in a different context)[435] and the innovation concerns were directed to areas broader than a specific product market. With respect to "competition to introduce new products in the area of European interest rate derivatives"[436] the Commission finds:

"In this context, it should be noted that this type of competition occurs in a broader space encompassing all European interest rate derivatives and therefore the question of whether the market should be further subdivided into STIR and LTIR derivatives is not relevant since it does not change the analysis."[437]

Even though the Commission looks at broader spaces, there is still a clear link to downstream markets.

Nevertheless, the Commission clearly distinguishes between the concept of potential competition[438] and of innovation competition:

"In conclusion, the Notifying Parties compete in product innovation in European interest rate derivatives, both by designing new products adjacent to their existing offerings and by upgrading these offerings in order to stay ahead of potential competition. In this regard, they are each other's closest competitor for the same reasons as this was concluded in respect of potential competition in the preceding Section, since success in new product innova-

433 Syngenta/Monsanto Decision, para 292; see also Syngenta/Monsanto Decision, para 246 et seq.

434 European Commission, Decision of 01.02.2012, C(2012) 440 final, OJ C 254, 05.08.2014, p. 8-18, Case No COMP/M.6166, *Deutsche Börse/NYSE Euronext* (hereinafter: "Deutsche Börse/NYSE Euronext Decision").

435 *„Within the European innovation space for equity indices thus defined, the Notifying Parties would have all the same advantages, and competitors suffer from all the same barriers to entry, as apply in European interest rates and European single stock derivatives."* Deutsche Börse/NYSE Euronext Decision, para 923.

436 Deutsche Börse/NYSE Euronext Decision, Section 11.2.1.4.4.

437 Deutsche Börse/NYSE Euronext Decision, para 802.

438 For the concept of potential competition see *Section II) G) 1)*.

tion in this space depends on exactly the same factors as those allowing an exchange to act as a potential competitor. This competition would be lost as a result of the notified transaction."[439]

Still, the Commission mainly uses the concepts of actual and potential competition to conclude that the transaction is likely to have an impact on innovation. Innovation competition is not assessed as a stand-alone factor:

"*The Commission therefore concludes that the notified transaction, by eliminating actual and potential competition between the Notifying Parties in European interest rate derivatives, equity derivatives and equity index derivatives, lessens the incentive which the merged entity would have to innovate in technology, process and market design in order to respond to these same competitive threats, and would result overall in less innovation being available to customers in those markets.*"[440]

According to the Commission, there would be

"*lower innovation in technology solutions, fewer new services, and less innovation in market design in respect of services for trading, registering and clearing European interest rate and equity derivatives.*"[441]

The Commission also incorporates the merger's impact on innovation activities of third parties:

"*Indeed, in this regard it should be noted that not only competition in innovation by the Notifying Parties would be adversely affected by the merger, but also that third parties (both index providers such as Russell and exchanges such as Chi-X Europe) might no longer have the means or incentive to innovate in this area post-merger, as they would face insurmountable barriers to entry given the combined margin pool of the merged entity and considering that the Notifying Parties would very likely be in a position to counter innovations from third parties with innovations of their own.*"[442]

Altogether, the *Deutsche Börse/NYSE Euronext* decision is the first decision in which the Commission relies on harm to innovation competition as an important parameter beyond specific defined product markets. It is even foreshadowed that there may be a reduction in innovation competition in the whole industry with respect to third parties –without, however,

439 Deutsche Börse/NYSE Euronext Decision, para 809.
440 Deutsche Börse/NYSE Euronext Decision, para 640.
441 Deutsche Börse/NYSE Euronext Decision, para 635.
442 Deutsche Börse/NYSE Euronext Decision, para 919.

further explaining that concern. Notably, the Commission's arguments are still directed towards specific market segments and incorporated in the assessment of actual and potential competition (rather being a means to determine competition on a downstream product market) and not a stand-alone criterion of merger control. Furthermore, there is no explanation of any underlying rationale that could justify the Commission's finding. In addition, the innovation concerns seem not to have been decisive for the Commission's final outcome.[443]

The Deutsche Börse/NYSE Euronext Decision has been confirmed by the General Court.[444]It should be noted, however, that the Court did not explicitly confirm the Commission's innovation theory, but rather rejected the claims of the parties on the basis of the specific way in which the Commission raised its concerns. The parties put forward two claims. In the first claim they argued that "*the Commission's conclusion that the competition between the parties to the concentration is the only driver of new product development is manifestly incorrect.*"[445] The General Court basically found that the Commission had not concluded that competition between the parties was the only driver of competition but took into account other factors as well.[446]

The parties further claimed that

> "*the Commission's conclusion that the concentration would eliminate any technological competition and would give rise to a reduction in the innovation available for consumers is manifestly incorrect and unsubstantiated.*"[447]

Here, the General Court also pointed to the specific finding of the Commission and concluded that the Commission had not set up the assumption that the concentration would eliminate any technological competition[448] and that the Commission had assessed the specific "*level of reduction in the area of innovation*".[449]

443 The concentration was declared to be incompatible with the internal market. Innovation concerns were not part of the Commission's conclusion.

444 General Court, Judgment of 09.03.2015, Case T-175/12, ECLI:EU:T:2015:148, *Deutsche Börse/Commission* (hereinafter: "GC, Deutsche Börse").

445 GC, Deutsche Börse, para 157.

446 GC, Deutsche Börse, para 162 et seq.

447 GC, Deutsche Börse, para 171.

448 GC, Deutsche Börse, para 172 et seq.

449 GC, Deutsche Börse, para 178.

In conclusion, the General Court did not assess the underlying rationale of the Commission's decision in *Deutsche Börse/NYSE Euronext* but basically rejected the parties' claims on the basis of formal grounds.

Novartis/Glaxo Smith Kline's Oncology Business:[450] In this decision, the Commission raised cannibalization concerns, and in a footnote referred to the application of the unilateral effects framework to innovation. However, the whole assessment was done with respect to observable "*competing clinical research programs*"[451] The Commission noted that in the pharmaceutical industry, it would typically be possible to identify those competing clinical research programs at an early stage.[452] The decision, accordingly, was about observable research towards a specific use and not about the abstract increase of innovation incentives on industry level. However, the remarks on cannibalization concerns are interesting.

The Commission finds:

> "*Therefore, the transaction brings together under the Notifying Party's ownership two among the only three competing clinical research programs based on the MEK and B-Raf inhibitors and pursuing to serve the same unmet medical needs. This is likely to diminish competition in innovation by curtailing the Notifying Parties' R&D efforts. Pre-transaction each party's incentive to invest in its clinical research program was driven by the future sales that the programme was expected to generate, without consideration of the fact that it could also be expected to reduce future sales of competing clinical research programs. Post-transaction, the Notifying Party will internalise that investing in one of the clinical research programs can be expected to cannibalise future sales of its other clinical research program. In light of the few competing research programs in this area, the transaction is likely to significantly reduce the Notifying Party's incentive to continue investing substantial amounts in R&D on both MEK and B-Raf clinical research programs in parallel.*"[453]

It further notes in a footnote:

> "*The cannibalisation effect on expected sales in competition in innovation is very similar to the mechanism by which internalisation of cannibalisation*

---

450 European Commission, Decision of 28.01.2015, C(2015) 538 final, OJ C 95, 21.03.2015, p. 14, Case No COMP/M.7275, *Novartis/GlaxoSmithKline Oncology Business* (hereinafter: "Novartis/GSK Decision").

451 See for example: Novartis/GSK Decision, para 104.

452 Novartis/GSK Decision, para 90.

453 Novartis/GSK Decision, para 104.

> *effects on sales lead merging firms to unilaterally increase prices on existing products. Here firms internalise an expected effect on sales that will materialise in the future, and modify their conduct today by reducing R&D investments instead of raising prices.*"[454]

The Commission also explains the need for an assessment of innovation competition beyond traditional approaches, especially in innovation-driven markets:

> "*In principle, the effects of a concentration on competition in innovation in this type of situation may not be sufficiently assessed by restricting the assessment to actual or potential competition in existing product markets.*"[455]

GE/Alstom:[456] Besides *Deutsche Börse/NYSE Euronext*, his is the second case that is closely related to *Dow/DuPont*.[457] In this decision, the Commission considered the effects of a "*credible innovator*"[458] being removed from the industry. The assessment was linked to the market of 50 Hz heavy duty gas turbines (HDGTs) and R&D activities with respect to GT 26 and GT36 turbines.[459] The Commission concludes:

> "*Therefore, the Commission considers that, by removing an important innovator in the market for 50 Hz HDGTs, the Transaction is likely to lead to significant and lasting harm on innovation.*"[460]

And with respect to third parties and innovation incentives at industry level:

> "*As such, the Transaction would remove an important innovator in the market for 50 Hz HDGTs, therefore reducing the overall competitive pressure on the remaining players, with a reduction in the overall incentives to invest*

---

454 Novartis/GSK Decision, para 104, fn. 59; the Commission also relied on the Horizontal Merger Guidelines for the assessment of competition in innovation, Novartis/GSK Decision, para 89, fn. 50.

455 Novartis/GSK Decision, para 89.

456 European Commission, Decision of 08.09.2015, C(2015) 6179 final, OJ C 139, 04.05.2017, p. 6-13, Case No M.7278, *General Electric/Alstom (Thermal Power – Renewable Power & Grid Business)* (hereinafter: "GE/Alstom Decision").

457 The Commission refers to the Deutsche Börse/NYSE Euronext Decision and the GE/Alstom Decision in the context of Dow/DuPont in European Commission, Competition Merger Brief, Article 1, Issue 2/2017- July, p. 8, available at: *ec.europa.eu/competition/publications/cmb/2017/kdal17002enn.pdf*.

458 GE/Alstom Decision, para 946, 955 et seq, 1493 et seq.

459 GE/Alstom Decision, para 1077, 1078.

460 GE/Alstom Decision, para 996.

significantly in innovation. The Commission concludes that, due to the very high barriers to entry in the market for 50 Hz HDGTs, by removing an important innovator, the Transaction is likely to lead to significant and lasting harm on innovation."[461]

Even though the Commission puts a focus on the market structure and the capability of the market players as innovators, the assessment is still linked to specific products. Furthermore, the Commission did not provide any theoretical basis for its concerns and conclusions.

(b) Intermediate result

As is usually the case with innovations, the theory of harm in *Dow/DuPont* did not come out of the blue but rather had predecessors in other Commission decisions. However, in *Dow/DuPont* the Commission has for the first time expressed concerns on mere innovation incentives without clear interrelation to product markets. The innovation spaces do not replace a product market, as has been shown above, most of all because the Commission did not provide any evidence or assessment on which of the innovation spaces could possibly be harmed. Most importantly, in *Dow/DuPont* there has been for the first time a theoretical background and a legal and economic assessment of innovation competition. The Commission's rationale that a merger between two out of a limited number of innovators in a market characterized by oligopolistic market structure and high barriers to entry as well as high appropriability may depress innovation incentives has no example in preceding decisions. All in all, even though the Commission's concern may have been foreshadowed[462] in prior case law, in *Dow/DuPont*, there is for the first time a manifest theory of harm and the explanation of an underlying rationale. There is a novel "theory" in the meaning of a definition and explanation of innovation concerns beyond specific product markets or observable research activities.

461 GE/Alstom Decision, para 999-1000.
462 *Jung/Sinclair*, 40 E.C.L.R. (2019) 266, 271.

2) Innovation Market Analysis

(a) Concept of the Innovation Market Analysis

Besides European Case Law, there has also been a theoretical approach in merger control incorporating innovation activities beyond specific product markets. *Gilbert* and *Sunshine*, at that time members of the U.S. Department of Justice, published an Article in 1995 about a concept of "Innovation Markets".[463] The authors consider research and development to constitute a market on its own, namely an input market as opposed to goods and services output markets.[464] They define an innovation market as "*a set of activities and a geographical area in which a hypothetical monopolist would impose at least a small but significant and nontransitory reduction in R&D effort.*"[465] Gilbert and Sunshine suggest a five-step analysis in order to assess "*market concentration, competitive effects on incentives to invest in R&D, and efficiencies resulting from a combination of R&D activities.*"[466] Those five steps are:[467]

1. Identification of overlapping R&D activities of the merging firms;
2. Identification of alternative sources of R&D;
3. Evaluation of actual and potential competition from downstream products;
4. Assessment of the increase in concentration in research and development and competitive effects on investment in R&D;
5. Assessment of R&D efficiencies.

The authors further examine how the innovation market approach could be incorporated into existing law. The relevant provision in U.S. Law is Section 7 of the Clayton Act, which provides that no person shall acquire the stock or assets of another person "*where in any line of commerce or in any activity affecting commerce in any section of the country, the effect of*

---

463 *Gilbert/Sunshine*, 63 Antitrust Law Journal (1995), 569.

464 *Gilbert/Sunshine*, 63 Antitrust Law Journal (1995), 569, 581.

465 *Gilbert/Sunshine*, 63 Antitrust Law Journal (1995), 569, 594; this is similar to the approach on product markets in the EU Market Definition Notice, para 15: "*The assessment of demand substitution entails a determination of the range of products which are viewed as substitutes by the consumer. One way of making this determination can be viewed as a speculative experiment, postulating a hypothetical small, lasting change in relative prices and evaluating the likely reactions of customers to that increase.*"

466 *Gilbert/Sunshine*, 63 Antitrust Law Journal (1995), 569, 595.

467 *Gilbert/Sunshine*, 63 Antitrust Law Journal (1995), 569, 595-597.

such acquisition may be substantially to lessen competition, or tend to create a monopoly."[468] Accordingly, an innovation market has to be a "line of commerce" or an "activity affecting commerce". *Gilbert* and *Sunshine* find:

> "*One way to do so would be to recognize an "upstream" innovation market or a defined set of technologies as a line of commerce. Under this method of analysis, innovation for a defined group of products would be considered an area of effective competition. If a transaction were to lessen substantially competition in such a market, it would be held unlawful. The product an geographic dimensions of the relevant market for innovation for a defined group of products will not necessarily correspond to the dimensions of the relevant market for those same products downstream. For example, given technology may be used to produce two different products which, for the purpose of manufacture and sale of those products downstream, compete in separate markets {…}. In this instance, there may be a unitary innovation market for the technology to produce the products, but multiple downstream markets for the products themselves. Similarly, the geographic market for a type of innovation may be worldwide while the downstream products that are the focus of the innovation trade in narrower markets (for example, because of the need for specialized distribution assets, freight costs, or regulatory and trade barriers).*"[469]

While the abovementioned reasoning corresponds to a "line of commerce" (comparable to a defined market in European Law), Gilbert and Sunshine also offer a second way of incorporating innovation concerns into merger control:

> "*An alternative way to fit the innovation markets framework within existing Section 7 case law is to treat the framework as a tool for identifying mergers with anticompetitive effects in output markets. The relevant output markets would be defined by commonly accepted principles of market definition. A merger would be held illegal if the innovation analysis revealed a substantial anticompetitive effect in an output market resulting from reduced innovation competition upstream. {…} The only requirement would be that the merging firms be significant competitors in innovation and that the reduction in innovation will have a harmful effect in an output market.*"[470]

---

468 15 U.S.Code § 18.

469 *Gilbert/Sunshine*, 63 Antitrust Law Journal (1995), 569, 600-601.

470 *Gilbert/Sunshine*, 63 Antitrust Law Journal (1995), 569, 601.

(b) Intermediate result

Even though there are major differences between the Innovation Market Analysis as suggested by *Gilbert* and *Sunshine* and the Commission's approach in *Dow/DuPont*, there are also commonalities. The five-step-analysis proposed by *Gilbert* and *Sunshine* points into the same direction as the Commission's assessment. The Commission also analyzes effects on concentration and partly also on R&D investment, even though the Commission's approach is broader, incorporating the number of innovation output targets. The identification of overlapping R&D activities of the merging firms and of alternative sources of R&D is part of the *Dow/DuPont* analysis, as well as possible efficiencies.

The actual or potential competition from downstream products is included in the Commission's cannibalization concerns. Gilbert and Sunshine find:

> "*In addition to competition from alternative technologies, a second reason why a reduction in R&D may be unprofitable for a hypothetical monopolist is actual and potential competition from downstream products. Innovation permits the hypothetical monopolist to increase its share of downstream markets and be more profitable.*"[471]

This relates to the product competition channel in the Dow/DuPont Decision, that, according to the Commission, is potentially ambiguous for innovation incentives. The Commission, however, expands the scope of its analysis from existing products to future products, that also can have an impact on the innovation incentives of the merging parties.

Furthermore, even though Gilbert and Sunshine recognize that the innovation efforts do not necessarily correspond to the downstream product markets, they do not give an explanation of the interrelation between innovation and the final product. The Commission refined that approach and introduced the concept of innovation spaces. However, concerning the five-step analysis proposed by Gilbert and Sunshine, one may very well conclude that the major thoughts have been transferred into *Dow/DuPont*,[472] even though the Commission puts a greater emphasis on market structure criteria.

---

471 *Gilbert/Sunshine*, 63 Antitrust Law Journal (1995), 569, 596.

472 The Head of Unit of the Merger Unit responsible for *Dow/DuPont*, Thomas Deisenhofer, referred to the paper of *Gibert* and *Sunshine* in a speech at the "Arbeitskreis Kartellrecht" of the FCO on 5 October 2017, see: www.d-kart.d

Gilbert and *Sunshine* still focus on specific research and development activities that are directed to future products (they mention "innovation for a defined group of products", see above), and not so much on a reduction of innovation incentives at industry level. Even though Gilbert and Sunshine claim that the only requirement for an anticompetitive effect in the downstream market would be that the parties were "*significant competitors in innovation*" and "*the reduction in innovation will have a harmful effect on an output market*", they give no explanation or instruction how to assess the importance as innovator and, most notably, how to account for negative effects on innovation incentives.

Despite similarities in the approach of *Gilbert* and *Sunshine* and the Commission in *Dow/DuPont*, the most important difference is the incorporation of innovation concerns into the legal framework. Whereas *Gilbert* and *Sunshine* analyze innovation as a market on its own, the Commission explicitly refers to innovation competition as a means that affects the market position of the merging parties. *Gilbert* and *Sunshine* somehow implied such an approach when stating that a merger could also be deemed illegal if the merger leads to a "*substantial anticompetitive effect in an output market resulting from reduced innovation competition upstream*", but did not further elaborate that approach. They mainly focus on "*delineating innovation markets*"[473].

(c) Critique on the Innovation Market approach

The Innovation Market Analysis as proclaimed by *Gilbert* and *Sunshine* has been subject to critique.[474] Since the critique partly is also relevant for the Commission's approach in *Dow/DuPont*, the main arguments will be analyzed in the following Section. The critique mainly focuses on three lines of argumentation:[475] First, commentators claim that there is no legal or economic link between market concentration and innovation. Second, the innovation market as proclaimed by *Gilbert* and *Sunshine* lacks the necessary features of a "market". And third, besides the innovation market

e/blog/2017/10/09/beschraenkung-von-innovation-kann-das-ein-siec-sein/; in addition, Annex 4 of the Dow/DuPont Decision cites the paper introducing the Innovation Market Analysis by *Gilbert* and *Sunshine*.

473 *Gilbert/Sunshine*, 63 Antitrust Law Journal (1995), 569, 570.

474 For an overview of possible lines of critique see *Barth*, Innovationsmärkte in der Fusionskontrolle, p. 100-109.

475 See *Gilbert/Sunshine*, 64 Antitrust Law Journal (1995), 75.

analysis, there are sufficient tools in competition law to assess innovation concerns.

With respect to the first argument, *Rapp* finds that: "*Neither economic theory nor any factual analysis of the connections between market structure, R&D, and innovation provides a persuasive basis for the innovation market approach, {…}.*"[476] *Rapp* focuses on the interrelation between competition and R&D expenditure and states that "*{i}ncreases in R&D concentration may or may not lead to less R&D, and cutbacks in R&D may or may not affect future prices and output quantities in product markets, {…}.*"[477]

Rapp further elaborates his critique:

> "*On average, the social returns to R&D exceed the private returns. This tells us that society gains, on average, when individuals invest in R&D. It is also true that, in theory, more inputs imply more output, to that a firm which outs in more R&D will get more innovation out, all things equal. These insights are an inadequate basis for innovation-oriented merger policy, however, because they abstract from quality considerations, duplication of effort, waste, bad decisions, and the opportunity cost of innovation activity.*"[478]

With respect to R&D expenditure, *Rapp* makes a valid point. It is indeed not certain that more money produces more new products. However, *Gilbert* and *Sunshine* do not solely rely on a reduction of R&D expenditure, but have the broader notion of a reduction of "*total R&D*"[479] or reduced innovation competition[480]. In fact, the incentive to perform R&D in order to be able to compete on markets implies that the R&D efforts are efficiently directed towards specific goals. In order to be able to successfully compete in innovation, firms must take into account the quality of their research efforts as well as possible duplication, waste and opportunity cost. Rivalry in innovation will not lead to random waste of R&D expenditure but rather to the best allocation of innovation effort. This can also

---

476 *Rapp*, 64 Antitrust Law Journal (1995) 19, 20; see also *Hay*, 64 Antitrust Law Journal (1995), 7, 16, who finds that: „*Suffice it to say that there is no solid basis in economic theory or empirical observation to reach the conclusion either that the likely result of the merger will be to reduce the incentive to engage in R&D or that, if duplicate R&D is reduced, that is necessarily a bad thing.*"

477 *Rapp*, 64 Antitrust Law Journal (1995) 19, 20, 27, 33.

478 *Rapp*, 64 Antitrust Law Journal (1995) 19, 33; *Hoerner* finds that there can also be too much R&D, „*as when its total cost to a firm exceeds the firm's total revenues on an ongoing basis.*", *Hoerner*, 64 Antitrust Law Journal (1995), 49, 52.

479 *Gilbert/Sunshine*, 63 Antitrust Law Journal (1995), 569, 590.

480 *Gilbert/Sunshine*, 63 Antitrust Law Journal (1995), 569, 601.

include a cut back of expenditure if the most promising path of research is not cost-intensive.[481] For that reason, the Commission in *Dow/DuPont* refers to "*innovation effort*"[482], less "*innovation output targets*"[483] and less "*innovation output levels*"[484] instead of mere R&D expenditure.

Furthermore, *Rapp's* comment that there is no clear connection between market structure and R&D must be approved. An interrelation between market concentration and innovation incentives in this generality does not exist or has at least not been proven until today. Additional factors are necessary to make a prediction as to an influence of concentration on R&D. Those additional factors have been taken into account in the Dow/DuPont Decision, as will be further explained in *Section II) H) 1) (b)-(e)*.

The second line of critique deals with the assessment of an innovation "market".[485] *Hoerner* finds that the Innovation Market Analysis as proposed by *Gilbert* and

> *Sunshine* "*violates the principle that there can be no "market" until there are buy/sell transactions. There are no buy/sell transactions involved in research and development solely for the internal use of the firm. It is not until the research and development produces innovation, and the innovation is offered for sale, that a "market" comes into play.*"[486]

In fact, it is difficult to assess a "market" if there is no opposite market side. Criteria for defining the market are hard to find and would suffer from a high degree of uncertainty. This may actually be one of the reasons why the Commission in *Dow/DuPont* did not assess a market on its own but defined innovation as a different level of competition influencing the market position in downstream product markets.[487]

The third line of critique refers to the need for an innovation market analysis. In most cases the use of the traditional approaches of potential

---

481 As is suggstested by *Rapp*, 64 Antitrust Law Journal (1995) 19, 36.

482 See for example Dow/DuPont Decision, para 348.

483 Dow/DuPont Decision, para 2396.

484 Dow/DuPont Decision, para 3223.

485 See also *Drexl*, Anti-Competitive Stumbling Stones, p. 11.

486 *Hoerner*, 64 Antitrust Law Journal (1995), 49, 51.

487 See *Section II) C) 4)*; *Chernenko* argues that because *Dow/DuPont* mirrors key aspects of the Innovation Market approach, the Commission assessed innovation as a market on its own; *Chernenko*, 40 E.C.L.R. (2019) 9, 19. However, this a circular argument. The criteria of a market were not fulfilled in *Gilbert* and *Sunshine's* approach in the first place and therefore the Commission basically incorporated a necessary correction when considering innovation with respect to the position on a market.

competition[488] and future markets[489] are deemed sufficient. *Hay* claims that the actual concern in the Innovation Market Analysis is the loss of competition on future markets:

> *"{...}, the factual basis for concern is the belief that, but for the merger, both firms would have been significant independent sellers of the product in question and after the merger there will be only the one. In my view the fact that the result of the merger will be that one of the firms will, in effect, abandon its R&D effort before he product has been created, instead of combining production and sales decisions after the product already exists, is of no great importance and does not, by itself, require a new analytic approach."*[490]

However, as pointed out in *Section II) C) 3)*, innovation concerns are not about competition on future markets but about incentives to perform research and development. Those incentives cannot be incorporated in the future markets approach and they do not fall within the potential competition doctrine.[491] In that respect, *Gilbert* and *Sunshine* themselves replied to the critique and stated:

> *"Because the innovation market analysis identifies welfare effects not reached by other models of analysis, it provides a tool to reach certain anticompetitive transactions that may not be reached by the traditional tools."*[492]

The requirement of an analysis beyond traditional approaches will be discussed further in the following Section.[493]

There has been an additional argument in the debate, relating to the identification of innovation competitors. It has been argued that important innovation competitors are hard to identify.[494] With respect to this argument, *Kern* rightly points out that innovation in most cases will not *"come out of the blue"*.[495] The Innovation Market Analysis can be used in

488 *Rapp*, 64 Antitrust Law Journal (1995) 19, 37 et seq.
489 *Hay*, 64 Antitrust Law Journal (1995), 7, 15.
490 *Hay*, 64 Antitrust Law Journal (1995), 7, 15.
491 See *Section II) G)*.
492 *Gilbert/Sunshine*, 64 Antitrust Law Journal (1995), 75, 82.
493 See *Section II) G)*.
494 *Carlton/Gertner*, Intellectual Property, Antitrust and Strategic Behavior, 29, 41 et seq.
495 *Kern*, Innovation Markets, Future Markets, or Potential Competition, p. 25.

cases in which research and development requires particular and specialized assets. As *Kern* puts it:

> *"These assets can also be understood as entry barriers for the participation in the process of innovation competition. Whenever these entry barriers can be characterized as being indispensable for the research and development in a certain field, as well as difficult to acquire and adopt in an adequate period of time, they can serve as a device for the identification of the relevant competitors."*[496]

This is precisely what the Commission does in *Dow/DuPont* when assessing entry barriers to research and development.[497]

G) *In need of a new theory?*

As has already been expressed in the scope of the Innovation Market Analysis,[498] one may argue that innovation incentives can be accounted for and protected with traditional analysis tools, such as potential competition or the future markets approach. As explained in *Section II) A) 2)*, innovation as the very reason behind research and development is protected under EU primary law. Therefore, the European Commission has to fully take into account factors that influence innovation when releasing decisions. This means that research and development shall not only be protected once it has started and is directed towards a specific product or product market, but that innovation has to be secured in a comprehensive way, including the mere incentives to perform research and development. Even though innovation concerns have been part of traditional concepts, those concepts have only covered part of the innovation process.

1) The potential competition doctrine

The original idea behind the concept of potential competition is that "*already the perceived threat for market entry has a disciplining effect on the incumbent firms which prevents them from (fully) exploiting their market pow-*

496 *Kern*, Innovation Markets, Future Markets, or Potential Competition, p. 25.
497 See *Section II) B) 3) and 4)*.
498 See *Section II) F) 2) (c)*.

er."[499] The doctrine may be divided into two separate forms, perceived potential competition and actual potential competition. A perceived potential entrant is a firm that may never enter the market, but has the potential to do so and this mere potential limits the ability of the market player(s) to raise prices or decrease innovation efforts.[500] An actual potential competitor is a "*particular firm, which is undertaking R&D in order to enter a certain product market*"[501]. Even though the EU Horizontal Merger Guidelines seem to mirror the two concepts when stating that the "*Commission examines whether entry is likely or whether potential entry is likely to constrain the behaviour of incumbents post-merger*"[502], they only give guidance on the assessment of actual potential competition. Accordingly, entry must be likely, timely and sufficient.[503] This implies that there have to be observable research and development activities directed towards a specific product market.[504]

2) The future markets concept

The future markets concept relates to product markets that do not yet exist but are likely to exist in the future.[505] There are two concerns associated with that concept:[506] First of all, that research and development activities towards that future product market would be abandoned, resulting in an innovation not coming to market. Second, there is the fear that there will be less competition on the future market if one of two products is not brought to market. Even though that approach refrains from current

---

499 *Kern*, Innovation Markets, Future Markets, or Potential Competition, p. 4; the original idea is from *John Bates Clark* who refers to „*the competition of the mill that is not yet built but will be built if the trust becomes too extortionate.*", *Clark*, 68 The Century Magazine (1904), 954, 955.

500 See *Kern*, Innovation Markets, Future Markets, or Potential Competition, p. 4-5; *Gilbert/Newberry*, 72 The American Economic Revue (1982), 514, especially p. 521.

501 *Kern*, Innovation Markets, Future Markets, or Potential Competition, p. 5.

502 Horizontal Merger Guidelines, para 69.

503 Horizontal Merger Guidelines, para 68.

504 See *Kern*, Innovation Markets, Future Markets, or Potential Competition, p. 6.

505 *Kern*, Innovation Markets, Future Markets, or Potential Competition, p. 6; FCO, Innovationen – Herausforderungen für die Kartellrechtspraxis, p. 31.

506 See *Kern*, Innovation Markets, Future Markets, or Potential Competition, p. 7; FCO, Innovationen – Herausforderungen für die Kartellrechtspraxis, p. 31.

product markets, there is still the need of observable research targeted towards specific products.[507]

The Commission has used the concept of future markets in its *Ciba-Geigy/Sandoz* Decision[508]. The Commission finds:

> *"In the pharmaceutical industry, a full assessment if the competitive situation requires examination of the products which are not yet on the market but which are at an advanced stage of development {…}. The Commission has to look at R&D potential in terms of its importance for existing markets, but also for future markets."*[509]

With respect to the definition of such future market, the Commission finds:

> *"In so far as research and development must be assessed in terms of its importance for future markets, the relevant product market must, by its very nature, be defined in a less clear-cut manner than in the case of existing markets. {…} Market definition can be based on the existing ATC classes only if existing products are to be replaced. Otherwise it must be guided primarily by the indications to which the future products are to be applied."*[510]

Accordingly, even though the definition of a future market may be broader or slightly different from the one of an existing market, the underlying principles for market definition remain the same. It is the question of whether products are interchangeable with one another that guides the definition of existing as well as future product markets.

3) Innovation competition

In contrast, the concept of innovation competition, as developed in *Dow/DuPont*, incorporates the mere innovation capacity and the innovation incentive beyond any specific (future) product or existing research activity. Whereas the other concepts do not at all include the initiation of

---

507 If the research was not directed towards a specific product than the authority would not be able to assess whether the future product was interchangeable with an existing product, thus falling within an existing market.

508 European Commission, Decision of 17.07.1996, OJ L 201, 29.07.1997, p. 1-47, Case No IV/M.737, *Ciba-Geigy/Sandoz* (hereinafter: "Ciba-Geigy/Sandoz Decision").

509 Ciba-Geigy/Sandoz Decision, para 42.

510 Ciba-Geigy/Sandoz Decision, para 44.

innovation activities (their scope begins way after the basic and broad research has started), the innovation competition approach focuses on the innovation incentives as protective goal. It is not about the final product but about the competitive pressure to generally start R&D.

In that respect, one may scrutinize *Kern's* categorization of the former concept of the Innovation Market Analysis[511]. *Kern* draws the following table[512]:

Table 2: Kern's Overview of the general applicability of the distinct approaches {content in brackets added}

	The merging firms are pre-innovation competitors {on current product markets}	The merging firms are not pre-innovation competitors {on current product markets}
'Unobservable' R&D projects	Innovation Markets	Perceived Potential Competition; Innovation Markets
R&D is expected to constitute a new relevant product market	Future Markets; Innovation Markets	Future Markets; Innovation Markets
R&D is not expected to constitute a new relevant product market	Innovation Markets	Actual Potential Competition; Innovation Markets

However, that categorization of the Innovation Market Analysis seems somewhat vague. Whereas the concept of innovation competition (in this respect comparable to the Innovation Market Analysis) may somehow be "used" in the respective scenarios, it is not at all the goal of the Commission's novel theory to assess observable or unobservable R&D projects. Furthermore, it is completely irrelevant if the firms concerned are competitors in existing product markets. It is just not the aim of the concept of innovation competition to assess specific research and development activities with respect to specific markets. It is about the competitive pressure between important innovators that leads to innovation incentives.

In that respect, it is also not useful to extend any of the traditional concepts of potential competition or future markets to try to cover "unobservable" R&D or undertakings not currently competing on existing product markets. The concept of innovation competition simply falls outside the scope of the traditional concepts and does not fit into the abovementioned table. Innovation competition is not an extension of the

511 See *Section II) F) 2)*.

512 Author's layout, but content taken from *Kern*, Innovation Markets, Future Markets, or Potential Competition, p. 20.

existing approaches, but rather an aliud. Accordingly, the overview of the applicability of different approaches covering innovation aspects must look as follows:

Table 3: Overview of the general applicability of different innovation approaches

	The merging firms are innovation competitors	The merging firms are pre-innovation competitors (on current product markets)	The merging firms are not pre-innovation competitors (on current product markets)
Innovation incentives	Innovation Competition		
'Unobservable' R&D projects			Perceived Potential Competition
R&D is expected to constitute a new relevant product market		Future Markets	Future Markets
R&D is not expected to constitute a new relevant product market			Actual Potential Competition

Since the protection of research and development is one of the aims of the European Treaties, it is necessary to develop and use a concept that preserves the incentives to perform that research and development. Since none of the traditional approaches achieves that goal with respect to general changes in market structure, the Commission's approach of assessing innovation competition is necessary.

H) Is the innovation competition approach valid?

The novel theory of harm in *Dow/DuPont* has been severely criticized. The main points in the discussion are that there is no definite link between market concentration and innovation, or even if there was a link, there is no presumption that an increase in concentration will lead to a decrease in innovation incentives. Also, possible efficiencies had not correctly been taken into account in *Dow/DuPont*. Additionally, it has been argued that the differences between the two features price and innovation prevent the Commission from using its traditional unilateral conduct assessment with respect to innovation competition. Finally, several authors found that the Commission improperly measured the innovation capacity of the relevant firms, negotiated overly far-reaching remedies and in total undermined legal certainty.

Some of that criticism can be countered by means of the abovementioned analysis and understanding of the rationale behind the Dow/DuPont Decision. The Commission did not set up a general rule that an increase in concentration always leads to a decrease in innovation incentives. Furthermore, it has to be kept in mind that specific products or pipeline projects were not the object of the Commission's assessment. However, some arguments may claim validity, especially with respect to the consideration of additional factors inciting innovation activities and possible efficiencies.

1) Link between innovation and competition

Numerous commentators[513] have argued or implied that the Commission has set up a general rule that effective competition leads to innovation or established that an increase in market concentration does depress innovation incentives. *Chernenko* finds that the "*assumption underlying these policy choices, of course, is that competition is 'beneficial for innovation without proviso'.*"[514] *Cary* explicitly criticizes the Dow/DuPont Decision and finds that

> "*an increase in concentration may either decrease or increase incentives to innovate, and thus there is no presumption of harm to innovation from increases in concentration.*"[515]

Until now, there has indeed not been a definite theoretical or empirical finding on the precise interrelation between competition and innovation incentives.[516] However, the Commission did not reach the conclusion in *Dow/DuPont* that there was such definite relationship between market con-

---

513 In addition to those mentioned below: *RBB Economics*, RBB Brief 54, p. 1, 3; with limitations: *Wirtz/Schulz*, NZKart 2019, 20, 22, *Thiede/Müller*, EuZW 2019, 628, 633; *Denicolò/Polo*, The innovation theory of harm, p. 2.

514 *Chernenko*, 40 E.C.L.R. (2019) 9; referring to *Mooji/Rusu*, 43 Legal Issues of Economic Integration (2016), 173, 174.

515 *Cary*, Festschrift für Dirk Schroeder, p. 184.

516 *Chernenko*, 40 E.C.L.R. (2019) 9, 11; *Cary*, Festschrift für Dirk Schroeder, p. 185; *Wirtz/Schulz*, NZKart 2019, 20, 22; Monopolkommission, XXII. Hauptgutachten, para 716; *RBB Economics*, RBB Brief 54, p. 3; *Thiede/Müller*, EuZW 2019, 628, 633; *Haucap*, Merger Effects on Innovation, p. 1, 5; *Kern*, Innovation Markets,

centration and innovation incentives in general. The Commission rather developed a theory of harm for a specific case, namely a merger between important innovators in a close oligopoly with high barriers to entry and a high level of appropriability. Under those circumstances, there is economic literature supporting the Commission's findings. It is particularly important to note that Annex 4 of the Dow/DuPont Decision includes literature on a general interrelation between market concentration and innovation. However, that specific literature mainly offers a background and a support for the Commission's assessment and may also serve to counter some of the parties' arguments.[517] The Commission explicitly mentions that Annex 4 sets out "*economic considerations related to the theory of harm on the likely effects of the current Transaction on innovation incentives.*"[518]

Before analyzing the validity of the economic background of *Dow/ DuPont*, there must be an assessment of the standard for incorporating economic models into competition law. Even though law is not independent of empirical scientific findings, it nevertheless has the peculiarity of the normative. Even in case there is no definite empirical or theoretical finding supporting a decision, the law nevertheless must find a solution to existing problems. Accordingly, there must be rules as to what extent competition law assessment should or can be based on economic findings.

(a) Standard for incorporating economic reasoning in competition law

In its *Tetra Laval* judgment, the ECJ has established criteria for the standard of incorporating economic evidence in merger review. The Court states:

> "*Whilst the Court recognises that the Commission has a margin of discretion with regard to economic matters, that does not mean that the Community Courts must refrain from reviewing the Commission's interpretation of information of an economic nature. Not only must the Community Courts, inter alia, establish whether the evidence relied on is factually accurate, reliable and consistent but also whether that evidence contains all the information which must be taken into account in order to assess a complex*

Future Markets, or Potential Competition, p. 26, 28; *Denicolò/Polo*, The innovation theory of harm, p. 1.

517 Cf. Annex 4, para 1.

518 Annex 4, para 1.

situation and whether it is capable of substantiating the conclusions drawn from it."[519]

Evidence is factually accurate if it correctly reflects the existing situation. The Commission may not rely on evidence that is manifestly incorrect. The principle of reliability "*aims to filter out ambiguous, equivocal or controversial economics from merger review.*"[520] The evidence has to be consistent, meaning that there may not be discrepancies in different pieces of evidence. Contradictory facts or facts contradicting the underlying rationale may not support a decision. Those three conditions overlap in a way, since contradictory evidence may also prove to be manifestly incorrect and not reliable.

In addition, the Commission must make a complete assessment, taking all information into account. This includes supportive as well as unsupportive information.[521] The criterion also refers to all relevant information in and outside the case file.[522] Accordingly, the Commission is not bound to the information the parties submit. It even has the duty to include further findings if relevant for the case.

The term "*information of economic nature*" is not restricted to facts of economic nature but also to the underlying economic theories.[523] This is comprehensible when taking into account that the Commission is issuing a decision based on legal grounds. In that respect, its discretion does not cover the appraisal of economic theory, models or methods. Scientific results, in general, represent the factual basis in legal decisions but are not part of the legal process of consideration. When economic results are incomplete or insecure, the usual legal methods for dealing with such factual deficiencies apply.

Notably, the Commission has to find a convincing way of relying on economic principles and theories.[524] As the General Court puts it:

---

519 ECJ, Judgment of 15.02.2005, Case C-12/03 P, ECLI:EU:C:2005:87, para 39, *Tetra Laval*; see also ECJ, Judgment of 26.03.2019, C-621/16 P, ECLI:EU:C:2019:251, para 104, *Commission/Italy*.

520 *Petit*, Innovation Competition, p. 45.

521 *Petit*, Innovation Competition, p. 48.

522 *Petit*, Innovation Competition, p. 48.

523 *Petit*, Innovation Competition, p. 39.

524 With respect to the Tetra Laval test, Petit finds: „*Moreover, the Tetra Laval test does not mean that the Commission is obliged to tell the best economic story, just a convincing one. This implies a certain amount of freedom to select economic models and other analytical tools to assess a merger.*“ *Petit*, Innovation Competition, p. 40.

> *"The Commission {…} enjoys a degree of latitude regarding the choice of economic instruments available to it and the choice of the appropriate approaches to the study of any matter, {…} provided that those choices are not manifestly contrary to the accepted rules of economic discipline and are applied inconsistently."*[525]

The ECJ emphasized the importance of consistency and persuasion in its *Impala* judgment:

> *"Furthermore, it is true that, as is apparent from the Court's case-law, the decisions of the Commission as to the compatibility of concentrations with the common market must be supported by a sufficiently cogent and consistent body of evidence {…}."*[526]

When there are different possible outcomes, the Commission has to rely on the most likely economic scenario:

> *"It follows that, where it has been notified of a proposed concentration pursuant to the Regulation, the Commission is, in principle, required to adopt a position, {…} in accordance with its assessment of the economic outcome attributable to the concentration which is most likely to ensue."*[527]

As a result, the economic principles and theories the Commission uses must be accurate, reliable, consistent and complete. The Commission must rely on the most likely outcome and provide a cogent assessment of the economic background.

At this point, it is important to distinguish the facts of the specific *Dow/DuPont* case from the general underlying theory. Whereas it is the goal of this thesis to scrutinize the underlying theory of harm in *Dow/DuPont* and assess whether this theory can be applied in scenarios other than a merger setting as well, it is not about a critique of the specific case. Admittedly, since the theory has been developed in a case, it cannot completely be separated from the underlying facts. However, the accuracy, reliability, consistency and completeness of the specific features of the crop protection industry and the economic data submitted in *Dow/DuPont* are

525 CFI, Judgment of 11 .07.2007, T-351/03, ECLI:EU:T:2007:212, para 132, *Schneider Electric.*

526 ECJ, Judgment of 10.07.2008, C-413/06 P, ECLI:EU:C:2008:392, para 50, *Impala.*

527 ECJ, Judgment of 10.07.2008, C-413/06 P, ECLI:EU:C:2008:392, para 52, *Impala*; see also GC, Judgment of 28.05.2020, Case T-399/16, ECLI:EU:T:2020:217, para 116, *CK Telecoms UK Investments.*

irrelevant for the general validity of the Commission's approach.[528] When *Petit* mentions a paper of the agrochemical industry and statistics that have not been taken into account in the Commission's assessment,[529] this only relates to the specific facts of the case and not the general underlying theory.

It will be discussed below whether the theory of harm the Commission has set up is based on an accurate, reliable, consistent and complete basis. The finding that innovation incentives will be reduced if two out of a limited number of innovators merge in a market with high barriers to entry as well as high appropriability and absent efficiencies must be most likely and cogent.

(b) The Schumpeter/Arrow controversy

It is indeed true that there is no definite general link between market concentration or competition intensity and innovation incentives. When looking at the arguments brought forward, one may, however, get an idea of the factors being important for a possible assessment of innovation incentives. Initially, the debate about an interrelation between innovation and competition has been part of the so-called *Schumpeter/Arrow controversy*.

Schumpeter found that a monopolist has the greatest incentive to invest in R&D because it is able to realize the entire value of an invention without others being able to free-ride on its efforts by copying the new product or service (so-called "spillover").[530] Accordingly, *Schumpeter* focuses on the notion of appropriability.[531]

Arrow, in contrast, found that a monopolist's inventions would likely only capture (i.e. "cannibalize") sales from its own existing products or services.[532] In consequence, a less concentrated market would increase innovation efforts because cannibalization effects decrease with the number of players. *Arrow* highlights the importance of cannibalization effects.[533]

528 *Petit*, Innovation Competition, p. 44.
529 *Petit*, Innovation Competition, p. 49.
530 *Schumpeter*, Capitalism, Socialism and Democracy, especially p. 87-107.
531 See *Cary*, Festschrift für Dirk Schroeder, p. 184.
532 *Arrow*, Economic Welfare and the Allocation of Resources for Invention, p. 619 et seq.
533 *Cary*, Festschrift für Dirk Schroeder, p. 184.

In *Dow/DuPont*, the Commission takes into account both effects. Cannibalization concerns are at the center of the Commission's reasoning. The merged entity is likely to decrease its innovation efforts because the number of current and future products that will likely be cannibalized increases with the size of the firm (provided that the merging parties are active on the same markets and invent with respect to the same targets). On the other hand, the Commission states that its theory is only valid if appropriability is high pre-merger. If an innovator does not have to be afraid of spillover effects, the reasoning of *Schumpeter* is less important.

(c) Notion of appropriability

However, the latter also depends on the notion of the term "appropriability". As Schumpeter puts it, appropriability is about "*realizing the value of an invention*". The parties' economists in *Dow/DuPont* used a similar notion according to which appropriability "*refers to the extent to which a firm can realise the benefits generated by its innovation efforts.*"[534] But the parties went on:

> "*However, over and about the existence of IPRs, the degree of appropriability also depends on other factors, such as on whether rivals are innovating (or perceived to be innovating) in the same area. A firm's perceived risk that too many rivals may also be investing in new products that would end up competing with, and therefore take away sales from, its planned innovation may discourage it from investing in the development of the new product.*"[535]

A reduction in the number of innovation competitors would thus increase the benefit a firm may obtain with a new product.[536]

However, this is a very wide understanding of appropriability that is not in line with *Schumpeter's* findings. In that respect, the Commission emphasizes that there is a difference between the value of an innovation and its appropriation:

> "*Clearly an innovation with many competing alternatives is less profitable than one which has none, all else given. But this is not because the innovator could not appropriate its value. It is rather because the value of that innova-*

534 *RBB Economics*, RBB Brief 54, p. 2.
535 *RBB Economics*, RBB Brief 54, p. 2.
536 See *RBB Economics*, RBB Brief 54, p. 2.

tion is lower when many rival firms can come up with a good alternative. An innovation is valuable to the extent it differentiates the innovative product from rival products that do not embedded it. No firm, whether it is in competition with other firms or it is a monopolist – that is to say irrespective of the product market structure – would invest in an innovation which does not provide a better value than an existing innovation to at least some customers."[537]

The Commission's analysis is in line with the theory of *Schumpeter*. It is not about preserving alleged "innovations" that add little or nothing new to existing products, but about setting incentives for firms to start innovation efforts to reach the best result they can. The parties' view would lead to firms starting innovation efforts towards future products that would not endure in a competitive setting. Also, this opinion does not have anything to do with spillovers. The parties have not argued that the particular invention would have been captured by others but that another invention would take away sales. But even a monopolist would only invest in innovations that would likely enable it to gain larger revenues and not just replace its own products without bringing additional profit. Thus, it is the aim of a firm to raise the value of an innovation in order to be able to appropriate that specific value. The prevention of competition in order to gain additional revenues without valuable inventions does not benefit society and is not the aim of competition policy.

If the Commission finds that appropriability is high pre-merger, the key argument of *Schumpeter* loses its relevance for the specific case. There are, however, additional factors that determine the interrelation between competition and innovation incentives.

(d) Additional factors determining the relation between innovation and competition

Besides appropriability and cannibalization concerns, several other factors determining the interplay between market concentration and innovation incentives have been mentioned in literature. *Cary* points to the time horizon as an important measure and finds that

"innovations that require lengthy investments over an extended period of time and whose success is uncertain evidence a greater potential for appropri-

537 Annex 4, para 175.

ability effects and a lower risk of negative cannibalization effects. In such a case, an innovator is uncertain of the competitive set, especially because in the interim competitors may enter the market, thus reducing the scale of cannibalization."[538]

One may add that the latter only is the case if entry is possible, meaning that the barriers to entry are not too high. Even more, innovations that require such lengthy investment are likely to create barriers to entry, because newcomers would have to have sufficient financial resources at their disposal a long time before they would for the first time gain revenues. Accordingly, the time horizon does not seem to play an important role because an increase in time to market will likely result in increased barriers to entry that prevent other undertakings from both free-riding on the innovator's invention and reducing the scale of cannibalization.

It may also be important if products are sufficiently differentiated.[539] In that case, the cannibalization effect is not as strong.[540] This refers to the value of innovation or the differentiation of research and development targets compared to existing products. The Commission takes up that point when assessing the closeness of the two merging parties with respect to existing products as well as research targets.

Finally, the relation between competition and innovation incentives also depends on the number of players in the industry as a whole, as well as with respect to specific research targets. Haucap finds that

"*both economic theory and empirical evidence suggests that 3-to-2 mergers tend to be more problematic than 5-to-4 mergers, not only in terms of price effects, but also due to their potentially adverse effects on innovation, at least in research intensive industries. In fact, with respect to 5-to-4 mergers there is not reliable general presumption on a merger's innovation effects. What makes a merger's impact on innovation even more difficult to evaluate is the fact that mergers typically concern multi-product firms which may often imply a 5-to-4 merger in one product market (where innovation effects may, therefore, be positive) and a 3-to-2 merger in another product market (where innovation effects may be negative).*"[541]

538 *Cary*, Festschrift für Dirk Schroeder, p. 186.

539 *Haucap*, Merger Effects on Innovation, p. 5; *Greenstein/Ramey*, 16 International Journal of Industrial Organization (1998), 285; *Gilbert*, Looking for Mr. Schumpeter, p. 167.

540 Cf. *Haucap*, Merger Effects on Innovation, p. 5; *Gilbert*, Looking for Mr. Schumpeter, p. 167.

541 *Haucap*, Merger Effects on Innovation, p. 7.

(e) Intermediate result

When looking at the abovementioned criteria important for the interrelation between competition and innovation incentives, the Commission has included all of them into its underlying theoretical foundation. The most important factor, the possibility of appropriating the value of an innovation, is explicitly mentioned in the Commission's theory of harm. In case appropriability is high, *Schumpeter's* finding – that competition is likely to decrease innovation incentives since firms fear spillovers in a competitive environment – loses much of its impact.[542] Furthermore, the Commission has been taking into account barriers to entry and closeness of the parties activities on existing markets as well as with respect to research and development targets. Special attention has been paid to the number of players in a market. The Dow/DuPont Decision precisely mirrors the research results by *Haucap* and *Stiebale*: In a 5-to-4 merger (which is the case in *Dow/DuPont*), there is no general presumption that the concentration results in a decrease of innovation efforts. But the merger concerns undertakings with activities in different innovation spaces. In those innovation spaces, the concentration is higher, resulting rather in a 3-to-2 merger, according to the Commission's factual analysis. This is comparable to the multi-product firm, mentioned by *Haucap* and *Stiebale*, that may raise competitive concerns in specific product markets where only three players are active pre-merger.

In conclusion, the Commission's assessment in *Dow/DuPont* concerning a possible link between market concentration and innovation incentives is accurate, reliable, consistent and complete. With respect to the specific setting, the relevant literature has been taken into account. In its Annex 4, the Commission also deals with divergent economic views. In fact, when looking at the arguments of commentators discussing *Dow/DuPont*, those commentators mainly claim that there is no definite link between market

542 In fact, there have been attempts to combine Schumpeter's and Arrow's reasoning; *Shapiro* finds that both approaches mainly focus on contestability, appropriability and possible synergies, *Shapiro*, Competition and innovation, p. 385 et seq; the Commission refers to Shapiro's findings in Annex 4, para 38 et seq and European Commission, Competition policy brief, EU merger control and innovation, 2016-01, April 2016, p. 2; available at: *ec.europa.eu/competition/publications/cpb/2016/2016_001_en.pdf*.

concentration and innovation. However, the Commission does not allege such a link in its generality.[543]

Furthermore, even the fact that the Commission in *Dow/DuPont* relied on factual written evidence concerning a reduction in R&D input as well as output does not counteract the abovementioned finding. In fact, the Tetra Laval criteria oblige the Commission to use all evidence available. This includes factual evidence supplementing the general theory behind a decision.

As a last point one may have a look at the counterfactual: not taking into account innovation concerns in an innovation driven scenario means taking it into account to the negative. In other words, it is impossible to exclude a merger's impact on innovation by simply ignoring innovation competition. If the Commission decided to refrain from assessing innovation concerns, this could lead to even greater harm to research and development incentives. The literature mentioned in Annex 4 as well as additional findings[544] imply that there is some kind of interrelation between market structure and innovation incentives even though the specific preconditions are not uncontroversial. When authors claim that there is no general link, this claim upon closer examination may lead to either outcome: on the one hand, since there seems to be some kind of interrelation, innovation competition would have to be taken into account; on the other, since there is no definite link, the Commission may not include it into its assessment.

Concerning the specific market features in *Dow/DuPont*, the Commission has made efforts to support its theory of harm with all economic findings available. This must be sufficient in light of the normativity of legal decisions.[545] The mere fact that there is no one-hundred-percent

543 Even with respect to a general link *Haucap* finds it is „*relatively weak*“, which implies that there may be a weak general link; see *Haucap*, Merger Effects on Innovation, p. 1.

544 See for example *Kern*, Innovation Markets, Future Markets, or Potential Competition; *Haucap*, Merger Effects on Innovation; there has also been an empirical study on the effects of concentration on innovation in the pharmaceutical industry that comes to the conclusion that in concentrated markets with high innovation intensity and a high degree of firm heterogeneity, patenting and R&D of the merged entity as well as of its non-merging rivals decline substantially after a merger, *Haucap/Stiebale*, How Mergers Affect Innovation.

545 In respect of the controversy about Dow/DuPont, *Ibáñez Colomo* emphasizes that commentators may ignore the legal dimension of merger control. *Ibáñez Colomo* finds that the European Commission is not required to show direct harm to innovation but may, to the requisite legal standard, rely on the assess-

scientific certainty about a specific result does not prevent an authority from taking a decision.[546]

2) Measuring innovation capacity

One of the most important points in the novel theory on innovation competition is how to determine "important innovators" and thus how to measure innovation capacity. The Commission used various factors to determine the parties' strength as innovators, for example expertise and assets, R&D input targets, output in the form of new and successful AIs, and the strength of the patent portfolios.[547] There is no specific focus on R&D expenditure as the Commission finds that the rate of expenditure may underestimate the importance of a firm as innovator.[548] The Commission rather points to the so-called pipeline productivity (that is pipeline products compared to R&D expenditure).[549] Furthermore, it is also important that the players are able to market an invention, for example by being vertically integrated.[550]

Commentators have argued that measuring innovation in the past, for example by patent shares and AI launches, does not say anything about

ment that a transaction will lead to a significant reduction of the competitive pressure faced by the parties, *Ibáñez Colomo*, 9 Journal of European Competition Law & Practice (2018), 561-562.

546 In fact, the GC states with respect to the standard of proof that "*the Commission is required to produce sufficient evidence to demonstrate with a strong probability the existence of significant impediments following the concentration.*" However, the standard of proof is less strict than „*being beyond all reasonable doubt*", GC, Judgment of 28.05.2020, Case T-399/16, ECLI:EU:T:2020:217, para 118, *CK Telecoms UK Investments*.

547 See *Esteva Mosso*, Innovation in EU Merger Control, p. 10; for the patent analysis see Dow/DuPont Decision, para 2428, 2493-2496: The Commission uses the number of citations accumulated by a patent, as this may better reflect the quality and technological significance of an innovation. Patent shares are reported separately for the whole industry and for herbicides, insecticides and fungicides. The Commission uses different criteria to narrow down its analysis, for example excluding mixture patents and internal citations, and distinguishes between different qualities of patent citations (all patens, top 50 %, top 25 % and top 10%).

548 See Dow/DuPont Decision, para 2426.

549 Dow/DuPont Decision, para 2400.

550 Dow/DuPont Decision, para 2193.

successful innovation in the future.[551] *Petit* finds that the Commission's model

> *"predicts a reduction of efforts in relation to R&D inputs which primarily consists of R&D expenditure. However, instead of measuring R&D inputs, the decision measures R&D outputs."*[552]

With respect to vertical integration *Cary* finds that the Commission in

> *Dow/DuPont "misses the point – the issue {…} is not whether a firm can compete in Europe as a marketer but whether a firm will continue to contribute to ongoing innovation in the industry."*[553]

The Commission's theory presumes that a merger of two important innovators will, under certain circumstances, lead to a reduction in innovation incentives. Accordingly, the Commission does not have to prove an actual reduction in R&D inputs as this reduction is already the core of the underlying theory. It is precisely the advantage of a presumption that it facilitates factual evidence in individual cases. The only thing the Commission must provide is an assessment of the importance of the players in a specific industry as innovators. Keeping in mind that it is about oligopolistic industries with high barriers to entry, it is indeed reasonable to assume that those undertakings that have recently been successfully innovating do have the highest incentives to discover and develop new products in the future too.[554] To date, they seem to have the best capabilities, assets, personnel and so on to successfully perform R&D. In that sense, *Kern* points out that innovations usually do not "*come out of the blue*" but require particular, specialized assets.[555] Notably, it may have to be taken into account if there have recently been any changes in R&D capabilities that could lead to less thriving R&D activities in the future. In *Dow/DuPont*, there have not been hints to such changes.

The underlying rationale in *Dow/DuPont* is that those undertakings with the highest R&D capabilities do have the highest incentives to innovate. In fact, if an undertaking is unable to perform the entire innovation process

551 *Petit*, Innovation Competition, p. 47; *Cary*, Festschrift für Dirk Schroeder, p. 189-191.

552 *Petit*, Innovation Competition, p. 47.

553 *Cary*, Festschrift für Dirk Schroeder, p. 191.

554 *Federico/Scott Morton/Shapiro* find that "*evidence on current product-to-pipeline or pipeline-to-pipeline overlaps may be a useful proxy for the overlap in the underlying R&D capabilities*", *Federico/Scott Morton/Shapiro*, Antitrust and Innovation, p. 19.

555 *Kern*, Innovation Markets, Future Markets, or Potential Competition, p. 25.

from discovery to marketing, it is unlikely to even start research and development activities. Incentives to innovate require the opportunity of success. In order to even be able to innovate, it is rather necessary to be in possession of a lot of knowledge and experience as well as testing facilities and communication platforms. That knowledge is not easy to obtain and may well show the importance of a firm as innovator.[556]

In line with the protective purpose of the innovation competition assessment in *Dow/DuPont*, namely the innovation incentive, it is important to note that the R&D capabilities of a firm do not stand for the likely success of innovation activities but for the likeliness of research and development efforts in the future. Indeed, if a company has never introduced an innovative product or at least not done so for a long period of time, it is unlikely that this company does have high incentives to perform research and development in the near future. At the very least, there will have to be special indications that such undertakings have serious intentions to innovate despite not having done so in the past.

In conclusion, the assessment of tangible and intangible assets in combination with past success of those assets is a valid measure of innovation capability and thus innovation incentives.

3) Differences between price and innovation

It has been argued that there are major differences between price and innovation that prevent the Commission from using its traditional unilateral effects model for innovation concerns. One of the main points of critique, namely that the link between market concentration and innovation is not as clear as the link between market concentration and price,[557] has been analyzed above.[558] The assessment of efficiencies in line with the Commission's Horizontal Merger Guidelines will be discussed below.[559] However, there are additional arguments in literature.

Petit finds that there is a *"structural rigidity of R&D resources"*[560] that prevents a firm from shutting down R&D programs immediately after a

556 In that sense also *Kern*, Innovation Markets, Future Markets, or Potential Competition, p. 25.
557 See for example *Cary*, Festschrift für Dirk Schroeder, p. 184.
558 See *Section II) H) 1)*.
559 See *Section II) H) 5)*.
560 *Petit*, Innovation Competition, p. 32.

merger.[561] Labor capacity, especially, is supposed to be fixed in the short term due to stringent labor regulation or imperfect labor mobility.[562] In addition, *Petit* finds that there may be *"post-merger intrafirm R&D competition in a same innovation space on account of the merged firms' organisational structure."*[563] In fact, DuPont had a decentralized R&D organization with different levels and units performing R&D.[564]

However, upon closer look, neither argument prevents the Commission from using the standard unilateral effects model with respect to innovation. The main goal of the Commission's assessment is the preservation of innovation incentives. Those incentives may decrease regardless of the specific personnel or assets. It is not only about continuing ongoing research activities in specific innovation spaces but also about the general effort put into R&D, namely in the form of output targets. Whereas it may be difficult to divest assets within a short period of time, the decision to decrease efforts is taken immediately at the time of the implementation of the merger. The harm occurs at that very moment even if it may take some time to dismiss personnel. In addition, *Petit* himself mentions that there may be a need to retain scientists to oversee the regulatory process over an extended period.[565] Accordingly, personnel could even stay in the respective undertaking but no longer be performing research and development with respect to new products. In respect to multi-product firms such as Dow and DuPont, one may also think of moving personnel to different industry sectors, such as seeds or gene editing.

With respect to intrafirm competition because of a firm's organizational structure, there is no difference between prices and innovation. Intrafirm competition may lead to a lower price level as well as increased innovation incentives. Furthermore, the organizational structure may not be changed through a merger. It is unlikely that intrafirm competition will outweigh the decrease of innovation incentives set by cannibalization concerns. When Petit finds that *"given that innovation is "stochastic", the post-merger incentive of a merged firm to promote a degree of intrafirm competition within the same innovation spaces increases"*[566], he does not take into account that this presupposes that the merged firm wants to successfully innovate in the

561 *Petit*, Innovation Competition, p. 26-27.
562 *Petit*, Innovation Competition, p. 26-27.
563 *Petit*, Innovation Competition, p. 30.
564 See *Petit*, Innovation Competition, p. 30; *Agyres/Silverman*, 25 Strategic Management Journal (2004), 929, 931.
565 *Petit*, Innovation Competition, p. 27.
566 *Petit*, Innovation Competition, p. 31.

first place. If a merged entity has no incentive to bring new products to market, it will also not engage in organizational intrafirm competition.

4) Presumption towards decreased innovation incentives: weighing of other factors

As mentioned above, there is a presumption that under specific circumstances a merger tends to lead to a decrease in innovation incentives. However, unlike with price, there are other factors impacting innovation incentives besides market concentration. In *Dow/DuPont*, regulatory issues and resistance of crops have been mentioned. Those factors are not efficiencies as they are not related to the merger. The Commission finds that generic entry, regulation and resistance are not altered by the transaction and are therefore not important in the innovation assessment of the transaction.[567]

Commentators have argued, however, that even though regulation and resistance may not be altered, they could nevertheless be the key drivers of innovation.[568] The Commission would at least have to assess and quantify other innovation-driving factors and set them in relation with market concentration.[569] As *Cary* puts it, a product may be ineffective or banned due to resistance or regulation and "*even if all other firms' ceased innovation efforts, the value of a firm's products will decline over time.*"[570]

It is indeed true that the mere fact that a driver of innovation is not altered does not say anything about its importance. And it also does not seem impossible that those factors may outweigh the negative effects of market concentration on innovation. This does not mean that resistance and regulation were the main innovation drivers in *Dow/DuPont*. But the Commission had to assess whether innovation incentives in the crop protection industry were mainly driven by factors other than market concentration.

Wirtz/Schulz suggest incorporating possible countervailing industry factors at the level of the "significance" of the SIEC test.[571] Whereas in case of market dominance, the criterion of significance is indicated by a position

567 Dow/DuPont Decision, para 2030.
568 *Cary*, Festschrift für Dirk Schroeder, p. 197; *RBB Economics*, RBB Brief 54, p. 2.
569 *Cary*, Festschrift für Dirk Schroeder, p. 197.
570 *Cary*, Festschrift für Dirk Schroeder, p. 197.
571 *Wirtz/Schulz*, NZKart 2019, 20, 27.

of structural market power, this is not the case with respect to non-market based innovation competition.[572] *Wirtz/Schulz* state:

> *"However, the decisive factor is whether the reduction in innovation incentives actually results in a significant impediment to effective innovation competition or whether sufficient innovation incentives remain despite reduced rivalry and increased cannibalization."*[573]

The consideration of other innovation-driving factors in the scope of "significance" is a possible way. Instead, one can already question whether there is an impediment at all. It is important at this point to work out at what level the SIEC test needs to be applied. Article 2 (3) EC Merger Regulation states: "*A concentration which would significantly impede effective competition, in the common market or in a substantial part of it, {...} shall be declared incompatible with the common market.*" However – and as the Commission explicitly points out –[574] innovation competition is not happening "in the common market" but rather at a different level only indirectly affecting competition on downstream product markets.[575] This means that the harm to innovation incentives must lead to a significant impediment to downstream or upstream product markets. But this does not imply that the impediment to "innovation competition" itself must be significant.[576] In fact, besides innovation competition there may be other factors impacting the overall innovation incentive. In case those other factors outweigh the reduction of rivalry on the innovation level, there will not even an impediment to effective competition on market level.

In any case, whereas price level depends to a high degree on market concentration and the level of competition,[577] innovation may also be

---

572 *Wirtz/Schulz*, NZKart 2019, 20, 27; *Montag/von Bonin* in MüKo, Art. 2 FKVO para 46 et seq.

573 *Wirtz/Schulz*, NZKart 2019, 20, 27; Author's translation from: *„Entscheidend ist aber, ob aus der Verringerung der Innovationsanreize auch tatsächlich eine erhebliche Behinderung effektiven Wettbewerbs folgt, oder ob trotz verringerter Rivalität und erhöhter Kannibalisierung ausreichende Innovationsanreize verbleiben."*

574 Dow/DuPont Decision, para 348.

575 See *Section II) C) 4)*.

576 Admittedly, the Commission concludes that there is a "*significant impediment to effective innovation competition*" without, however, explaining why the SIEC standard is applied at this level; see Dow/DuPont Decision, para 1998, 2599 and Headline 8.9.

577 Even cost savings may not automatically be passed on to consumers if the level of competition on a market is very low, see also Horizontal Merger Guidelines, para 84.

incentivized by other factors. For a complete assessment of innovation competition, those factors not only have to be taken into account but also have to be put in relation to market concentration.[578]

With respect to the Commission's assertion that those additional factors may not be altered through the merger, it has to be kept in mind that in traditional merger assessment, the Commission is taking into account buyer power or the extent of entry barriers as countervailing factors.[579] However, buyer power or entry barriers are also not changed through a merger. It is not important for factors countervailing possible anti-competitive effects to be altered through a merger as long as their effect is sufficiently strong pre-merger. Thus, the Commission must assess the significance of factors such as regulation or resistance in the crop protection industry and relate it to the negative effects arising from reduced competitive pressure.

Admittedly, the Commission somehow made an argument on the impact of additional factors on innovation incentives. Namely, in its Annex 4, the Commission referred to regulatory pressure, resistance and generics and argued that in the crop protection industry companies would regularly bring to market innovative products a long time before older products being rendered obsolete due to resistance of regulation.[580] However, this finding is only included in the Annex and not the text of the legal decision. It also contradicts the Commission's finding that factors besides market concentration are not decisive for innovation incentives because those factors are not altered by the transaction.

In conclusion, when analyzing innovation competition, the Commission must take into account possible innovation incentives regardless of whether they are altered through the merger or not, and must set them in relation to the increase in concentration.

5) Efficiencies

Besides the link between market concentration and innovation and the weighing of other innovation incentivizing factors, one of the main points

578 In that sense see *Cary*, Festschrift für Dirk Schroeder, p. 199.

579 Horizontal Merger Guidelines, para 12.

580 Annex 4, para 171.

in the discussion has been the assessment of efficiencies in *Dow/DuPont*.[581] Commentators mainly claim that the assessment used for efficiencies in the Horizontal Merger Guidelines is not fit for analyzing efficiency claims with respect to innovation. First of all, the burden of proof of the merging parties set up in the Horizontal Merger Guidelines is supposed to be invalid with respect to innovation incentives.[582] *Cary* finds with respect to the unilateral effects test:

> *"This test subjects efficiencies to a high burden. While this arguably makes sense in the context of price competition where increases in concentration are presumed to lead to upward pricing pressure, it makes no sense when assessing innovation {...} where the tools for assessing procompetitive potential are the same as those used to assess anticompetitive effects."*[583]

Second, commentators argue that the Commission applies a lower burden of proof to anticompetitive effects than it does to procompetitive effects. It has been found that while the Commission did not specify in which innovation spaces possible harm would occur, the parties had to prove efficiencies with respect to specific innovation activities.[584]

Third, it is said that the criteria mentioned in the Horizontal Merger Guidelines for assessing efficiencies do not fit the conditions of innovation competition.[585] With respect to innovation competition, it is impossible to show that efficiencies are beneficial to consumers, merger-specific and verifiable. With respect to verifiability, *Haucap* finds that

> *"while mergers may result in innovation efficiencies, these may be difficult to demonstrate, given that the European Commission requires the efficiencies*

581 *Petit*, Innovation Competition, p. 32; *Jung/Sinclair*, 40 E.C.L.R. (2019) 266, 275; *Cary*, Festschrift für Dirk Schroeder, p. 197-199; *Wirtz/Schulz*, NZKart 2019, 20, 28; *Götz* and *Weiß* at the 2. Kölner Kartellrechtsgespräche, see *Hasselhorn*, NZKart 2019, 546, 547; *Haucap*, Merger Effects on Innovation, p. 1, 9-10; *RBB Economics*, RBB Brief 54, p. 2, Footnote 8; *Chernenko*, 40 E.C.L.R. (2019) 9, 20, 23.

582 *Cary*, Festschrift für Dirk Schroeder, p. 198; *Götz* at the 2. Kölner Kartellrechtsgespräche, see *Hasselhorn*, NZKart 2019, 546, 547; *Jung/Sinclair*, 40 E.C.L.R. (2019) 266, 275.

583 *Cary*, Festschrift für Dirk Schroeder, p. 198.

584 *Cary*, Festschrift für Dirk Schroeder, p. 197; *Chernenko*, 40 E.C.L.R. (2019) 9, 20-21; *Wirtz/Schulz*, NZKart 2019, 20, 28; see also *Haucap*, Merger Effects on Innovation, p. 9-10.

585 *Chernenko*, 40 E.C.L.R. (2019) 9, 20; *Cary*, Festschrift für Dirk Schroeder, p. 199; *Weiß* at the 2. Kölner Kartellrechtsgespräche, see *Hasselhorn*, NZKart 2019, 546, 547; *Haucap*, Merger Effects on Innovation, p. 1, 9-10.

to accrue in a timely fashion, i.e., within two to four years after the merger. This contrasts with the timespan applied to the theories of harm which the Commission itself employs."[586]

In addition,

"*the condition of verifiability may prove to be even more problematic for demonstrating innovation efficiencies, given the inherently uncertain nature of R&D and innovation.*"[587]

(a) Efficiencies in the Horizontal Merger Guidelines

According to Recital 29 of the EC Merger Regulation, efficiencies should be taken into account when analyzing possible anticompetitive effects of a merger. The Commission is obliged to publish guidance on how the efficiencies are assessed. This has been done in para 76 et seqq. of the Horizontal Merger Guidelines as well as in para 52 et seqq. of the Non-Horizontal Merger Guidelines. The Horizontal Merger Guidelines state:

"*In order to assess the foreseeable impact of a merger on the relevant markets, the Commission analyses its possible anti-competitive effects and the relevant countervailing factors such as {…} possible efficiencies put forward by the parties.*"[588]

Efficiencies are supposed to counteract otherwise existing negative effects on competition:

"*It is possible that efficiencies brought about by a merger counteract the effects on competition and in particular the potential harm to consumers it might otherwise have.*"[589]
"*The Commission considers any substantiated efficiency claim in the overall assessment of the merger. {…} This will be the case when the Commission is in a position to conclude on the basis of sufficient evidence that the efficiencies generated by the merger are likely to enhance the ability and incentive of the merged entity to act pro-competitively for the benefit of*

586 *Haucap*, Merger Effects on Innovation, p. 1.
587 *Haucap*, Merger Effects on Innovation, p. 10.
588 Horizontal Merger Guidelines, para 12.
589 Horizontal Merger Guidelines, para 76.

> *consumers, thereby counteracting the adverse effects on competition which the merger might otherwise have.*"[590]

For counteracting the negative effects of a merger, efficiencies must cumulatively benefit consumers, be merger-specific and verifiable.[591]

The criterion of benefit to consumers is explained as follows:

> "*The relevant benchmark in assessing efficiency claims is that consumers will not be worse off as a result of the merger. For that purpose, efficiencies should be substantial and timely, and should, in principle, benefit consumers in those relevant markets where it is otherwise likely that competition concerns would occur.*"[592]
> "*Consumers may also benefit from new or improved products or services, for instance resulting from efficiency gains in the sphere of R & D and innovation.*"[593]
> "*In general, the later the efficiencies are expected to materialise in the future, the less weight the Commission can assign to them. This implies that, in order to be considered as a counteracting factor, the efficiencies must be timely.*"[594]

Efficiencies are verifiable, according to the Horizontal Merger Guidelines, if they are clearly identifiable and at best quantifiable. It is upon the merging parties to show that the efficiencies are likely to be realized and likely to countervail possible negative effects:

> "*Efficiencies have to be verifiable such that the Commission can be reasonably certain that the efficiencies are likely to materialise, and be substantial enough to counteract a merger's potential harm to consumers. {...} Where reasonably possible, efficiencies and the resulting benefit to consumers should therefore be quantified. When the necessary data are not available to allow for a precise quantitative analysis, it must be possible to foresee a clearly identifiable positive impact on consumers, not a marginal one. {...}*"[595]
> "*Most of the information, allowing the Commission to assess whether the merger will bring about the sort of efficiencies that would enable it to clear a merger, is solely in the possession of the merging parties. It is, therefore, incumbent upon the notifying parties to provide in due time all the relevant*

590 Horizontal Merger Guidelines, para 77.
591 Horizontal Merger Guidelines, para 78.
592 Horizontal Merger Guidelines, para 79.
593 Horizontal Merger Guidelines, para 81.
594 Horizontal Merger Guidelines, para 83.
595 Horizontal Merger Guidelines, para 86.

information necessary to demonstrate that the claimed efficiencies are merger-specific and likely to be realised. Similarly, it is for the notifying parties to show to what extent the efficiencies are likely to counteract any adverse effects on competition that might otherwise result from the merger, and therefore benefit consumers."[596]

In conclusion, the rationale behind efficiency claims in the Horizontal Guidelines is that there is competitive harm through a merger in the first place and that this harm can be counterbalanced by quantifiable efficiencies. As the relevant benchmark for the Horizontal Merger Guidelines is the consumer in the relevant market, the efficiencies must be quantified in respect to their impact on that very market. Furthermore, the efficiencies must be timely. Due to the underlying presumption that there is competitive harm in the first place, the likeliness and significance of the efficiencies must be proven by the merging parties. Even though the Horizontal Merger Guidelines mention efficiency gains in R&D and innovation as possible benefits for consumers, the abovementioned preconditions for efficiencies do not seem to fit into the Commission's assessment of innovation competition as used in *Dow/DuPont*.

(b) Efficiency assessment in Dow/DuPont

In *Dow/DuPont*, the parties submit several efficiency claims. They argue that the merger may reduce spillovers, resulting in a reduced risk of imitation (that is a higher lever of appropriability).[597] The merger would lead to an increase of returns to innovation by capturing greater sales and accordingly appropriating more of the value of the innovation.[598] Also, post-merger the parties would be able to combine complementary products in a way not feasible pre-merger.[599] In the specific context, the merger would allow a greater pool of AIs for mixtures.[600] In that case dependency on third parties would be reduced and returns for innovation efforts would be enhanced leading to increased investment incentives.[601] The parties also argue that through the merger it would be possible to

596 Horizontal Merger Guidelines, para 87.
597 Dow/DuPont Decision, para 3267.
598 Dow/DuPont Decision, para 3268.
599 Dow/DuPont Decision, para 3269.
600 Dow/DuPont Decision, para 3269.
601 Dow/DuPont Decision, para 3270.

eliminate redundant assets, retaining the more efficient capabilities.[602] Furthermore, the transaction would enable the merged entity to use existing capabilities more efficiently:

> *"if different assets are used at different stages of an AI's journey through the pipeline, then developing a larger number of AIs would allow the merged entity to ensure that its assets are not under-used."*[603]

Finally, the parties submit that the transaction would allow the combination of complementary strengths.[604]

However, the Commission finds that the alleged efficiencies do not fulfill the criteria set out in the Horizontal Merger Guidelines:

> *"All the efficiencies alleged by the Parties depend on future strategic decisions by the companies and on detailed knowledge of companies' assets and capabilities and of the function of the industry and its dynamics. They likely take place in the long-term based on a complex and long chain of events. The efficiencies are thus difficult for the Commission to verify on its own and the submissions by the Parties do not provide any concrete evidence on how these efficiencies are being planned and how much they would improve the productivity of the merged entity."*[605]
> *"The Parties have not provided any evidence that these efficiencies would be passed on to consumers to a sufficiently large extent."*[606]

With respect to the merger-specificity of the efficiencies, the Commission refers to the possibility of R&D cooperation:

> *"The Parties have not provided any evidence that these efficiencies can only be achieved with the Transaction. On the contrary, it seems that a number of these alleged benefits can be achieved through other means (for example R&D agreements) and do not require a merger between the Parties."*[607]
> *"In the absence of any substantiated submission and proof, the Commission cannot assess whether the claimed efficiencies are likely, verifiable, merger-specific and beneficial to consumers. Accordingly, the Commission cannot*

602 Dow/DuPont Decision, para 3271.
603 Dow/DuPont Decision, para 3271.
604 Dow/DuPont Decision, para 3272.
605 Dow/DuPont Decision, para 3280.
606 Dow/DuPont Decision, para 3283.
607 Dow/DuPont Decision, para 3282.

conclude that the alleged efficiencies would countervail the reductions of innovation competition that are likely to result from the Transaction."[608]

In conclusion, the Commission refers to the abovementioned arguments of the parties as being traditional efficiencies for which the merging parties bear the burden of proof and which must benefit consumers, be merger-specific and be verifiable.

The Commission gives an explanation as to why the arguments of the parties are considered as being efficiencies within the meaning of the Horizontal Merger Guidelines:

"*At the outset, the Commission notes that according to its assessment, all the channels set out by the Parties rely on merger efficiencies. This is because each of the channels is based on a mechanism conceptually distinct from the loss of competition between the Parties brought about by the merger itself. In other words, these channels are not necessarily specific to a merger or linked to the elimination of competition between the Parties. While a reduction in imitation (or free-riding) by rival firms may, for example, generate an offsetting pro-innovation effect (by allowing the merging parties to internalise a positive externality that was not being internalised absent the merger), it can be logically distinguished from the effect of the loss of competition between the Parties. This is because a reduction in imitation risk does not automatically follow from a loss of competition between the Parties. The reduction in this risk can - at least in principle - be achieved by strong (enforcement of) IPR, high degree of secrecy or other business strategies by the industry participants.*"[609]

(c) Appraisal

(1) Efficiencies are part of the underlying theory of harm: no burden of proof with the parties

Concerning the first claim made in the literature – namely that the burden of proof should not be with the parties or that the parties' arguments stated above are not traditional efficiencies but rather part of the theory of harm itself – there are good reasons for it being valid. Two points must be considered to conclude that the treatment of pro-innovation effects of a

---

608 Dow/DuPont Decision, para 3284.
609 Dow/DuPont Decision, para 3275.

merger does not fit into the traditional setting of efficiencies and that the Commission itself is obliged to prove the non-existence of pro-innovation effects.

First of all, one must recall the rationale behind *Dow/DuPont*. The Commission refers to the following thesis:

> "*Economic principles indicate that a merger between two out of a limited number of significant innovators is likely to reduce product innovation when appropriability is high (that is, when IPRs are effective), and when there are no merger-specific efficiencies associated with the merger.*"[610]

This indicates that the competitive harm (reduction of product innovation or rather reduction of incentives to product innovation) will only occur if there are no efficiencies. Without the assessment of efficiencies, there cannot be an ascertainment as to possible negative effects on innovation. The mere assessment of the limited number of significant innovators in a specific market setting with high appropriability does not lead to the conclusion that innovation incentives are reduced. Even though there is, under specific circumstances, a link between market concentration and innovation incentives, the final assessment of a reduction of the very innovation incentives relies on the incorporation of possible innovation-enhancing effects.[611] Unlike concentration on product markets that has a high likelihood of leading to increased prices,[612] this is not automatically the case with respect to innovation. This is reflected in one of the papers issued by the Chief Economist team where it reads:

> "*{…} the merger leads to lower innovation incentives for the merged entity, absent cost efficiencies and knowledge spillovers.*"[613]
> "*We also consider innovation-related efficiencies that a merger may release, including reductions in R&D costs and merger-specific enhancements in the effectiveness of innovation. {…} Both the results on innovation incentives and on consumer welfare can be overturned if there are sufficiently large R&D efficiencies.*"[614]

610 Dow/DuPont Decision, para 2042.

611 *Kern* finds that the consideration of efficiencies serves as a necessary corrective to the rather weak presumption in favor of competition, *Kern*, Innovation Markets, Future Markets, or Potential Competition, p. 33.

612 See *Cary*, Festschrift für Dirk Schroeder, p. 184; *Federico/Scott Morton/Shapiro*, Antitrust and Innovation, p. 5.

613 *Federico/Langus/Valletti*, Horizontal Mergers and Product Innovation, p. 1.

614 *Federico/Langus/Valletti*, Horizontal Mergers and Product Innovation, p. 2.

Even though the term "overturned" is somehow misleading (as it presupposes a negative effect in the first place), it becomes clear from the above-mentioned statements that a merger assessment concerning innovation incentives cannot be complete without an assessment of efficiencies. Imagine the parties not bringing forward any efficiency claims (for whatever reason) even though post-merger there would be extremely large cost efficiencies and a high reduction of knowledge spillover. In that case, if a Commissions' merger assessment does not take into account those effects by itself (without the parties invoking it), it would lead to a completely flawed outcome, even eminently decreasing innovation incentives. This refers to the potentially ambiguous relationship between market concentration and innovation incentives. Whereas market concentration will in general lead to higher prices,[615] the link between concentration in innovation and innovation incentives is only valid under specific circumstances. Those circumstances include the absence of innovation-specific efficiencies.

The latter becomes apparent with respect to the Commission's assessment of appropriability. Whereas the existing level of appropriability is part of the Commission's theory of harm that is assessed ex officio, an increase of the level of appropriability is treated as merger-specific efficiency. But if a high level of appropriability is prerequisite for the possible harm to innovation, it is by no means comprehensible why an increase should not be part of the Commission's theory of harm anymore. The latter distinction seems to imply that there is an optimal level of appropriability from which point forward an increase is no longer important. However, there is no argument or theory that refers to that optimal height of appropriability. Accordingly, the Commission will always have to assess whether a merger can increase appropriability, even without the parties invoking it.

The same is true with respect to cost savings due to a merger. One of the thoughts behind the Commission's theory of harm is that increased cannibalization post-merger may lead to decreased innovation incentives. This is due to the fact that the merged entity is more likely to capture sales from own products. Thus, innovation does not "pay out", because it does not lead to a greater stream of revenues. However, if there are sufficient cost efficiencies with respect to R&D, innovation activities may be profitable, as they outweigh the captured sales from a company's own products. In that respect, cost efficiencies not only counteract lost returns

615 Regardless of the specific market features; the effect may just be overturned with respect to specific efficiency effects.

to innovation but they prevent losing returns in the first place. It should be kept in mind that the reasoning behind cannibalization and its relation to innovation incentives is not that a firm wants to prevent taking sales from own products but rather that it wants to prevent losing revenues. It is not in the specific interest of a firm to protect old products but to maximize income.

In that respect, it seems artificial to separate the concern of cannibalization of own products from the merger-specific cost savings that both occur at the very same time. A firm will not concern itself first with losing sales from own products and then find that this does not matter as there are cost savings that outweigh the cannibalized sales. In practice a firm will rather look at whether its final income will decrease or increase if it invests in R&D. In that respect, one cannot separate the increased cannibalization concerns from the increased cost savings post-merger. In order to come to a realistic picture of the innovation incentives post-transaction, the Commission is obliged to assess both. Leaving out the cost savings (because the parties do not rely on those) would not only lead to an incomplete picture but in fact to a false result.

In addition, there is one big difference between price and innovation in terms of possible efficiencies: In general, a higher market share may give the merged entity the ability to increase prices or limit production without losing income. On the other hand,

> "*cost savings in production or distribution may give the merged entity the ability and incentive to charge lower prices following the merger.*"[616]

However, the

> "*incentive on the part of the merged entity to pass efficiency gains on to consumers is often related to the existence of competitive pressure from the remaining firms in the market and from potential entry.*"[617]

This means that besides cost savings there need to be additional factors that put pressure on the merged firm to not raise prices. Apart from those additional factors, the merged entity would have no incentive to pass on cost savings to consumers. The decision to raise prices is to a large extent determined by competitive pressure from third parties. Even if there remain other players on the market, the merged entity may still have an

616 Horizontal Merger Guidelines, para 80.
617 Horizontal Merger Guidelines, para 84.

incentive to raise prices if those players do not sufficiently restrict that incentive.

This is different with respect to innovation incentives. The decision to innovate is driven by the prospect to raise income. Any additional income will be sufficient to decide to innovate. This means that even if the competitive pressure of third parties is low, there will still be innovation incentives as long as a new product will gain any revenues from other market participants. Only in the case of a merger to monopoly will there not be a way of gaining more revenues from third parties, and it will depend on competitive pressure – for example by perceived potential entrants – to set incentives to innovate.

Accordingly, the biggest difference between price and innovation with respect to efficiencies is that efficiencies will not automatically incentivize lower prices, whereas in most cases they will automatically lead to innovation incentives as long as the efficiencies are large enough to outweigh cannibalization concerns. Whether cost efficiencies lead to lower prices depends on third party competitive pressure. Whether cost efficiencies lead to increased innovation incentives is to a high degree independent of competitive pressure from third parties.

The same holds true for appropriability effects. As the Commission points out

> *"a reduction in imitation (or free-riding) by rival firms may, for example, generate an offsetting pro-innovation effect (by allowing the merging parties to internalise a positive externality that was not being internalised absent the merger) {…}."*[618]

The same effect, namely the internalization of a positive externality, applies to the increase in appropriability as it holds for general cannibalization concerns. Again, it depends on the sum of both internalization effects if a merger leads to a decrease or increase in innovation incentives. This is independent of competitive pressure by other market participants.

The second reason why the treatment of pro-innovation effects does not fit into the traditional efficiency analysis is reflected in the wording of the Horizontal Merger Guidelines. According to the Guidelines, the Commission analyses *"possible anti-competitive effects and the relevant countervailing factors such as {…} possible efficiencies put forward by the parties."*[619] The

618 Dow/DuPont Decision, para 3275.
619 Horizontal Merger Guidelines, para 12.

efficiencies may "*counteract the effects on competition and in particular the potential harm to consumers it might otherwise have.*"[620]

This implies that there must be an anti-competitive effect in the first place. But as shown above, this is not the case. There is no presumption that an increase in concentration will lead to a decrease in innovation incentives independent of efficiencies. In that respect, the Horizontal Merger Guidelines start from a perspective that does not fit innovation concerns.

For that reason, the burden of proof that traditionally lies with the parties[621] must be shifted to the Commission concerning innovation competition. Since innovation-enhancing effects cannot be separated from innovation-depressing effects, the Commission must incorporate both in its assessment regardless of the parties invoking possible benefits.[622]

This outcome is not changed by the fact that the information necessary for assessing possible efficiencies is usually "*solely in the possession of the merging parties.*"[623] This is not different with respect to the information necessary to assess the whole transaction. The Commission has the right to request information according to Article 11 of the EC Merger Regulation. This instrument suffices to get access to all material relevant for the analysis of possible efficiencies. Since undertakings are generally required to hand in comprehensive information, it is unlikely that they have any additional material available to prove possible efficiencies.

(2) Efficiency criteria of the Horizontal Merger Guidelines are not fit for innovation competition

As mentioned above, the assessment of efficiencies in the Horizontal Merger Guidelines does not fit with respect to innovation competition. This is

620 Horizontal Merger Guidelines, para 76 and 77.

621 Horizontal Merger Guidelines, para 85, 87.

622 In a recent judgment, the General Court even found that there generally has to be a distinction between those efficiencies mentioned in the Horizontal Cooperation Guidelines and "*those specific to each concentration*". As far as efficiencies are part of the theory designed to establish whether there are restrictive effects of a merger, they have to be taken into account "*prior to the overall competitive appraisal as provided for in paragraph 76 of the Guidelines.*" GC, Judgment of 28.05.2020, Case T-399/16, ECLI:EU:T:2020:217, para 279, *CK Telecoms UK Investments*.

623 Horizontal Merger Guidelines, para 87.

not only true for the burden of proof but also for the specific criteria to assess efficiencies.

This refers to the second and third line of critique by commentators.[624] They found that the Commission would apply a lower burden of proof to anticompetitive than to procompetitive effects. In addition, the standard of the Horizontal Merger Guidelines – that efficiencies have to be beneficial to consumers, merger-specific and verifiable– is deemed to be invalid with respect to innovation competition.

Those two arguments have to be read in conjunction: the criteria in the Horizontal Merger Guidelines for assessing efficiencies do not fit innovation competition. And because of that, the Commission ends up in *Dow/DuPont* in imposing a higher standard to the parties for proofing efficiencies than it does for the original assessment of competitive harm.

This finding is due to the fact that the Commission does not assess innovation competition as happening in a market but rather on a different level as an input activity. When the Horizontal Merger Guidelines state that efficiencies should "*benefit consumers in those relevant markets where it is otherwise likely that competition concerns would occur*"[625], it is obvious that this benchmark is not applicable to effects beyond market level.

In fact, it seems impossible that in an assessment based on concentration of innovation competitors and importance of innovators, there may be any factor directly affecting consumers in a market. As mentioned above,[626] the protective goal of Commission action is the innovation incentive. This is mainly due to the fact that competition policy cannot intervene into the relation between R&D activity and innovation outcome. Competition does not alter the stochastic process of innovation. In that respect, it cannot be expected of the parties to submit findings concerning any effect on the innovation outcome. It may be that more innovation activity leads to more new products. However, the only thing that can be influenced in this context is the incentive to start R&D. Accordingly, when the harm may be a decrease in innovation incentives, possible efficiencies also have to relate to those very innovation incentives.

In that respect, the claim in *Dow/DuPont* that the parties would be able to combine complementary products in a way not feasible pre-merger[627] is not related to innovation incentives but rather to the R&D outcome. It

---

624 See *Section II) H) 5)*.

625 Horizontal Merger Guidelines, para 79.

626 See *Section II) C) 3)*.

627 Dow/DuPont Decision, para 3269.

is thus not a possible efficiency. However, the two most important efficiencies mentioned in the literature, namely an increase in appropriability and cost savings in R&D,[628] are both related to innovation incentives.

The finding that the innovation efficiencies mentioned above cannot benefit consumers directly is not changed by the statement in the Horizontal Merger Guidelines that consumers "*may also benefit from new or improved products or services, for instance resulting from efficiency gains in the sphere of R & D and innovation.*"[629] This does not relate to the rationale in *Dow/DuPont*, where the goal of protection is not the innovative product but the innovation incentive.

Even though it seems likely to prove that innovation efficiencies are merger-specific, it seems impossible to show a specific consumer benefit.[630] With respect to verifiability, it seems unlikely that the standard of the Horizontal Merger Guidelines may be fulfilled. First of all, the Horizontal Merger Guidelines require with respect to verifiability that

> "*the efficiencies are likely to materialise, and be substantial enough to counteract a merger's potential harm to consumers. {...} Where reasonably possible, efficiencies and the resulting benefit to consumers should therefore be quantified.*"[631]

A consumer benefit can, by its very nature, not be substantiated for a setting beyond existing markets. Second, it may be difficult to precisely quantify, for example, the level of appropriability post-merger. Hence, it must be sufficient to prove that there will be higher appropriability and

628 *Denicolò/Polo* also mention the coordination of R&D projects and sharing of technological knowledge as possible positive effects of a merger on innovation incentives, *Denicolò/Polo*, The innovation theory of harm, p. 4 et seq, 12 et seq, 27; whereas the coordination of R&D projects rather seems to lead to cost savings, sharing of technological knowledge may to a large extent be important with respect to innovation optimizing production processes or be captured with the mechanism of coordination in the product market, see *Section II) D) 1)*; see also *Federico/Scott Morton/Shapiro*, Antitrust and Innovation, p. 8.

629 Horizontal Merger Guidelines, para 81.

630 In *Dow/DuPont*, the parties also seem to mainly criticize this point when stating that it would be impossible to prove and quantify for example pass-on to consumers, Dow/DuPont Decision, para 3278; *Todino/van de Walle/Stoican* find that "*the criteria the Commission has established for an efficiency defense to succeed with respect to product and price competition simply cannot apply to innovation competition, where it is impossible to prove and quantify the pass-on.*", *Todino/van de Walle/Stoican*, 64 The Antitrust Bulletin (2019), 11, 28.

631 Horizontal Merger Guidelines, para 86.

that this will likely outweigh an increased concentration with respect to innovation.

Concerning the criterion of timeliness[632], it should be noted that there will be increased incentives to innovate due to expected cost savings and increased appropriability at the time of the implementation of the merger. This mirrors the point in time in which the possible harm would occur. Since it is not about long-term effects on innovative products but about the short-term incentives to perform R&D,[633] efficiencies manifest themselves immediately with the prospect of cost savings and reduced spillover.

In addition, the Commission's finding in *Dow/DuPont* that the efficiencies brought forward by the parties are not merger-specific is inconsistent. The underlying rationale in *Dow/DuPont* points to firms being important innovators if they are vertically integrated from basic research until marketing.[634] It remains completely unclear why possible efficiencies "*can be achieved through other means (for example R&D agreements) and do not require a merger between the Parties.*"[635] If the strength as innovator depends on the interplay between marketing experience and research approach, it seems unlikely that this strength can be achieved through a mere partnership.[636] Cooperation can usually be terminated and in that case even increase spillover effects.[637] Structural changes are by far more efficient to realize cost advantages and decreased spillover.

(d) Conclusion on efficiencies

Efficiencies such as cost savings or increased appropriability are part of the Commission's theory of harm in *Dow/DuPont*. Accordingly, the Commission is obliged to assess those efficiencies ex officio. Otherwise, the

---

632 See Horizontal Merger Guidelines, para 83.

633 See *Section II) C) 3)*.

634 See *Section II) C) 1)*.

635 Dow/DuPont Decision, para 3282.

636 In that sense *Cary*: „*The Decision, however, discounts such partnerships as not providing the same benefits of an internal program when it discounts non-vertically integrated innovators as not being „R&D players.*", *Cary*, Festschrift für Dirk Schroeder, p. 199.

637 The partners will have fundamental knowledge about the underlying invention and, beyond existing IPR, be able to develop solutions based on the jointly developed technology.

Commission's outcome with respect to innovation incentives would not only be incomplete but bears the risk of being manifestly wrong.

With respect to efficiencies, the standard in the Horizontal Merger Guidelines is only partly fit to cover innovation competition. Whereas is seems likely to show that effects are merger-specific, it is impossible to quantify benefits for consumers. The level of verifiability has to be adjusted to the specific efficiency.

6) General requirements of the SIEC test

In the landmark *CK Telecoms UK Investments* judgment of 28 May 2020, the General Court has set up requirements for an analysis of unilateral effects in an oligopolistic market under the SIEC test.[638] According to the General Court, the SIEC test has been established to cover concentrations in oligopolistic markets that, although not creating or strengthening a dominant position, affect the market in a way equivalent to the creation of dominance.[639] In that regard,

> "*the mere effect of reducing competitive pressure on the remaining competitors is not, in principle, sufficient in itself to demonstrate a significant impediment to effective competition in the context of a theory of harm based on non-coordinated effects.*"[640]

Under certain circumstances, it may be sufficient for a significant impediment to effective competition if a transactions removes an "important competitive force" from the market. However, such an "important competitive force" has to stand out from its competitors in terms of its impact on competition. The General Court finds:

> "*It is apparent from the contested decision that, as regards the elimination of an 'important competitive force', the Commission is of the opinion that the mere decline in the competitive pressure which would result, in particular, from the loss of an undertaking having more of an influence on competition*

638 GC, Judgment of 28.05.2020, Case T-399/16, ECLI:EU:T:2020:217, para 85, *CK Telecoms UK Investments*.

639 GC, Judgment of 28.05.2020, Case T-399/16, ECLI:EU:T:2020:217, para 90, *CK Telecoms UK Investments*.

640 GC, Judgment of 28.05.2020, Case T-399/16, ECLI:EU:T:2020:217, para 97, *CK Telecoms UK Investments*.

than its market share would suggest is sufficient, in itself, to prove a significant impediment to effective competition."[641]

{...}

> "*It follows that the Commission made an error of law and an error of assessment, in recital 326 of the contested decision, in finding that an 'important competitive force' does not need to stand out from its competitors in terms of impact on competition, particularly in so far as such a position would allow it to treat as an 'important competitive force' any undertaking in an oligopolistic market exerting competitive pressure.*"[642]
> "*As the applicant has rightly pointed out, that would amount to allowing the Commission to prohibit, by that fact alone, horizontal concentrations in such markets and would infringe the principle of legal certainty, since the Commission could thus omit to analyse the possible elimination of the important competitive constraints that the merging parties exert upon each other in favour of a theory of harm based solely on a reduction of competitive pressure on the remaining competitors.*"[643]

Generally, "closeness of competition" is an acceptable assessment criterion, particularly in case of unilateral effects in an oligopoly.[644] However, there has to be a detailed analysis that the merging parties are particularly close competitors. The General Court points out:

> "*However, most of the examples mentioned in the contested decision are not intended to identify how close the parties are, or to show that they exerted important competitive constraints on each other, but are aimed above all at showing that Three and O2 are 'close competitors' rather than 'particularly close competitors'. Thus, the Commission seems more to analyse the closeness of competition between Three and O2, on the one hand, and the other two mobile network operators, on the other. It concludes, in recital 1183 of the*

641 GC, Judgment of 28.05.2020, Case T-399/16, ECLI:EU:T:2020:217, para 171, *CK Telecoms UK Investments*.

642 GC, Judgment of 28.05.2020, Case T-399/16, ECLI:EU:T:2020:217, para 174, *CK Telecoms UK Investments*.

643 GC, Judgment of 28.05.2020, Case T-399/16, ECLI:EU:T:2020:217, para 175, *CK Telecoms UK Investments*.

644 GC, Judgment of 28.05.2020, Case T-399/16, ECLI:EU:T:2020:217, para 236, 239, 241, *CK Telecoms UK Investments*.

> *contested decision, that the four mobile network operators, and not only Three and O2, 'compete closely'."*[645]
>
> *"Although it may indeed be established that Three and O2 are relatively close competitors in some of the segments of a concentrated market comprising four mobile network operators, that factor alone is not sufficient to prove, in the present case, the elimination of the important competitive constraints which the parties to the concentration exerted upon each other and cannot suffice to establish a significant impediment to effective competition; if that were not the case, any concentration resulting in a reduction from four to three operators would as a matter of principle be prohibited."*[646]

In addition, the General Court finds that the cursory reference to the elimination of a competitive force, the closeness of the parties and a large market share is not sufficient to conclude that unilateral effects are "*significant*".[647]

One may wonder whether the Dow/DuPont Decision meets the requirements laid down by the General Court. In fact, the Commission relied to a large extent on the reduction of the number of competitors in the industry. However, the General Court explicitly pointed out that the mere elimination of a competitor (or of competitive pressure on the remaining competitors in general) in an oligopoly is not sufficient to lead to a significant impediment to effective competition.

Having said this, there are two main arguments why the Commission's theory in *Dow/DuPont* is likely to fulfill the General Court's requirements. First, the criterion of "significance" can only be determined on a case-by-case basis. There is no theory on when an effect is "significant". The General Court set up a benchmark for the factual assessment in the specific case but it did not say when a theory of harm itself may support a significant impediment. There is not such a thing as a *per se* significance and the underlying theory of a case cannot be examined on the basis of the General Court's criteria.

Transferred to the individual *Dow/DuPont* case this means that the underlying rationale (that a merger of two out of a limited number of impor-

645 GC, Judgment of 28.05.2020, Case T-399/16, ECLI:EU:T:2020:217, para 242, see also para 434, *CK Telecoms UK Investments*.

646 GC, Judgment of 28.05.2020, Case T-399/16, ECLI:EU:T:2020:217, para 249, *CK Telecoms UK Investments*.

647 GC, Judgment of 28.05.2020, Case T-399/16, ECLI:EU:T:2020:217, para 288, 289, *CK Telecoms UK Investments*.

tant innovators leads – under additional circumstances –[648] to reduced innovation incentives) may support an impediment to effective competition. Whether this impediment is significant depends on the implementation of the theory in the specific case. Or in other words: whereas the underlying rationale suggests that there is a decrease in innovation incentives, the extent of the decrease is a question of the individual case. As mentioned above,[649] this thesis is not about the assessment of the specific *Dow/DuPont* case but about scrutinizing its underlying rationale. The General Court's analysis is not a very suitable starting point for this purpose.

Second, even when looking at the specific assessment in *Dow/DuPont*, there are good reasons to believe that the General Court's conditions are met. The Commission has not limited itself to finding that competitive pressure was removed from the remaining competitors. It also did not base its analysis on the mere reduction of players in the industry. Instead, the Commission performed a very detailed analysis to show that Dow and DuPont were the most important and closest innovation competitors in the industry[650] that "stand out" against their competitors. In addition, the Commission focused on very specific industry features[651] – namely that innovation is the key parameter of competition and that barriers to entry as well as the level of appropriability are high – that have to be met in order to conclude that there is harm to innovation incentives. It is not just about the reduction of competitors in an oligopoly. In that regard, it seems likely that the General Court's criteria for assessing "significance" are even fulfilled in the specific *Dow/DuPont* case.

7) Legal Certainty and the right to realize concentrations of undertakings

Another argument raised in the context of the validity of the Commission's approach in *Dow/DuPont* is the question of legal certainty and the right to realize concentrations of undertakings. Commentators find that the Commission's theory contains "*significant uncertainties*" with respect to a case-by-case assessment.[652] First, it is considered unclear how to define

---

648 See *Section II) C) 1)*.

649 See *Section II) H) 1) (a)*.

650 Dow/DuPont Decision, para 2396 et seq, 2499, 2517, 2531, 2532, 2533, 2547, 2600 et seq.

651 See also *Section II) C) 1)*.

652 *Wirtz/Schulz*, NZKart 2019, 20, 22; see also *Spangler/Heppner*, PharmR 2018, 522, 523.

specific innovation spaces.[653] In fact, the Commission used crop/pest combinations similar to the downstream product markets as well as broader ranges of pests without connection to specific crops (broader than product markets).[654] There are no specific criteria for the definition of innovation spaces in the Dow/DuPont Decision.

Second, there are insecurities on the undertakings in the innovation spaces as well as on industry level that can be considered important innovators.[655] This becomes apparent with respect to Monsanto, which has been analyzed as not being an important innovator in *Dow/DuPont*.[656] The Commission referred to its herbicide Glyphosate as not being innovative.[657] In addition, the Commission found that Monsanto only had a limited role in the research for crop protection chemicals.[658] In the subsequent *Bayer/Monsanto* merger, however, the Commission found that Monsanto was an important innovator because it would continuously innovate with respect to new mixtures and formulas for Glyphosate.[659] This shows that the assessment of important players in innovation spaces – such as mixtures and formulas for Glyphosate – may vary. In addition, it is supposed to be even more difficult to analyze the relative importance of the innovators in an industry.[660]

Specifically, it has been claimed that R&D activities in early stages are usually internal and thus difficult to assess for competitors.[661] With respect to the Commission's extensive investigations in *Dow/DuPont*, incorporating information from competitors and market participants, patent analysis, and data on past innovation races as well as industry development, it has been argued that such assessment cannot be realized by small innova-

653 *Wirtz/Schulz*, NZKart 2019, 20, 28.

654 Dow/DuPont Decision, para 311, 351.

655 *Wirtz/Schulz*, NZKart 2019, 20, 24; FCO, Innovationen – Herausforderungen für die Kartellrechtspraxis, p. 37; *Thiede/Müller*, EuZW 2019, 628, 633; *Fort* at the 2. Kölner Kartellrechtsgespräche, see *Hasselhorn*, NZKart 2019, 546.

656 Dow/DuPont Decision, para 2205, 2230 et seq, 2242; Commission Decision of 21.03.2018, C(2018) 1709 final, OJ C 459, 20.12.2018, p. 10-23, Case M.8084, para 166, *Bayer/Monsanto*.

657 Dow/DuPont Decision, para 2232.

658 Dow/DuPont Decision, para 2232-2233.

659 Commission Decision of 21.03.2018, C(2018) 1709 final, OJ C 459, 20.12.2018, p. 10-23, Case M.8084, para 1600 et seq, 1614 et seq, 1623 et seq, 1776, *Bayer/Monsanto*; see also *Wirtz/Schulz*, NZKart 2019, 20, 25.

660 *Wirtz/Schulz*, NZKart 2019, 20, 24.

661 *Wirtz/Schulz*, NZKart 2019, 20, 24, 28.

tors.[662] In that regard the *Dow/DuPont* criteria could put a high burden on undertakings willing to merge.[663]

(a) Constitutional basis

The right to realize concentrations of undertakings falls within the freedom to conduct a business according to Article 16 of the Charter of Fundamental Rights of the European Union ("CFR") and the right to property according to Article 17 CFR.[664]

In addition, the general principles of Union Law including the principle of legal certainty and the related principle of precision are also applicable in the case of merger assessment. With respect to legal certainty, the ECJ has ruled in

> *Gondrand Frères*: "*The principle of legal certainty requires that rules imposing charges on the taxpayer must be clear and precise so that he may know without ambiguity what are his rights and obligations and may take steps accordingly.*"[665]

Concerning the principle of respect for legitimate expectations, the ECJ found:

> "*{…}, the field of application of this principle cannot be extended to the point of generally preventing new rules from applying to the future effects of*

---

662 *Thiede/Müller*, EuZW 2019, 628, 633.

663 See *Thiede/Müller*, EuZW 2019, 628, 633; *Wirtz/Schulz*, NZKart 2019, 20, 23, fn. 30.

664 Advocate General *Kokott* in *Impala*: "*Thus, while the commercial freedom of the participating undertakings and the property rights of their shareholders (Articles 16 and 17 of the Charter of fundamental rights) undoubtedly include the right to realize concentrations of undertakings, this applies only in so far as certain conditions or obligations on, or even the prohibition of, the concentration in question are not necessary for protecting competition from distortion.*", Opinion of Advocate General *Kokott* delivered on 13.12.2007, Case C-413/06 P, ECLI:EU:C:2007:790, para 214, *Impala*; Sceptical with respect to protection of enterprises under Article 17 CFR: *Jarass*, Charta der Grundrechte der Europäischen Union, Art. 17 para 13; *Wollenschläger* in von der Groeben/Schwarze/Hatje, Europäisches Unionsrecht, Art. 17 GRC para 16.

665 ECJ, Judgement of 09.07.1981, Case 169/80, ECLI:EU:C:1981:171, para 17, *Gondrand Frères*.

> *situations which arose under the earlier rules in the absence of obligations entered into with the public authorities.*"[666]

Detached from definite "rules", the ECJ has found:

> "*Since Community institutions enjoy a margin of discretion in the choice of the means needed to achieve their policies, traders are unable to claim that they have a legitimate expectation that an existing situation which is capable of being altered by decisions taken by those institutions within the limits of their discretionary power will be maintained.*"[667]

In conclusion, the Commission is not prevented from introducing new theories into its Decisions.[668] In that respect, it is at the Commission's discretion how to enforce its policies, namely with regard to the appraisal of the development of technical and economic progress in Article 2 (1) EC Merger Regulation. In addition, the term "innovation" is mentioned in the Horizontal Merger Guidelines. Those Guidelines, despite not being a formal law, set binding principles for the Commission and reference for companies. Accordingly, it is foreseeable that the Commission may take into account innovation concerns.

However, when introducing new principles, the criteria must be clear and precise and enable the addressees to asses rights and obligations. This is even more the case with respect to a possible interference with fundamental rights such as Article 16 and 17 CFR.

(b) Application in Dow/DuPont

With that in mind, one may question whether the criteria in *Dow/DuPont* are clear and precise. In fact, it seems difficult to predict the amount of innovation competitors in an industry and the specific definition of innovation spaces. *Wirtz/Schulz* claim that the parties of a transaction would

666 ECJ, Judgement of 16.05.1979, Case 84/78, ECLI:EU:C:1979:129, para 21, *Tomadini*; see also ECJ, Judgment of 05.05.1981, Case 112/80, ECLI:EU:C:1981:94, para 48, *Dürbeck*.

667 ECJ, Judgment of 15.07.1982, Case 245/81, ECLI:EU:C:1982:277, para 27, *Edeka Zentrale/Germany*.

668 The General Court finds that "*the mere fact that a theory of harm formulated by the Commission in a decision is innovative does not, in itself, lead to the conclusion that it is, as such, unlikely or unfounded*", GC, Judgment of 28.05.2020, Case T-399/16, ECLI:EU:T:2020:217, para 331, *CK Telecoms UK Investments*.

have to be able to assess the "*key decision determinants*" with a "*reasonable degree of certainty*" before a planned transaction.[669] *Chernenko* emphasizes that if there is a "*discrepancy between soft law and practice*"[670] this may impose "*real economic costs on parties by undermining a previously-negotiated allocation of risk.*"[671] As *Chernenko* rightly points out, the regulatory risk is part of the negotiation of the purchasing price.[672] Business risk is increased and budget planning is made complicated if a merger is prohibited by a competition authority and the parties (or rather their advisers) are not able to predict that outcome.

Nevertheless, two things should be kept in mind with respect to legal certainty and merger assessment: First, the mere fact that the outcome of a merger assessment is hard to predict is not a severe interference with fundamental rights. The final prohibition decision is definitely a severe interference into the right to realize concentrations of undertakings. The same, even though less pronounced, is true for conditions and obligations.[673] But the mere fact that this outcome cannot be predicted does not have a comparable severity. Increased costs may not even be part of the protective scope of Article 16 and 17 CFR, because negative economic consequences or financial losses are not protected by those fundamental rights.[674] In this respect the ECJ found:

> "*If laws of ownership are protected by the constitutional laws of all the Member States and if similar guarantees are given in respect of their right freely to choose and practice their trade of profession, the rights thereby guaranteed, far from constituting unfettered prerogatives, must be viewed in the light of the social function of the property and activities protected thereunder. For this reason, rights of this nature are protected by law subject always to limitations laid down in accordance with the public interest. Within the Community legal order it likewise seems legitimate that these rights should, if necessary, be subject to certain limits justified by the over-*

669 *Wirtz/Schulz*, NZKart 2019, 20, 23, fn. 30: authors translation from *„wesentliche Entscheidungsdeterminanten"* *„brauchbares Maß an Sicherheit"*.

670 *Chernenko* finds that the innovation concerns in *Dow/DuPont* are outside the scope of the Horizontal Merger Guidelines, *Chernenko*, 40 E.C.L.R. (2019) 9, 19; see also fn. 487.

671 *Chernenko*, 40 E.C.L.R. (2019) 9, 23.

672 *Chernenko*, 40 E.C.L.R. (2019) 9, 22.

673 See Opinion of Advocate General *Kokott* delivered on 13.12.2007, Case C-413/06 P, ECLI:EU:C:2007:790, para 214.

674 *Wollenschläger* in von der Groeben/Schwarze/Hatje, Europäisches Unionsrecht, Art. 15 GRC para 30, Art. 16 GRC para 10.

all objectives pursued by the community, on condition that the substance of these rights is left untouched. As regards the guarantees accorded to a particular undertaking, they can in no respect be extended to protect mere commercial interests or opportunities, the uncertainty of which are part of the very essence of economic activity."[675]

It is not entirely clear if investments with respect to a merger can be designated as commercial interests or opportunities. The wording seems to rather refer to the risk on a market and not the risk of the insecure outcome of an authority assessment. The latter may likely not be part of the very essence of economic activity. However, even when assuming that the increased risk and associated cost resulting from the novel theoretic approach in *Dow/DuPont* somehow fall within Article 16 or 17 CFR, it will very likely be justified by the public interest as well as community objectives. It is not about the prohibition of the transaction (that may be subject to a different weighing of rights and objectives) but about increased efforts and possibly increased duration of proceedings. On the other hand, there is the risk of decreased innovation incentives that may harm society and economy. It is in the public interest as well as a community objective to keep industries innovative. The interest of a less complicated merger control procedure finds its limitations in the abovementioned principles.

Second, the filing and approval procedure in merger control alters the level of precision of assessment criteria. It is a general rule that a person must be able to align his or her behavior with the existing legal provisions. A person or legal entity must be able to foresee what is forbidden or allowed. However, with respect to merger control, it is forbidden to not file a concentration that fulfills the filing requirements, implement a concentration before approval or in case of declaration of incompatibility, not to comply with conditions or obligations or to break rules of procedure.[676] Most of those provisions depend on turnover of the undertakings concerned,[677] the correct definition of a concentration[678] or a specific Commission decision. None of them deals with the question of whether competition is significantly impeded. Whether or not a company correctly analyzes innovation competition is irrelevant for an infringement of competition law. Accordingly, with respect to merger control, what matters are precise rules for filing and procedure. Whether or not a company can

675 ECJ, Judgement of 14.05.1974, Case 4/73, ECLI:EU:C:1974:51, para 14, *Nold.*
676 Cf. Article 14 EC Merger Regulation.
677 Cf. Article 1 EC Merger Regulation.
678 Cf. Article 3 EC Merger Regulation.

predict the final outcome of the Commission's substantive assessment is irrelevant with respect to legal certainty and the principle of precision.

8) Appropriate remedies

It has been argued that the remedies related to innovation competition cases are overly broad.[679] *Fort* found that personnel and laboratory capacities were usually not exclusively allocated to a specific line of research. Accordingly, it would be unrealistic to assume the existence of clearly defined lines of research that could be sold in order to dispel concerns with respect to innovation competition.[680]

However, this critique refers to a rather traditional understanding of innovation competition. As mentioned above,[681] the assessment in *Dow/DuPont* is not about specific innovation activities that could be defined in line with traditional market analysis. It is rather about the innovation capacity and the corresponding incentives to perform R&D. The concept of innovation spaces refers to a concretization of the innovation capacity at industry level. The specific innovation spaces serve as examples of innovation targets and provide a more accurate picture with regard to innovation in specific parts of the industry.

In fact, it is impossible to allocate innovation assets to specific lines of research or even innovation spaces. But such allocation is not necessary to define appropriate remedies. It is not about the preservation of specific lines of research or early pipeline products but about preventing a decrease of innovation incentives in the entire industry. Only the divestment of the R&D organization, representing the innovation capacity of a company, would eliminate such industry-wide innovation concerns.

Another question is whether the divestment of an R&D organization to another important innovator in an oligopoly will eliminate the Commission's concerns on increased innovation concentration.

Purchasers fulfilling the Commission's criteria will only be the other big R&D-integrated companies in the crop protection oligopoly (especially with regard to necessary financial resources, expertise and the need to be already active in crop protection). Despite the divestment, the merger is likely to reduce the number of global R&D-integrated companies from

679 *Fort* at the 2. Kölner Kartellrechtsgespräche, see *Hasselhorn*, NZKart 2019, 546.
680 *Fort* at the 2. Kölner Kartellrechtsgespräche, see *Hasselhorn*, NZKart 2019, 546.
681 See *Section II) C) 3)-5)*.

five to four. One may well argue that the divestment to another big player may not counteract the alleged reduction of competitors resulting in a reduction in innovation. This would be different if a new entrant was to purchase the divested business. Nonetheless, competition is not only about the number of players but also about the competitive pressure they exert on one another. Rivalry may be increased by enabling one of the big R&D-integrated players to better catch up with the new merged entity.

In the course of the *Dow/DuPont* merger, DuPont's R&D organization was divested to FMC. FMC was considered to not be one of the big vertically-integrated R&D players in crop protection,[682] mainly because of its lack of significant discovery activities.[683] But if FMC is considered to have sufficient financial resources and expertise to exercise a competitive constraint on the remaining four R&D players after the purchase of DuPont's assets, it is not quite clear why FMC has not been considered a potential competitor with respect to innovation competition before.

In conclusion, one may scrutinize whether in a close oligopoly with high barriers to entry (as is prerequisite for the Commission's theory of harm in *Dow/DuPont*) the divestment of an R&D organization may in fact create a new innovation player. In any case, even the exercise of additional pressure from a pre-existing innovation player may at least reduce harm to innovation competition.

I) Conclusion

In *Dow/DuPont*, the Commission set up a novel theory of harm based on the finding that a merger between two out of a limited number of important innovators is likely to reduce innovation when appropriability is high and when there are no merger-specific efficiencies. Protective purpose of the Commission's theory is the preservation and promotion of innovation incentives. Any decrease in innovation incentives will take place immediately after the implementation of the transaction due to decreased rivalry, and may therefore be considered a short-term effect. Innovation is not treated as a market of its own but rather as a parameter determining the market position on downstream or upstream markets. The same holds true for innovation spaces, which mainly serve the purpose of specifying innovation concentration in certain parts of an industry. Neither specific

682 Dow/DuPont Decision, paras 2205, 2258.
683 Dow/DuPont Decision, para 2246.

products nor specific pipeline activities are at the core of the Commission's innovation competition analysis. The Commission's approach fits into Article 2 (3) EC Merger Regulation. The Commission's approach in *Dow/ DuPont* does not constitute an unwritten element in the legal framework but is a means of determining a „dominant position" or a „significant impediment to effective competition".

For the most part, the Commission's approach is valid. Attention must be paid to other factors besides rivalry that may influence innovation incentives in an industry. In addition, the traditional efficiency analysis is not fit for innovation concerns. Since efficiencies are part of the underlying rationale itself, the Commission bears the burden of proof of possible innovation-enhancing effects. Furthermore, the standard in the Horizontal Merger Guidelines must be altered with respect to innovation competition. It is impossible to quantify specific benefits for consumers beyond market level. The standard for verifiability must be adjusted on a case-by-case basis.

The novel approach in *Dow/DuPont* is in line with the European Treaties. Innovation is one of the objectives of the TEU and TFEU. Innovation and competition are both pillars of the internal market. In addition, innovation is an important driver of competition. The Commission's comprehensive approach in the Dow/DuPont Decision is therefore anchored in the provisions of the Treaties. The Commission must take into account innovation incentives when issuing merger decisions in order to be in line with the objectives of the Treaties. It is not sufficient for the preservation of innovation to consider only research and development activities with respect to defined markets; there is also the need to secure the entire innovation process, from the basic incentive to the final marketed product. The Commission therefore only puts into practice what is stated in primary law. *Dow/DuPont* does not mark a shift in the triangle of the internal market, the competition rules and the rules on innovation, but realizes its full potential.

III) Innovation Competition and the scope of its application in EU Competition Law

This part will be dedicated to possible fields of application of the concept of innovation competition as developed in *Dow/DuPont*. I will assess whether the rationale in *Dow/DuPont* can be used in the scope of Article 101 and 102 TFEU as well.

A) *Restrictive Agreements according to Article 101 TFEU*

One may think of applying the Commission's rationale in *Dow/DuPont* to restrictive agreements under Article 101 TFEU. As an example, one may consider a hypothetical cooperation between Dow and DuPont concerning the exploration of possible treatments against a newly emerged pest (against which there is currently no protection or cure). As the law stands, this cooperation would likely be exempted according to the research and development Block Exemption Regulation ("R&D BER")[684] regardless of the market share on existing markets or the innovation capacity of the undertakings involved.[685]

According to Article 4 (1), 2 R&D BER, research and development agreements are exempted if the parties are not competing undertakings for the duration of the research and development and, in case of joint exploitation, for an additional seven years from marketing. Article 1 (1) lit r) R&D BER defines "competing undertaking" as an actual or potential competitor. The definitions of actual or potential competitor in Article 1 (1) lit s) and t) R&D BER both presuppose an existing market at the time the research and development starts, and there have to be research

684 Commission Regulation (EU) No 1217/2010 of 14.12.2010 on the application of Article 101 (3) of the Treaty on the Functioning of the European Union to certain categories of research and development agreements, OJ L 335, 18.12.2010, p. 36-42.

685 *Drexl* uses a similar example with car manufacturers cooperating with respect to batteries, *Drexl*, Anti-Competitive Stumbling Stones, p. 4, 22-24; *Fuchs* is also critical on the non-existence of an "innovation market" in the R&D BER, *Fuchs* in Immenga/Mestmäcker, Wettbewebsrecht EU, Art. 4 FuE-GVO para 3, 7.

activities in the direction of that market.[686] However, with respect to the abovementioned example, there is not such an existing market. There is no treatment for the new pest yet that could be substituted with a new chemical. Accordingly, Dow and DuPont would be treated as non-competitors and would be able to conduct joint research on a large scale for a long period of time. The lead time to market of a new chemical in the crop protection sector is about eleven years.[687] In case there is joint exploitation of the invention, the R&D BER provides for the active ingredient for an additional seven years being exempted from Article 101 (1) TFEU. As a result, two of the most important innovators are, on first sight,[688] allowed to perform joint research and development for a period of eighteen years with respect to treatments for a new pest, even though there may be no other innovation players targeting the same disease.

With respect to the outcome in the *Dow/DuPont* merger, this is a startling result. In case of a merger, DuPont had to divest almost its entire R&D organization. In case of joint research, assessing an individual exemption according to Article 101 (3) TFEU is not even needed. This is all the more surprising as the difference between merger and cooperation may be rather small. On EU level, it may be about the full-functionality of a joint venture. In fact, according to Article 3 (4) of the EC Merger Regulation, only a joint venture performing on a lasting basis all the functions of an autonomous economic entity shall be treated as a concentration that fulfills the filing requirements.

The decisive factor for full-functionality is market relevance.[689] According to para 94 of the Commission's Jurisdictional Notice[690]: "*Full function character essentially means that a joint venture must operate on a market, performing the functions normally carried out by undertakings operating on the same market.*" According to para 95 of the Jurisdictional Notice, joint

686 Cf. *Drexl*, Anti-Competitive Stumbling Stones, p. 22-23.

687 Dow/DuPont Decision, para 161, 168.

688 There is the possibility of withdrawal of the exemption according to Article 29 (1) of Council Regulation (EC) No 1/2003 of 16.12.2002 on the implementation of the rules on competition laid down in Articles 81 and 82 of the Treaty, OJ L 1, 04.01.2003, p. 1-25 (hereinafter: "Regulation 1/2003"); see also Recital 19-22 of the R&D BER for further criteria.

689 Cf. *Körber* in Immenga/Mestmäcker, Wettbewerbsrecht Fusionskontrolle, Art. 3 FKVO para 130.

690 Commission Consolidated Jurisdictional Notice under Council Regulation (EC) No 139/2004 on the control of concentrations between undertakings, OJ C 95, 16.04.2008, p. 1-48.

ventures limited to R&D or production are usually not full-function. Accordingly, whether the establishment of a research and development joint venture falls within the EC Merger Regulation or not may depend on the existence of an independent marketing organization. On first sight, the mere absence of such marketing organization may not rule out the need to apply the criteria mentioned in the *Dow/DuPont* merger. It will have to be discussed if a new entity may only harm innovation competition in reducing innovation incentives if it is able to independently market possible new products. In line with this, *Gilbert* and *Sunshine* suggested the application of the Innovation Market Analysis[691] not only in case of a merger but also in case of joint ventures and other R&D arrangements.[692]

One may also think of using the rationale behind *Dow/DuPont* in the scope of technology transfer agreements. Those agreements may impact further research and development activities of the licensor as well as the licensee. It must be analyzed whether technology transfer may reduce innovation competition.

1) Possible starting points for innovation competition concerns in Article 101 TFEU

As mentioned above,[693] the Commission's innovation competition approach in *Dow/DuPont* affects the position of an undertaking. The Commission does not define an own innovation market but rather uses the innovation capacity of an undertaking to determine its innovative strength in relation to upstream or downstream markets. With respect to Article 101 (1) TFEU, the position of companies in innovation competition may thus determine whether an agreement between them has a restrictive effect. In addition, one may think of an exemption according to Article 101 (3) TFEU due to improved production of goods or promotion of technical or economic progress without eliminating competition.

The innovation competition approach does not cover restriction by object settings. In case, two or more independent undertakings agree on restricting their own research and development activities or innovation activities of third parties, this may constitute a restriction by object in

691 See *Section II) F) 2)*.

692 *Gilbert/Sunshine*, 63 Antitrust Law Journal (1995), 569, 594; see also *Drexl*, Anti-Competitive Stumbling Stones, p. 11.

693 See *Section II) C) 4)*.

the scope of Article 101 (1) TFEU.[694] However, the approach developed in *Dow/DuPont* is neither necessary nor helpful in those cases. It covers the communitization of innovation assets leading to effects on innovation incentives and capabilities. Those effects do not depend on any explicit agreement on lessening innovation activities but on structural changes in the possession of assets. They are independent of the objectives of any agreement or concerted practice.

In the following part, specific starting points for incorporating innovation competition into Article 101 TFEU will be presented.

(a) Innovation aspects in Article 101 TFEU

Article 101 (1) TFEU states that

> *"all agreements between undertakings, decisions by associations of undertakings and concerted practices which may affect trade between Member States and which have as their object or effect the prevention, restriction or distortion of competition within the internal market"*

shall be prohibited. Article 101 (1) TFEU further mentions examples fur such prohibited behavior in lit a) to e).

Article 101 (3) TFEU sets up criteria for the exemption of behavior falling within Article 101 (1) TFEU. Such behavior may be permissible if:

1. it "*contributes to improving the production or distribution of goods or to promoting technical or economic progress*";
2. "*while allowing consumers a fair share of the resulting benefit*";
3. it does not "*impose on the undertakings concerned restrictions which are not indispensable to the attainment of these objectives*"; and
4. it does not "*afford such undertakings the possibility of eliminating competition in respect of a substantial part of the products in question.*"

Article 101 (1) lit b) TFEU explicitly mentions "*technical development*" as one of the goals of protection of competition law. Article 101 (3) TFEU states that an agreement may only be exempted if there is improvement of production or distribution of goods or promotion of technical or

694 European Commission, Guidance on restrictions of competition „by object" for the purpose of defining which agreements may benefit from the De Minimis Notice, SWD(2014) 198 final, p. 12; Article 5 (a) of the R&D BER.

economic progress. In line with the general Union policy,[695] innovation concerns must be taken into account in the scope of Article 101 TFEU.

(b) Competition in innovation in Regulations and Guidelines on Article 101 TFEU

While undertakings originally had to notify agreements, decisions and practices to the Commission in order to receive a formal decision on the exemption,[696] Regulation 1/2003[697] established a system of legal exception. Undertakings must now self-assess whether their behavior falls within Article 101 (1) TFEU and is exempted according to Article 101 (3) TFEU.

In addition to an individual exemption, Article 101 (3) TFEU also allows for "categories" of agreements, decisions or concerted practices to be exempted from Article 101 (1) TFEU. The Commission has issued Block Exemption Regulations ("BER") for certain categories, amongst which are the R&D BER and the Technology Transfer BER[698]. In addition, the Commission has set up numerous Guidelines on behavior falling within the Block Exemption Regulations as well as for the assessment of an individual exemption. Even though the Block Exemption Regulations and the Guidelines concretize the preconditions for exemption,[699] the burden of assessment still lies with the undertakings.

Approaches of the concept of innovation competition have found their way into the R&D BER as well as into Commission's Guidelines.

Even though the R&D BER does not rely on innovation capacity or innovation activity in the past with respect to the preconditions for an exemption, there is a hint to innovation competition with respect to the possibility of withdrawal of the exemption. Recital 21 of the R&D BER states:

---

695 See *Section II) A) 2) and 4)*.

696 Article 4, 5 of Council Regulation 17: First Regulation implementing Article 85 and 86 of the Treaty, OJ P 13, 21.02.1962, p. 204-211.

697 See fn. 688.

698 Commission Regulation (EU) No 316/2014 of 21.03.2014 on the application of Article 101 (3) of the Treaty on the Functioning of the European Union to categories of technology transfer agreements, OJ L 93, 28.03.2014, p. 17-23 (hereinafter "Technology Transfer BER").

699 Cf. *Nordeman/Nyberg* in Loewenheim/Meessen/Riesenkampff/Kersting/Meyer-Lindemann, Kartellrecht, Art. 101 Abs. 3 AEUV para 9; *Ellger* in Immenga/Mestmäcker, Wettbewerbsrecht EU, Art. 101 Abs. 3 AEUV para 346, 349.

> *"The benefit of this Regulation could be withdrawn pursuant to Article 29 of Regulation (EC) No 1/2003, for example, where the existence of a research and development agreement substantially restricts the scope for third parties to carry out research and development in the relevant field because of the limited research capacity available elsewhere, {…}, or where the existence of the research and development agreement would restrict competition in innovation or eliminate effective competition in research and development on a particular market."*

The R&D BER, however, neither defines the terms "competition in innovation" or "competition in research and development" nor sets up criteria for assessing a restriction or elimination of such kind of competition. What is interesting to note is that the R&D BER incorporates third party incentives by taking into account the possibly "limited research capacity" in a specific field.

The Technology Transfer BER, in contrast, does not mention competition in innovation. According to Recital 17, the Commission may withdraw the benefit of the BER "*in particular where the incentives to innovate are reduced or where access to markets is hindered.*" However, this seems to refer to specific actions or agreements of the parties directly preventing innovation activities rather than to a reduction of competition on the innovation level. Recital 17 of the Technology Transfer BER should be read in conjunction with Recital 4 and 15 that deal with the balancing of innovation incentives of the licensee and the licensor in respect of the specific agreement.

In addition, the Commission's Horizontal Cooperation Guidelines[700] mention competition in innovation. Para 119 of the Horizontal Cooperation Guidelines reads:

> *"R&D co-operation may not only affect competition in existing markets, but also competition in innovation and new product markets. This is the case where R&D co-operation concerns the development of new products or technology which either may – if emerging – one day replace existing ones or which are being developed for a new intended use and will therefore not replace existing products but create a completely new demand. The effects on competition in innovation are important in these situations, but can in some*

700 Communication from the Commission - Guidelines on the applicability of Article 101 of the Treaty on the Functioning of the European Union to horizontal co-operation agreements, OJ C 11, 14.01.2011, p. 1-72 (hereinafter: "Horizontal Cooperation Guidelines").

cases not be sufficiently assessed by analysing actual or potential competition in existing product/technology markets. In this respect, two scenarios can be distinguished, depending on the nature of the innovative process in a given industry."

The Horizontal Cooperation Guidelines further distinguish between differently structured industries:

> *"In the first scenario, which is, for instance, present in the pharmaceutical industry, the process of innovation is structured in such a way that it is possible at an early stage to identify competing R&D poles. Competing R&D poles are R&D efforts directed towards a certain new product or technology, and the substitutes for that R&D, that is to say, R&D aimed at developing substitutable products or technology for those developed by the co-operation and having similar timing. In this case, it can be analysed whether after the agreement there will be a sufficient number of remaining R&D poles. The starting point of the analysis is the R&D of the parties. Then credible competing R&D poles have to be identified. In order to assess the credibility of competing poles, the following aspects have to be taken into account: the nature, scope and size of any other R&D efforts, their access to financial and human resources, know-how/patents, or other specialised assets as well as their timing and their capability to exploit possible results. An R&D pole is not a credible competitor if it cannot be regarded as a close substitute for the parties' R&D effort from the viewpoint of, for instance, access to resources or timing."*[701]

With respect to this first scenario, the Commission also finds that "*{b}esides the direct effect on the innovation itself, the co-operation may also affect a new product market.*"[702]

Accordingly, the Commission seems to distinguish between effects "on the innovation" and effects on the product market. However, as will be explained,[703] both effects are related to the final product and not the innovation incentive or process itself.

The Commission also mentions a second scenario in which

> *"the innovative efforts in an industry are not clearly structured so as to allow the identification of R&D poles. In this situation, in the absence of exceptional circumstances, the Commission would not try to assess the*

701 Horizontal Cooperation Guidelines, para 120.
702 Horizontal Cooperation Guidelines, para 121.
703 See *Section III) A) 1) (d)*.

> *impact of a given R&D co-operation on innovation, but would limit its assessment to existing product and/or technology markets which are related to the R&D co-operation in question.*"[704]

The Horizontal Cooperation Guidelines seem to distinguish between competition on existing as well as new (future) product markets and competition in innovation. However, it is important to note that the R&D poles necessary for the assessment of competition in innovation are described as (identifiable) R&D efforts towards a specific product or technology and with similar timing. Since the Guidelines refer to the R&D being "substitutable" to other products or technologies, they seem to rely on the principle of demand substitution traditionally used to define markets.[705] The Guidelines continue on analyzing the credibility of the R&D poles using measures such as competing R&D poles and access to resources traditionally used to assess the market position of an undertaking.[706]

The latter finding may be due to the fact that a previous version of the Horizontal Cooperation Guidelines referred to an actual innovation market.[707] It seems as if in the current version the Commission removed the term "innovation market" but maintained the underlying market based approach.

The Commission further clarifies its approach in the examples in para 147 and 148 of the Horizontal Cooperation Guidelines. Example 1 deals with observable R&D efforts towards specific products. The R&D poles in Example 2 rather refer to specific pipeline activity at the development stage ("*There exist two other poles of research with other companies at approximately the same stage of development using the same basic new technology.*"). Example 4 also uses poles of research towards a specific blockbuster medicine that appear to be out of the scope of potential competition ("*but it is not yet clear that they will reach industrial production*"). All in all, there is a focus on specific research and development activities towards a defined product or technology.

---

704 Horizontal Cooperation Guidelines, para 122.

705 See Market Definition Notice, para 13, 15-19.

706 Cf. Market Definition Notice, para 53-55.

707 Commission Notice - Guidelines on the applicability of Article 81 of the EC Treaty to horizontal cooperation agreements, OJ C 3, 06.01.2001, p. 2-30, para 60, 73.

Competition in innovation is also incorporated into the Commission's Technology Transfer Guidelines.[708] Para 26 of those Guidelines states:[709]

> *"Some licence agreements may affect competition in innovation. In analysing such effects, however, the Commission will normally confine itself to examining the impact of the agreement on competition within existing product and technology markets. Competition on such markets may be affected by agreements that delay the introduction of improved products or new products that over time will replace existing products. In such cases innovation is a source of potential competition which must be taken into account when assessing the impact of the agreement on product markets and technology markets. In a limited number of cases, however, it may be useful and necessary to also analyse the effects on competition in innovation separately. This is particularly the case where the agreement affects innovation aiming at creating new products and where it is possible at an early stage to identify research and development poles. In such cases it can be analysed whether after the agreement there will be a sufficient number of competing research and development poles left for effective competition in innovation to be maintained."*

The Technology Transfer Guidelines also point to the importance of the number of independent technologies in para 157:

> *"{T}he Commission takes the view that outside the area of hardcore restrictions Article 101 of the Treaty is unlikely to be infringed where there are four or more independently controlled technologies in addition to the technologies controlled by the parties to the agreement that may be substitutable for the licensed technology at a comparable cost to the user. In assessing whether the technologies are sufficiently substitutable the relative commercial strength of the technologies in question must be taken into account."*

Para 26 of the Technology Transfer Guidelines refers to para 157. Accordingly, the sufficient number of competing research and development poles

708 See fn. 177.

709 In the previous version of the Technology Transfer Guidelines, the Commission also used the term "*innovation market*", see para 25 of the Guidelines on the application of Article 81 of the EC Treaty to technology transfer agreements, OJ C 101, 27.04.2004, p. 2-42. The term was deleted in the current version of the Guidelines and, in contrast to the Horizontal Guidelines, there is also no market assessment with respect to innovation in the Technology Transfer Guidelines.

is also supposed to be four or more.[710] Unlike in the Horizontal Cooperation Guidelines, there is, however, no definition or example for those innovation poles.

A structural approach to competition in innovation can be found in paras 129 and 130 of the Technology Transfer Guidelines with respect to exclusive grant backs (that is, any direct or indirect obligation of the licensee to grant an exclusive license to the licensor in respect of its own improvements to, or its own applications of, the licensed technology, Article 5 (1) lit a) of the Technology Transfer BER[711]). The possible harm of exclusive grant back is explained in para 129:

> "*An obligation to grant the licensor an exclusive licence to improvements of the licensed technology or to assign such improvements to the licensor is likely to reduce the licensee's incentive to innovate since it hinders the licensee in exploiting the improvements, including by way of licensing to third parties.*"[712]

Para 130 underlines the interrelation between market position and innovation incentives:

> "*In the assessment of exclusive grant backs outside the scope of the block exemption the market position of the licensor on the technology market is also a relevant factor. The stronger the position of the licensor, the more likely it is that exclusive grant back obligations will have restrictive effects on competition in innovation. The stronger the position of the licensor's technology the more important it is that the licensee can become an important source of innovation and future competition.*"

Para 130 assumes an effect of the market position in existing technology markets on competition in innovation. Here it is more about different "sources" of innovation and, accordingly, about the incentive and ability to perform research and development.

---

710 *Chernenko*, 40 E.C.L.R. (2019) 9, 14.

711 See fn. 698.

712 A similar approach with respect to cross-licensing in settlement agreements can be found in para 241 of the Technology Transfer Guidelines.

(c) Innovation Markets in U.S. Guidelines

In addition to the Commission's Guidelines, U.S. Guidelines may give a hint on how to incorporate innovation concerns into the setting of cooperation between undertakings.

The U.S. Intellectual Property Guidelines[713] integrate the concept of innovation markets. The Guidelines state:

> *"If a licensing arrangement may adversely affect competition to develop new or improved goods or processes, the Agencies may analyze such an impact as a competitive effect in a separate research and development market. A licensing arrangement may have competitive effects on research and development that cannot be adequately addressed through the analysis of goods or technology markets. For example, the arrangement may affect innovation that is related to research to identify a commercializable product or to the development of particular goods or services. Alternatively, the arrangement may affect the development of new or improved goods or processes in geographic markets where there is no actual or potential competition in the relevant goods."*[714]

The Guidelines set up a safe harbor:

> *"Regarding potential effects in a research and development market, the Agencies, absent extraordinary circumstances, will not challenge a restraint in an intellectual property licensing arrangement if (1) the restraint is not facially anticompetitive and (2) four or more independently controlled entities in addition to the parties to the licensing arrangement possess the required specialized assets or characteristics and the incentive to engage in research and development that is a close substitute of the research and development activities of the parties to the licensing agreement. In evaluating close substitutes, the Agencies may consider numerous factors including the following: the nature, scope and magnitude of the R&D efforts of the other independently controlled entities; their access to financial support, intellectual property, skilled personnel or other specialized assets; their timing; and their ability, either acting alone or through others, to successfully commercialize innovations."*[715]

---

713 See fn. 175.
714 U.S. Intellectual Property Guidelines, p. 11.
715 U.S. Intellectual Property Guidelines, p. 25.

The U.S. JV Guidelines[716] follow a similar approach. According to those Guidelines,

> "*{a}n innovation market consists of the research and development directed to particular new or improved goods or processes and the close substitutes for that research and development. The Agencies define an innovation market only when the capabilities to engage in the relevant research and development can be associated with specialized assets or characteristics of specific firms.*"[717]

The JV Guidelines also contain a safe harbor concerning innovation market activities:

> "*Absent extraordinary circumstances, the Agencies do not challenge a competitor collaboration on the basis of effects on competition in an innovation market where three or more independently controlled research efforts in addition to those of the collaboration possess the required specialized assets or characteristics and the incentive to engage in R&D that is a close substitute for the R&D activity of the collaboration. In determining whether independently controlled R&D efforts are close substitutes, the Agencies consider, among other things, the nature, scope, and magnitude of the R&D efforts; their access to financial support; their access to intellectual property, skilled personnel, or other specialized assets; their timing; and their ability, either acting alone or through others, to successfully commercialize innovations.*"[718]

Even though the U.S. Guidelines seem to be broader in scope and cover, for example, "research to identify a commercializable product" (that can be understood as happening before the actual research on a specific product), they nevertheless focus on identifiable research activities towards a specific (future) product. Especially the precondition of a "close substitute" for R&D activities requires identifiable research efforts that can be assigned to a certain product.

716 DOJ and FTC, Antitrust Guidelines for Collaborations among Competitors, April 2000 (hereinafter: "U.S. JV Guidelines").

717 U.S. JV Guidelines, p. 17.

718 U.S. JV Guidelines, p. 26-27.

(d) Differences between existing concepts and innovation competition approach in Dow/DuPont

There are differences between "competition in innovation" – as mentioned in the R&D BER and the Commission's Guidelines – and the innovation competition approach in *Dow/DuPont*.

First of all, competition in innovation seems to still be closely related to the Innovation Market Analysis by *Gilbert* and *Sunshine*.[719] Accordingly, the Horizontal Cooperation Guidelines seem to apply usual market assessment criteria to innovation.[720] *Mestmäcker/Schweitzer* point out that the approach on R&D activities in the Horizontal Cooperation Guidelines is about "*assessing the impact of the R&D efforts on the competitive positions of the parties and rival firms in future markets.*"[721] Accordingly, the concept of competition in innovation refers to markets. In contrast, innovation competition as developed in *Dow/DuPont* does not relate to specific products or markets but to innovation incentives in general.[722]

Second, "R&D poles" as mentioned in the Guidelines do not correlate with "innovation spaces" in the Dow/DuPont Decision.[723] This is for two reasons: According to their treatment in the Horizontal Cooperation Guidelines, R&D poles relate to specific products. The Guidelines define R&D poles as efforts directed towards a certain new product or technology. In contrast, innovation spaces can be defined as the spaces in which goals broader than a specific product are targeted. In addition,

---

719 See *Section II) F) 2)*.

720 Cf. *Wollmann/Herzog* in MüKo 2015, Art. 101 AEUV para 206.

721 *Mestmäcker/Schweitzer*, Europäisches Wettbewerbsrecht, § 32 para 16; authors translation from: „Es geht darum, die Auswirkungen der F&E-Anstrenungen auf die Wettbewerbspositionen der beteiligten und der rivalisierenden Unternehmen auf Zukunftsmärkten zu beurteilen."

722 See *Section II) C) 3)-5)*.

723 *Todino/van de Walle/Stoican* find that innovation spaces could be qualified as R&D poles, because the Commission did employ a structured approach identifying and analyzing development-to-development and development-to-product overlaps, *Todino/van de Walle/Stoican*, 64 The Antitrust Bulletin (2019), 11, 24. However, the fact that the Commission performs a structured analysis does not say anything about a qualification of innovation spaces as R&D poles. As mentioned in *Section II) C) 4)*, the assessment of innovation spaces only serves as an example of the competitive conditions in specific areas of research and does not represent activities towards specific products; see also *Federico/Scott Morton/Shapiro* who find that the innovation competition approach is "*analytically similar*" to R&D poles without, however, giving a reason for that conclusion, *Federico/Scott Morton/Shapiro*, Antitrust and Innovation, p. 20.

R&D poles require existing research and development activity. According to the Horizontal Cooperation Guidelines, there have to be R&D efforts with a "similar timing", and only targeted activities can have a certain timing. Also, the examples in the Guidelines exclusively rely on existing research and development activities towards specific products. The same is true with respect to the Technology Transfer Guidelines that deal with "innovation aiming at creating new products".

As a result, even though the Horizontal Cooperation Guidelines mention existing markets, future markets and competition in innovation, they basically only set up criteria for the first two concepts. The conditions mentioned in connection with competition in innovation can almost entirely be incorporated into the future markets approach.[724] That concept relates to activities towards products or technologies that are not substitutable to existing products and therefore belong to a new market. Efforts directed towards a new product, as mentioned in the Horizontal Cooperation Guidelines, may either affect an existing or a future market.[725] With respect to existing markets, the (possibly extended) potential competition doctrine will serve as a starting point. In the case of future markets, the future markets approach will lead to sufficient results.[726] In those settings, the assessment of competition in innovation is not necessary.

In any case, there is nothing in the Commission's Guidelines up to date that points in the direction of innovation competition as developed in *Dow/DuPont*. One should recall that the innovation competition concept is about innovation incentives that may be decreased or increased through changes in the market structure. It is not about specific targets or research activities but rather about the general pressure to perform research and development. The approach in *Dow/DuPont* is not related to identifiable products or technologies.

---

724 See *Section II) G) 2)*.

725 *Schroeder* seems to use the term „innovation market" as a synonym for a future market when stating that a technology market may either be an existing or an innovation market, *Schroeder* in Wiedemann, Handbuch des Kartellrechts, § 9 para 121.

726 In fact, *Mestmäcker/Schweitzer* refer to „quality and diversity of future products and technologies", *Mestmäcker/Schweitzer*, Europäisches Wettbewerbsrecht, § 32 para 24; *Fuchs* finds that „Innovation Markets" or „R&D Markets" relate to the development of entirely new product or technology, *Fuchs* in Immenga/Mestmäcker, Wettbewerbsrecht EU, FuE-GVO, I. Einführung, para 2; none of the abovementioned authors gives an explanation of why those activities should relate to innovation markets instead of future product or technology markets.

The Technology Transfer Guidelines take into account the market position of the licensor in case of exclusive grant backs that may prevent the licensee from becoming an important source of innovation.[727] This is at least a hint to the interplay between the importance as innovator and incentives to innovate. However, this approach is not further elaborated upon. Up to date, there is no case law on the approach of competition in innovation or R&D poles. The Commission has not decided on such a case yet.

Even though the U.S. Guidelines are broader in scope, they nonetheless also rely on the innovation market approach. They can, therefore, not serve as a basis for how to incorporate the concept of innovation competition as developed in *Dow/DuPont* into the assessment of restrictive agreements.

2) Applicability of innovation competition in the scope of Article 101 TFEU

Since there is no hint to innovation competition in existing legislation or Commission practice, one may wonder if it is possible or even necessary to incorporate the *Dow/DuPont* rationale into the assessment of Article 101 TFEU. This could be particularly appropriate with regard to R&D cooperation and technology transfer.

(a) R&D cooperation

One may think of transferring the concept behind *Dow/DuPont* to R&D cooperation. Taking into account the rationale behind *Dow/DuPont*, this would lead to the following hypothesis:

> "An R&D cooperation between two out of a limited number of significant innovators is likely to reduce the incentives for product innovation when appropriability is high and when there are no cooperation-specific efficiencies."[728]

At first sight, this approach is much stricter than the concept in the Horizontal Cooperation Guidelines. The Horizontal Cooperation Guidelines

727 Technology Transfer Guidelines, para 130.
728 Cf. Dow/DuPont Decision, para 2042 and *Section II) C) 1)*.

only require a sufficient number of R&D poles[729] remaining after the R&D agreement without, however, setting up a general presumption that a cooperation will reduce research and development incentives. On the other hand, the Horizontal Cooperation Guidelines are broader in the sense that they do not require oligopolistic market features with high barriers to entry or a high level of appropriability.

The rationale in *Dow/DuPont* can be transferred if there is a link between R&D cooperation and innovation incentives.

(1) Negative effects on innovation incentives

Innovation incentives can be divided into two types: the incentives to start research and development activities and the incentive to continue ongoing research and development activities. An R&D cooperation may influence those incentives either with respect to the cooperating parties or with respect to third undertakings.

(aa) Innovation incentives of the cooperating parties

First of all, the incentive to start R&D with respect to a specific research activity is embodied in the R&D agreement itself. Obviously, the parties want to start innovation activities. Otherwise, they would not have engaged in setting up a joint project. In addition, it is unlikely that the parties would stop to continue joint ongoing activities due to an R&D cooperation. This is independent of possible hardcore cartels that might be concealed by an R&D cooperation. If undertakings decide to set up an agreement with the aim of not pursuing certain research and development activities, that is simply not an R&D agreement but a cartel within the meaning of Article 101 (1) lit b) TFEU (limitation of technical develop-

729 Typically two to four remaining poles besides the cooperating parties, *Fuchs* in Immenga/Mestmäcker, Wettbewerbsrecht EU, I. Einführung, para 52.

ment).[730] By its very definition[731], it is the goal of an R&D cooperation to perform research and not to prevent it. Usually, the parties of an R&D agreement do have the incentive to conduct innovation activities.

This intuitive finding is substantiated by an analogy to the mechanisms driving innovation incentives as elaborated in *Dow/DuPont*: the cannibalization mechanism, the product market mechanism and appropriability.[732]

For the first mechanism, an undertaking is likely not to perform R&D activities if the amount of own sales it "cannibalizes" is higher than the amount of sales it captures from third parties.[733] In a merger setting, the increase of cannibalization concerns may lead to a reduction of innovation incentives. However, with respect to R&D cooperation, this concern is not valid. The respective companies have already assessed possible cannibalization mechanisms and have obviously come to the conclusion that it is profitable for them to perform R&D. Moreover, cannibalization is not increased because the amount of products or pipeline products that could be cannibalized does not grow by means of an R&D cooperation. There remain two independent industry players with their respectively own product and research portfolio. That product and research portfolio is not affected by the cooperation.

If at all, the negative externality imposed on one another is internalized only for the specific cooperation project in question. With respect to that project, however, the parties already decided that it is profitable to them to perform R&D. Otherwise, they would not have started the cooperation. It is important to understand that R&D cooperation takes place after the

730 To that aspect *Mestmäcker/Schweitzer* find that R&D cooperation might set the basis for price fixing, output or quality reduction, *Mestmäcker/Schweitzer*, Europäisches Wettbewerbsrecht, § 32 para 11; however, the fact that a cooperation may serve as a shield for anticompetitive practices does not say anything about the lawfulness of the cooperation itself; every lawful kind of cooperation may serve as a starting point for hardcore cartels; still the general prohibition of cooperation would strongly harm competition.

731 Article 1 (1) lit c) of the R&D BER defines research and development as the acquisition of know-how relating to products, technologies or processes and the carrying out of theoretical analysis, systematic study or experimentation, including experimental production, technical testing of products or processes, the establishment of the necessary facilities and the obtaining of intellectual property rights for the results. An agreement aiming at preventing any of the abovementioned actions would not be considered to be a research and development agreement.

732 See *Section II) D) 1)*.

733 See *Section II) D) 1) (a)*.

innovation incentive has manifested itself in the plan to jointly perform R&D. Accordingly, the incentive to start innovation activities cannot be decreased by the cooperation.

In addition, the parties retain the option to terminate cooperation in case it is no longer profitable to them. If there is a fear of cannibalizing own products or research activities, the respective undertaking could decide to terminate either its own efforts or the cooperation. This decision will depend on the specifics in the individual case and does not presume a general reduction in R&D activities. The cannibalization concern does not support the finding that R&D cooperation reduces innovation incentives.

The same is true with respect to the product market channel. Market power on product markets may incentivize research and development activities because of a higher impact on pricing of the final product.[734] Two undertakings are able to coordinate their price setting, resulting in higher revenues. This leads to better exploitation of the final result of R&D. This is true for mergers as it is for R&D cooperation if the parties decide to jointly exploit the final results.[735] However, the decision of whether the product market channel promises a high level of revenues has already been made at the stage of entering into an R&D agreement. It is at least not altered through the cooperation.[736]

Appropriabilty may only serve as a decisive factor if the level is not already high pre-cooperation. In case of effective IP rights or marketing strategies, it may not affect the innovation incentive.

In addition, there is no theory of harm that presumes harm to competition or innovation through the mere combination of R&D assets. The rationale in *Dow/DuPont* is based on cannibalization concerns as mentioned above. The reasoning in the Horizontal Cooperation Guidelines seems to refer to assets necessary for developing and marketing a specific product that has basically already been discovered. The mere combination of assets necessary to perform basic discovery work neither decreases innovation incentives nor has any measurable impact on (existing or future) product markets taking into account the highly stochastic process of research and development.[737]

---

734 See *Section II) D) 1) (b)*.

735 Article 5 lit c) of the R&D BER permits certain levels of price fixing in case of joint exploitation of the results.

736 It may of course be altered due to other kinds of market development, for example the development of market power of other market participants.

737 Cf. *Krauß* in Bunte, Kartellrecht, § 1 GWB para 268; *Braun* finds that R&D cooperation in early stages may not affect competition because there is no

Commentators have argued that cooperation in R&D might harm innovation incentives. In the course of dealing with R&D cooperation, *Mestmäcker/Schweitzer* argue that communitization of R&D may lead to a slowdown of research activities because it is no longer possible for either of the participating parties to gain competitive advantages.[738] The degree of concentration in innovation driven industries and the associated limitation of technological knowledge to a few companies is supposed to increase the tendency to limit technical progress as a means of competition.[739] In case of market power, there is the risk of a restriction of competition impacting innovation activities in particular resulting in a slowdown.[740] *Kerber/Schwalbe* explain that in a rivalry process, there is a strong incentive for companies to invest in new products and technologies to gain highly profitable competitive advantages through innovation, or at least to avoid high losses if competitors introduce new better products and displace the company's own products. Accordingly, increased competitive pressure generally leads to higher investment in R&D and thus accelerates the innovation process. R&D cooperation may reduce or eliminate competitive pressure, leading to a reduction in R&D investment and thus a slowdown in the innovation process.[741]

Besides the fact that a reduction in R&D investment does not necessarily lead to less or slower innovation (reduction of R&D investment may also be associated with better allocation of efforts), there is no indication that R&D cooperation actually leads to a slowdown in innovation activities. The abovementioned arguments may claim validity with respect to structural changes such as a merger. In that setting, the findings are merely in line with the Commission's assessment in the *Dow/DuPont* merger. However, there is no explanation for why they should claim validity in a cooperation setting. It is true that it is no longer possible to gain a competitive advantage over the R&D cooperation partner once the coop-

---

activity on the product market yet, *Braun* in Bunte, Kartellrecht, Nach § 2 GWB para 106; this argument misses, however, that there may be competition beyond market level as set out in the *Dow/DuPont* Decision, cf. *Section II) C) 4)*.

738 *Mestmäcker/Schweitzer*, Europäisches Wettbewerbsrecht, § 32 para 11; see also *Kerber/Schwalbe* in MüKo, B. ökonomische Grundlagen des Wettbewerbsrechts, para 376; *Fuchs* in Immenga/Mestmäcker, Wettbewerbsrecht EU, FuE-GVO, I. Einführung, para 3, 6; *Hengst* in Bunte, Kartellrecht, Art. 101 para 463.

739 *Mestmäcker/Schweitzer*, Europäisches Wettbewerbsrecht, § 32 para 13.

740 *Mestmäcker/Schweitzer*, Europäisches Wettbewerbsrecht, § 32 para 26.

741 On the aforementioned *Kerber/Schwalbe* in MüKo, B. ökonomische Grundlagen des Wettbewerbsrechts, para 376.

eration has started. But the decision on competitive advantages is made before entering into the agreement. Further, it seems rather unlikely for an undertaking to decide on establishing an R&D cooperation just to slow down the research process if it could have accelerated the process outside the cooperation (and thus taken sales from its competitor). Again, whereas after a merger the decision to perform R&D is taken within the newly merged entity, in case of a cooperation two independent legal entities decide on how to perform R&D. They will each decide on the way most profitable to them. If there is a competitive advantage in separately performing R&D, this will be the way taken. If it is more profitable to cooperate, the undertakings will decide on setting up an R&D agreement. Accordingly, in a free market, the R&D cooperation itself is the competitive advantage.

It is also true that concentration may lead to a tendency to limit innovation as well as a slowdown in research and development activities. But this is only true for structural concentration, meaning a decrease in the number of independent companies. As long as the separate firms decide on which way of research and development is the most profitable to them, there are no hints for a decrease in innovation incentives or slowdown of the research and development process.

It is far from clear that cooperation actually reduces the need to constantly innovate. The parties remain competitors. They will decide on continuing the cooperation. In case a cooperation is no longer efficient, it may be terminated. This is a major difference compared to a merger that cannot easily be undone after its implementation.

Commentators also mention coordination of market behavior and market foreclosure as possible negative effects of R&D cooperation.[742] However, it has to be kept in mind that the starting point of the concept of innovation competition as developed in *Dow/DuPont* is the innovation incentive beyond specific research and development activities.[743] At the point in time when the discovery process has led to activities towards a somehow identifiable product, the concepts of potential competition and future markets are most suitable to cover competition aspects. When the innovation competition concept would be useful, there are no identifiable markets yet where behavior could be coordinated or that could be fore-

---

742 *Hengst* in Bunte, Kartellrecht, Art. 101 para 463; *Braun* in Bunte, Kartellrecht, Nach Art. 101 para 156; *Kerber/Schwalbe* in MüKo, B. ökonomische Grundlagen des Wettbewerbsrechts, para 377.

743 See *Section II) C) 3)*.

closed. One could think of already preventing effects on markets that are not yet identifiable. However, at the starting point of the research and development process it is so uncertain whether there will ever be a marketable product, and if the innovating parties will have any market power on the respective market, that it is not useful to apply the innovation competition concept in such cases.

All in all, the incentive of the cooperating parties to generally perform R&D is not altered through an R&D agreement. In this respect, there is no need of incorporating the innovation competition theory in *Dow/DuPont* into the assessment of R&D cooperation.

(bb) Third party incentives

The effects on innovation incentives of third parties must also be taken into account. *Mestmäcker/Schweitzer* find that the formation of strong R&D communities may deter outsiders from undertaking their own research activities and create or raise barriers to entry.[744] In addition, Recital 21 of the R&D BER mentions as a reason for withdrawal of the exemption a possible restriction of the scope for third parties to carry out research and development because of limited available research capacity.

With respect to the limited research capacity in a certain field, it is not quite clear how a cooperation might influence that capacity. Generally, the number of assets remains the same pre- and post-cooperation agreement. In case one of the two cooperating parties is in the possession of assets absolutely necessary for third parties to perform R&D, there may be a right of access[745] regardless of a possible cooperation.

In addition, the determent of innovation incentives for outsiders as well as the creation of barriers to entry depends on the stage at which cooperation takes place. In the very early research phase, where companies test a broad range of possible solutions for their research targets, there

---

744 *Mestmäcker/Schweitzer*, Europäisches Wettbewerbsrecht, § 32 para 11.

745 For example, on the basis of the so-called essential facilities doctrine. The ECJ set up criteria for granting access to facilities in its *Bronner* decision: The refusal of access has to be likely to eliminate all competition in the downstream market on the part of the person requesting access; the refusal must be incapable of being objectively justified; and the facility has to be indispensable to carrying on the requesting person's business, meaning that there is no actual or potential substitute, ECJ, Judgment of 26.11.1998, Case C-7/97, ECLI:EU:C:1998:569, para 41, *Bronner*; see also *Section III) B) 3) (b) (1)*.

are no hints that this could deter third parties from own R&D activities. First of all, specific research activities at this stage usually do not become publicly known and can thus not set any incentives for third parties. Second, even if third undertakings were to know the mere existence of an R&D cooperation, the rather broad research approach at this stage is unlikely to affect any third party incentives. If the existence and mode of action of any possible solution are not yet clear, third parties are unlikely to be deterred from performing own efforts.

This is different with respect to cooperation that starts at a late stage of development shortly before marketing. At this point, third parties may very well refrain from starting or continuing R&D that aims at the same solution. However, at this point in time, the innovation competition approach is not necessary. As will be further elaborated upon,[746] the concept of potential competition as well as that of future markets[747] are sufficient to prevent harm to competition and innovation at this point in time.

Generally, there are no indications that the mere existence of an R&D cooperation will prevent third parties from performing R&D in the same sector. The difference between cooperation and merger is the incentive of the merging versus the incentive of the cooperating parties. Whereas the merging parties have fewer incentives to start and maintain research and development post-merger, the innovation incentives of the cooperating parties are not changed through the conclusion of an R&D agreement. This difference also influences third parties' research and development. In a merger setting the reduced incentives of the merging parties lead to a general decrease in competitive pressure on the innovation level.[748] The merging parties have less incentives to perform R&D. Accordingly, they are also less likely to introduce new products and exert competitive pressure on rivals. This in turn leads to third parties' reduced innovation incentives since they do not have to fear the merged entity to cannibalize their sales. All in all, innovation incentives decrease in the industry (or at least in certain innovation spaces).

But this effect does not arise in a cooperation setting. As mentioned above, the innovation incentive of the cooperating parties does not decrease through the R&D agreement.[749] Since the general level of competi-

746 See *Section III) A) 2) (a) (3)*.

747 See for both concepts *Section II) G) 1) and 2)*.

748 See to this also *Section II) D) 1) (a)*.

749 See *Section III) A) 2) (a) (1) (aa)*.

tive pressure on the innovation level is not altered, third parties' research and development incentives remain the same.

In conclusion, an R&D cooperation is unlikely to decrease innovation incentives of the cooperating undertakings as well as those of third parties.

(cc) Economic findings on the interrelation between cooperation and innovation

In a recent economic paper, *Federico*, *Scott Morton* and *Shapiro* comment on R&D joint ventures. They state:

> *"One of the robust lessons from thus literature is that competition from rival innovators acts as a powerful incentive for innovation. A secure incumbent would invest less on R&D than a threatened incumbent, because it does not need to fear losing its business to rivals. Likewise, in the literature on R&D joint ventures, absent spillovers, cooperation between rivals leads to lower innovative efforts because it internalizes the business-stealing effects on innovation."*[750]

The authors rely on a paper by *d'Aspremont* and *Jacquemin*[751] and another paper by *Lopez* and *Vives*[752]. However, the papers relied on do not support the author's conclusion in this generality.

d'Aspremont and *Jacquemin* examine the effects of cooperative and non-cooperative R&D efforts in a duopoly with spillovers. They set up three different scenarios: noncooperative R&D (1) , cooperation only at the precompetitive stage (meaning that there is no cooperation in the market-place) (2) and R&D cooperation including common policies at the product level (3).[753]

When appraising the results of the paper, one must first consider that the authors set up a very specific model. In case of cooperation in a duopoly, there is no competitive pressure left at all if the two market players cooperate. This may lead to findings that not only reflect the loss of rivalry between the duopolists but the loss of rivalry in the industry as a whole. In fact, *d'Aspremont* and *Jacquemin* do not rely on a cannibal-

---

750 *Federico/Scott Morton/Shapiro*, Antitrust and Innovation, p. 4.

751 *d'Aspremont/Jacquemin*, Cooperative and Noncooperative R&D in Duopoly with Spillovers.

752 *Lopez/Vives*, Overlapping Ownership, R&D Spillovers, and Antitrust Policy.

753 *d'Aspremont/Jacquemin*, Cooperative and Noncooperative R&D, p. 1.

ization theory, but rather find that the solutions obtained in scenario (2) "*correspond to an internalization of the R&D external effects through joint decision on the levels of R&D expenditures.*"[754] However, what the authors do not take into account at this point is that this joint decision only takes place as long as cooperation is in total more beneficial for the partners than noncooperative research. Even though the authors mention that "*the noncooperative choice could always be adopted by cooperating firms, if more profitable*"[755], they do not incorporate this option into their model. In this context the authors also explicitly point out:

> "*However, in order to compute explicitly and to classify our various types of subgame-perfect solutions, our analysis has been very partial and based on a model ignoring many crucial aspects of R&D activities.*"[756]

As a second point, the paper does not support the finding that cooperation between rivals leads to lower innovative efforts. *d'Aspremont* and *Jacquemin* rather find:

> "*For large spillovers {…}, the amount of research which is the closest to the social optimum is the one achieved by firms' cooperating in both output and research, and the most distant, the one obtained by cooperative behavior.*"

For small spillovers, cooperative behavior in output and research leads to the "*second-best*" result. The authors conclude that "*cooperative behavior can play a positive role in industries having a few firms and characterized by R&D activities generating spillovers.*"[757] This is supposed to be in line with the European antitrust approach that allows cooperation in research and output.[758]

Admittedly, low spillovers (being a part of "appropriability"[759]) have been a precondition of the rationale in *Dow/DuPont*. In that regard, the findings of *d'Aspremont* and *Jacquemin* would indicate that cooperation is only the second-best option. However, there remain the abovementioned points of critique on the general duopoly setup and the non-incorporation of the option to terminate cooperation.

---

754 *d'Aspremont/Jacquemin*, Cooperative and Noncooperative R&D, p. 4.
755 *d'Aspremont/Jacquemin*, Cooperative and Noncooperative R&D, p. 4.
756 *d'Aspremont/Jacquemin*, Cooperative and Noncooperative R&D, p. 8.
757 On the aforementioned *d'Aspremont/Jacquemin*, Cooperative and Noncooperative R&D, p. 7.
758 *d'Aspremont/Jacquemin*, Cooperative and Noncooperative R&D, p. 8.
759 See *Section II) D) 1) (c) and Section II) H) 1) (c)*.

The paper of *Lopez* and *Vives* deals with the effects of overlapping ownership on R&D in an oligopoly model.[760] The authors find that increases in overlapping ownership "*increase (decrease) R&D and output for high (low) enough spillovers*"[761]. While, again, the theory in *Dow/DuPont* rests on the notion that there are already low spillovers, the finding of the authors nonetheless does not support the finding that cooperation decreases innovation efforts.

This is because overlapping ownership is at crucial points different from mere contractual cooperation. In fact, overlapping ownership rather corresponds to a merger than to cooperation. Overlapping ownership, in the form of cross-shareholding agreements among firms or common ownership,[762] is a structural element leading to a change in the decision-making power of firms. Even though overlapping ownership may not be of a permanent manner, it nevertheless restrains the decision-making power of the firms' management. The discretion to start or end R&D cooperation is influenced. In that setting, cannibalization may also play a role. If firm A brings to market an innovative product that cannibalizes sales from firm B, then this may have a negative effect on the common owner of firm A and B. That common owner will likely not have an interest in marketing innovative products that capture sales from any of the firms in which he holds shares.[763] Managers of the respective firms take that into account in their decisions.[764] This effect does not occur in mere cooperation settings without any structural relation between the cooperating undertakings. The general finding of the paper can thus not be transferred to mere R&D cooperation.

In a paragraph, *Lopez* and *Vives* mention that there should generally be no separation between coordination in R&D and output, "*whether because of overlapping ownership or because R&D cooperation naturally extends to prod-*

760 *Lopez/Vives*, Overlapping Ownership, p. 1.

761 *Lopez/Vives*, Overlapping Ownership, p. 1.

762 *Lopez/Vives*, Overlapping Ownership, p. 2, 7; investors' acquisition of firms' shares in an industry is called common ownership; a firms' acquisition of other firms' shares is called cross-ownership.

763 See for this effect also Dow/DuPont Decision, para 2348-2352; *Section II) D) 1) (a)*.

764 In fact, *Lopez/Vives* assume in their paper „*that the manager of a firm takes into account shareholders' incentives (through the control weights) and maximizes a weighted average of the shareholders' portfolio profits.*" *Lopez/Vives*, Overlapping Ownership, p. 7.

uct market cooperation"[765]. They find that R&D cooperation will in any case extend to the product market[766] and rely on empirical evidence and antitrust cases.[767] However, the authors do not give any explanation for why coordination in R&D and output should be treated the same regardless of whether there is overlapping ownership or mere cooperation. In fact, in light of the abovementioned arguments, it seems unlikely that factual or contractual cooperation can be compared with structural overlapping ownership. This is mainly because mere cooperation lacks the restraint on firms' management to take account of the interests of common shareholders and its own cross-shareholding. In the case of mere cooperation there is likely no increased cannibalization that has to be taken into account.

In addition, R&D cooperation as such is widely considered to be pro-competitive.[768] In a recent paper, *Motta* and *Tarantino* come to the conclusion that R&D cooperation is superior to a merger and may, under certain circumstances, increase consumer surplus as well as R&D investments.[769]

(2) Reduced number of entities performing R&D

On first sight, a reduction in the number of entities performing R&D may delay the discovery of innovative products. In fact, evolutionary theory and associated empiric studies indicate that heterogeneity of research approaches increases the likeliness of success.[770] This effect must be distinguished from a deliberate slowdown of research activities by the cooperating parties that has been discussed above.[771]

Instead of several possible solutions that could be found by each company separately, there is the chance of only one solution in case of R&D

765 *Lopez/Vives*, Overlapping Ownership, p. 39.
766 *Lopez/Vives*, Overlapping Ownership, p. 38.
767 *Lopez/Vives*, Overlapping Ownership, p. 39.
768 See for example Recital 6 of the R&D BER; Horizontal Cooperation Guidelines, para 141; *Chrocziel/Giedke* in MüKo, FuE-GVO, Einleitung, para 1,3; *Kerber/Schwalbe* in MüKo, Grundlagen, para 368, 30 et seq; *Fuchs* in Immenga/Mestmäcker, Wettbewerbsrecht EU, FuE-GVO, I. Einführung, para 4; *Schütze* in Loewenheim/Meessen/Riesenkampff/Kersting/Meyer-Lindemann, Kartellrecht, FuE-GVO, Einführung, para 1.
769 *Motta/Tarantino*, The Effect of Horizontal Mergers, When Firms Compete in Prices and Investments, p. 32-32.
770 See *Section II) D) 3)*.
771 See *Section III) A) 2) (a) (aa)*.

cooperation.[772] Alternative approaches remain undiscovered.[773] The probability of finding innovative solutions to existing problems may decrease.[774]

However, as already mentioned above,[775] evolutionary theory would in its final consequence lead to the finding that every kind of concentration or cooperation would harm innovation regardless of possible positive effects of communitization. A reduction in the number of market players researching independently always results in a decrease in diverse research approaches. In this respect it does not matter if there remain four or twenty independent entities performing research, because in the latter case it may well be that the twenty-first attempt would have been successful. Furthermore, the only determinant of the evolutionary approach is the number of players regardless of competitive pressure. But despite a reduction of the number of innovators, cooperation as well as concentration may lead to increased innovation incentives by creating a credible rival. It is by no means clear if the advantage of a higher number of independent research paths will outweigh a low competitive pressure to perform innovation activities. In addition, cooperation as well as concentration may lead to efficiencies that may also enhance innovation incentives.

Having said that, there are indeed differences regarding the point in time the cooperation takes place. Whereas in the early stages of the research process the abovementioned arguments claim validity, development activities close to the marketing of a product have to be assessed differently. The Commission's focus must shift from the preservation of innovation incentives to saving competition in current or future product or technology markets. In the development phase of a product, the stochastic discovery process is almost terminated and a product may with a relatively high degree of certainty reach the market. At this point in time it arguably makes sense to preserve a sufficient number of R&D poles.

Nonetheless, there is no need to apply the concept of innovation competition. Since markets can already be defined (be it existing or emerging markets), the concept of potential competition and the future markets

772 *Mestmäcker/Schweitzer*, Europäisches Wettbewerbsrecht, § 32 para 11; see also *Kerber/Schwalbe* in MüKo, B. ökonomische Grundlagen des Wettbewerbsrechts, para 378.
773 *Fuchs* in Immenga/Mestmäcker, Wettbewerbsrecht EU, FuE-GVO, I. Einführung, para 5.
774 *Kerber/Schwalbe* in MüKo, B. ökonomische Grundlagen des Wettbewerbsrechts, para 378.
775 See *Section II) D) 3)*.

approach[776] suffice to preserve a competitive environment. The innovation competition approach as developed in *Dow/DuPont* aims at preventing decreased innovation incentives that are due to an increase in concentration of innovation capacity. There is no need to apply this approach with respect to observable research and development activities towards defined markets. Furthermore, the innovation competition concept with its relation to R&D assets is not even fit to cover competition aspects at the late development stage. Innovation competition focuses on the assets necessary to perform R&D – namely personnel, facilities, patents and so on. But when preserving a market, it seems necessary to take into account marketing, distribution and production assets. It is no longer important who the most important innovator is, but rather which undertaking is powerful in a specific market.

(3) No adjustment of Guidelines

The concept of R&D poles as mentioned in the Horizontal Cooperation Guidelines seems to expand the potential competition doctrine and the future markets approach in terms of timing. The Horizontal Cooperation Guidelines point out in para 120 that R&D poles are efforts directed towards a certain new product or technology and the substitutes for that R&D. The approach already incorporates specific new products. However, the concept of potential competition as applied by the Commission requires timeliness of entry.[777] Normally, entry is considered timely if it occurs within two years.[778] In the pharmaceutical industry, that is mentioned in the relevant para 120 of the Horizontal Cooperation Guidelines, the development phase may well exceed two years due to complicated regulatory processes. However, the final product is already definable once the regulatory process starts. Accordingly, the protection of the future or existing market must start at that point too. For that reason, the Guidelines aim at expanding the scope of the traditional concepts with respect to entry that is more than two years away without, however, giving up the basic principles of those market related concepts.

The Commission even explicitly mentions in para 121 of the Horizontal Cooperation Guidelines that the analysis of a future market is difficult,

---

776 See for both approaches *Section II) G) 1) and 2)*.

777 See for example Horizontal Merger Guidelines, para 74.

778 Horizontal Merger Guidelines, para 74.

and may therefore be implicitly incorporated in the analysis of the Commission's notion of competition in innovation. The aim is not the innovation process itself but the final product and the respective market.

As a result, the Horizontal Cooperation Guidelines acknowledge in para 122 that if the innovation efforts in an industry are not structured in a way that allows the identification of R&D poles, the Commission will "*in the absence of exceptional circumstances*" not assess the impact of an R&D cooperation on innovation. As long as R&D efforts cannot be related to specific products, the Commission's approach of analyzing impacts on existing or future product markets is not applicable. Even though the Horizontal Cooperation Guidelines use the term "competition in innovation", they rather refer to competition in markets that may in specific industries already be assessed during the research and development process.

Overall, the Horizontal Cooperation Guidelines are stringent and consistent.[779] At first sight, the proposed assessment of the credibility of competing poles in para 120 of the Horizontal Cooperation Guidelines seems somehow incongruous. In order to analyze that credibility, the Horizontal Cooperation Guidelines refer to the nature, scope and size of any other R&D efforts, access to financial and human resources, know-how/patents, or other specialized assets as well as timing and capability to exploit possible results. Taking into account that R&D poles heading towards an identifiable product require that the basic discovery work has already been done, it is not quite clear why financial and human resources as well as know-how/patents are necessary to assess competitive strength. However, the Horizontal Cooperation Guidelines seem to refer to the assets necessary to perform the regulatory process and marketing activities rather than assets necessary for discovery.

In conclusion, the innovation competition approach as developed in *Dow/DuPont* is not applicable in the scope of R&D agreements. Innovation incentives are not decreased through mere cooperation. In addition, the fear that a reduction of the number of entities performing R&D leads to less innovation would prevent any kind of cooperation regardless of possible positive effects.

Since the concept of competition in innovation and the related notion of R&D poles in the Horizontal Cooperation Guidelines rather expand

779 Differing view: *Fuchs* who finds that the restrictions on the use of „innovation markets" are not convincing; *Fuchs* in Immenga/Mestmäcker, Wettbewerbsrecht EU, FuE-GVO, I. Einführung, para 47.

the scope of potential competition and future markets, the Guidelines may remain unchanged.

(b) Technology transfer

In contrast to R&D agreements, technology transfer takes place chronologically before the decision to start innovation activities. The primary purpose of licensing agreements is to enable the licensee to use the technology for the production of goods or services.[780] Nonetheless, since a technology is an "asset", a licensing agreement may have an impact on the innovation capacity of an undertaking. The licensed technology may increase the ability and therefore also the incentive of the licensee to innovate. These considerations are implicitly acknowledged in Article 5 (1) lit a) Technology Transfer BER and the Technology Transfer Guidelines with respect to exclusive grant backs. Para 129 of the Technology Transfer Guidelines states:

> "*An obligation to grant the licensor an exclusive licence to improvements of the licensed technology or to assign such improvements to the licensor is likely to reduce the licensee's incentive to innovate since it hinders the licensee in exploiting the improvements, including by way of licensing to third parties.*"

This implies that the licensed technology may be used for further improvements and the development of new products. In addition, technology transfer can set incentives for the initial research and development of the licensor.[781]

Another difference between R&D cooperation and technology transfer is that the latter is far more structural. When granting an exclusive license, the licensee may, depending on the specific form of the arrangement, enter into a position of having the licensed technology at its disposal. The respective technology may be considered an "own" asset of the licensee.

---

780 At least this is what the Technology Transfer BER covers, see Recital 7 and Article 1 (1) lit c) i) of the Technology Transfer BER that defines technology transfer agreement as *„a technology rights licensing agreement entered into between two undertakings for the purpose of the production of contract products by the licensee {...}*“; see also para 1, 58 et seq of the Technology Transfer Guidelines.

781 Recital 4 of the Technology Transfer BER and para 17 of the Technology Transfer Guidelines.

Accordingly, one may initially think of applying the Commission's innovation competition approach as developed in *Dow/DuPont* in the more structural setting of technology transfer.

However, attention must be paid to the specific reasoning behind *Dow/DuPont* and the differences with respect to a licensing agreement. The first line of argumentation refers to the communitization of assets. The licensed technology is not actually communitized in the sense of being a jointly exploited asset. Depending on the characteristics of the specific arrangement, one, both or even more parties can use the licensed technology. However, their decisions on how to use the technology for the purpose of further research and development are usually independent. This does not mean that one of the parties to the agreement may not be restricted from fully using the technology for its own research.[782] But this decision is usually made in advance of any concrete research activity and basically just limits the scope of the parties' innovation assets. If an undertaking may not fully use the licensed technology, its innovation capacity is limited. But the decision to perform R&D is still taken unilaterally.

Accordingly, even though technology transfer can impact the innovation capacity of an undertaking, it does not lead to joint decisions on whether and how to perform research activities. There is no "concentration" of decision-making processes as in a merger setting. Even though certain actions with respect to the use of the licensed technology may hinder innovation activities,[783] the structural communitization approach of the innovation competition assessment as used in *Dow/DuPont* does not fit a technology transfer agreement.

Mirroring the reasoning with respect to R&D agreements, the second line of argumentation deals with cannibalization concerns. It has been established that increased cannibalization of a company's own current or future sales is likely to decrease innovation incentives. However, cannibalization concerns are not increased through obtaining a license. Even though the licensee is unlikely to perform research and development in the direction of the licensed technology, the decision to obtain a license

782 However, according to Article 4 (1) lit d) of the Technology Transfer BER, the restriction of the ability to carry out research and development is usually considered a hardcore restriction if the parties to the agreement are competitors. In case of non-competitors, the restriction of research and development activities is excluded from the exemption, Article 5 (2) Technology Transfer BER, and has to individually be assessed; see also para 115, 141-143 of the Technology Transfer Guidelines.

783 This is explicitly mentioned in the R&D BER in Recital 15 and Article 5.

is, as in case of R&D cooperation, a unilateral decision of an undertaking balancing the risks and benefits of own research activities against obtaining a license for the desired technology. At the point in time when the firm decides whether to start research or to enter into a technology transfer agreement, cannibalization concerns are not important, as there are no additional sales yet that could be taken away. In addition, the decision could be reversed in the case of an increased profitability of own research activities. In any case, the respective firm still has an incentive to perform research in order to obtain a solution that could replace the licensed technology and safe license fees.[784] This is explicitly acknowledged in para 129 and 130 of the Technology Transfer Guidelines. In that respect, technology transfer agreements may even enhance innovation incentives, as they increase knowledge of a specific technical solution and may build a basis for further research.

Consequently, as is the case with respect to R&D cooperation, the Technology Transfer Guidelines use a concept of "competition in innovation" that rather refers to the potential competition or future markets approach. The Guidelines state at para 26 that in some cases competition in innovation must be analyzed separately. This is, according to the Guidelines, particularly the case where the agreement "*affects innovation at creating new products and where it is possible at an early stage to identify research and development poles.*" Structured research activities targeting a specific new product, however, may best be analyzed by means of the product-related future markets concept.[785] In contrast, the innovation competition approach as used in *Dow/DuPont* deals with structural changes leading to reduced innovation incentives beyond specific research activities or even identifiable products.

Para 26 of the Technology Transfer Guidelines continues that it is important for the assessment that there will be "*a sufficient number of competing research and development poles left*" after the technology transfer. Para 26 refers in a Footnote[786] to para 157. The latter paragraph sets up a safe harbor if there are four or more independently controlled technologies in addition to the technologies controlled by the parties that "*may be substitutable for the licensed technology at a comparable cost to the user.*" In

784 It is possible to obtain research results leading to the solution of a specific problem that do not infringe existing IP rights for that very problem. Patents, for example, usually only cover a specific technical solution for a problem.

785 For the future market concept see *Section II) G) 2)*.

786 Para 26, fn. 28 of the Technology Transfer Guidelines.

that respect, the "*relative commercial strength*" of the technologies must be considered. The Guidelines do not mention how the number of independent technologies refers to the research and development poles. Also, the relative commercial strength seems not to be a valid criterion for assessing research poles that are far away from any commercialization.

The U.S. IP Guidelines are a bit more precise at that point.[787] They find that four or more independently controlled entities in addition to the parties must possess the assets and the incentive to perform research and development "*that is a close substitute of the research and development activities of the parties to the licensing agreement.*" However, it is not said that the parties of a licensing agreement perform any research and development activities at the time of the conclusion of the licensing agreement. They nonetheless may have incentives to start not yet identifiable innovation activities later on. The U.S. IP Guidelines, like the EU Horizontal Cooperation Guidelines with respect to R&D cooperation,[788] seem to refer to an extended concept of potential competition and future markets.

All in all, the innovation competition concept as developed in *Dow/DuPont* is not yet reflected in the rules and Guidelines on technology transfer agreements. There is also no European case law on this point. However, since an innovation competition assessment does not fit the specific circumstances of technology transfer, no change is required.

3) Conclusion

The concept of innovation competition as developed in *Dow/DuPont* does not fit into the specific setting of cooperation. First of all, in case of a cooperation the parties remain independent market players. Even though they may align their research and development activities with respect to certain targets, they decide independently whether and how to begin and continue the cooperation. Secondly, cannibalization as the major rationale behind *Dow/DuPont* is not increased through cooperation. The number of products or research activities that could be cannibalized does not increase in case of a cooperation. Those two points have been illustrated above in case of R&D agreements as well as with respect to technology transfer. They claim general validity in case of a cooperation. As opposed to a merger, cooperating parties remain structurally independent. This means

787 See U.S. Intellectual Property Guidelines, p. 25.
788 See *Section III) A) 1) (b) and (d).*

that there is always the possibility to terminate a cooperation. In addition, the number of products or services that can be cannibalized generally does not increase for each cooperating party.

With regard to R&D agreements, the number of independent research and development activities may be decreased. This may limit the number of possible solutions to a problem. However, this argument would counteract any kind of concentration or cooperation regardless of possible pro-innovation effects. In addition, the focus on the mere number of independent approaches ignores any pro-competitive effects of cooperation. R&D agreements are generally considered harmless to competition.[789] Accordingly, the focus on the mere number of independent research and development activities cannot be considered as being a decisive factor for the legitimacy of R&D cooperation at a very early stage. As far as certain research activities are already directed towards specific markets, this may be different. However, at this point in time, there is no need for the innovation competition approach. The concepts of potential competition and future markets are sufficient to cover effects on competition in identifiable markets.

In conclusion, what seemed to be a contradiction in the first place may be adequately explained on a closer look. It is in fact a difference if undertakings decide to merge instead of cooperating. Whereas a structural merger of Dow and DuPont, finally leading to a new legal and economic entity, may decrease innovation incentives, a cooperation is unlikely to do so. Even though an R&D agreement may lead to the alignment of firms with respect to specific activities, the cooperating parties remain independent entities. Cannibalization of a company's own products is not significantly increased in that setting. In addition, the parties of an agreement could also terminate the cooperation in case independent research seems to be more profitable. This is different in a merger setting.

Concerning the apparent ambiguity in case of the creation of a joint venture,[790] it cannot be the solution to apply the innovation competition concept to a cooperation. It is rather advisable to not use the criteria established in *Dow/DuPont* with respect to full-function joint ventures (that fall

789 See Recital 6 of the R&D BER that states that joint research and development generally does not fall within the scope of Article 101 (1) TFEU; Recital 2 of the R&D BER further refers to Article 179 (2) of the TEU that protects research and development cooperation.

790 See *Section III) A)*.

within the scope of the EC Merger Regulation)[791] as well. Even though joint ventures may lead to a certain communitization of activities, there remain however two or more independent parent companies. As long as there is still some competition between those parent companies, the rationale behind *Dow/DuPont* does not claim validity.

B) Abuse of a dominant position according to Article 102 TFEU

One may think of applying the rationale behind *Dow/DuPont* in the scope of abuse of a dominant position according to Article 102 TFEU. Especially with respect to conduct related to hindering innovation, the innovation capacity of an undertaking might better reflect its competitive position than market shares on existing markets. Imagine DuPont (that pre-merger was supposed to be the most important innovator in the crop protection industry)[792] engaging in refusal to deal with respect to the license of an innovation. Under specific circumstances, market dominant undertakings do have to license their IP rights to third parties if otherwise competition and innovation on upstream or downstream markets were impeded.[793] However, according to the assessment in *Dow/DuPont*, DuPont was mainly not market dominant with respect to market shares on existing markets.[794] Still, taking into account DuPont's importance as innovator, the license to its innovative solutions could be even more important for competition as

---

791 See Article 3 (4) EC Merger Regulation.

792 Cf. Dow/DuPont Decision, para 2400-2413, 2499 et seq; *Todino/van de Walle/Stoican*, 64 The Antitrust Bulletin (2019), 11, 21.

793 This is the case if the licensed product or service is indispensable for the market entry in upstream or downstream markets and there is the development of a new product or service; ECJ, Judgment of 29.04.2004, Case C-418/01, ECLI:EU:C:2004:257, para 38, *IMS Health*; CFI, Judgment of 17.09.2007, Case T-201/04, ECLI:EU:T:2007:289, para 647, 665, *Microsoft*; Communication from the Commission – Guidance on the Commission's enforcement priorities in applying Article 82 of the EC Treaty to abusive exclusionary conduct by dominant undertakings, OJ C 45, 24.02.2009, p. 7-20 (hereinafter "**Priority Guidance**"), para 81, 87.

794 DuPont ranked sixth in terms of sales in the crop protection industry, see Dow/DuPont Decision, para 2206-2208; *Cary*, Festschrift für Dirk Schroeder, p. 186. With respect to specific defined markets see Dow/DuPont Decision, para 702, 868, 957, 1025, 1101, 1143, 1251, 1350, 1373, 1397, 1422, 1476, 1490, 1503, 1523, 1542, 1554, 1558, 1647, 1718, 1726, 1781 et seq, 1836, 1840, 1851, 1922, 1926, 1931; in some very narrowly defined markets, however, DuPont has a high market share.

well as innovation in the industry than the license of a currently dominant but not very innovative company.

In that regard, one may think of supplementing the concept of market dominance. In fact, the market share in existing markets is not the only factor that determines market power. Even though an undertaking may not have high market shares in existing markets, its competitive position may well be determined by its innovation capacity.

With this in mind, the criteria used in the Dow/DuPont Decision may serve as a starting point for assessing a firm's position on existing markets on the basis of its importance as innovator.

1) Possible starting points for innovation competition concerns in Article 102 TFEU

Innovation competition as mentioned in *Dow/DuPont* may alter or determine the market position of an undertaking and thus influence the scope of Article 102 TFEU. This does not mean that an innovation market shall be established, but that power in an existing product market may not only depend on market shares but also on the innovation capacity of an undertaking.[795]

(a) Legal basis for incorporating innovation concerns

Article 102 (1) TFEU states that the abuse of a dominant position within the internal market or a substantial part of it shall be prohibited. The assessment of an abuse of dominance consists of four steps:[796] First, the relevant market must be defined. Second, the undertaking concerned must hold a dominant position on that defined market. As a third point, the market dominant undertaking must abuse its position. And finally, the abuse may not be justified.

Innovation concerns may be incorporated when analyzing market dominance (that is the second step of the assessment). The term market domi-

---

795 Cf. *Dreher*, who finds that innovation potential or innovation capacity is merely and element to determine market dominance and that there is no need for a separate innovation market, *Dreher*, ZWeR 2009, 149, 167.

796 In EU law, the behavior also has to affect trade between Member States according to Article 102 TFEU.

nance is not legally defined in European law. Article 102 (1) TFEU does not set up criteria for the assessment of a dominant position. When taking into account the examples of prohibited behavior mentioned in Article 102 (2) TFEU, it becomes clear that the protection of innovation incentives is one of the goals of the provision.[797] Accordingly, innovation concerns also have to play a role in the assessment of a dominant position.

Article 102 (2) lit b) states that an abuse may, in particular, consist in limiting technical development to the prejudice of consumers. This refers to conduct by a dominant undertaking that prevents access to, use or further development of a given level of research and development.[798] Internal restrictions as well as restrictions at the expense of third parties are included.[799] In any event, the prevention of access to and use of new technologies may cause even greater harm if the acting undertaking is an important innovator. Accordingly, when Article 102 TFEU addresses dominant undertakings, the notion of dominance must take into account the protective purpose of the provision. There is an interaction between abusive behavior and dominance.[800]

This approach is mirrored in the Commission's Priority Guidance[801]. In the context of assessing market power, the Commission finds that:

> "*{…} an undertaking which is capable of profitably increasing prices above the competitive level for a significant period of time does not face sufficiently effective competitive constraints and can thus generally be regarded as dominant. In this Communication, the expression 'increase prices' includes the power to maintain prices above the competitive level and is used as shorthand for the various ways in which the parameters of competition — such as prices, output, innovation, the variety or quality of goods or services — can be influenced to the advantage of the dominant undertaking and to the detriment of consumers.*"

Accordingly, the possibility of influencing innovation is an important parameter already at the level of market power and may not only be taken into account with respect to a potentially abusive behavior. Nevertheless, the power to alter the level of innovation is particularly important in the

797 And generally is a protective goal in European Law, see *Section II) A) 2)*.

798 *Bulst* in Bunte, Kartellrecht, Art. 102 AEUV para 204.

799 *Bulst* in Bunte, Kartellrecht, Art. 102 AEUV para 204.

800 See Section {...}; cf. *Mestmäcker/Schweitzer*, Europäisches Wettbewerbsrecht, § 17 para 38.

801 See fn. 793.

context of refusal to supply and margin squeeze situations[802]. In those situations, the Guidance states:

> "*The Commission considers that consumer harm may, for instance, arise where the competitors that the dominant undertaking forecloses are, as a result of the refusal, prevented from bringing innovative goods or services to market and/or where follow-on innovation is likely to be stifled. This may be particularly the case if the undertaking which requests supply does not intend to limit itself essentially to duplicating the goods or services already offered by the dominant undertaking on the downstream market, but intends to produce new or improved goods or services for which there is a potential consumer demand or is likely to contribute to technical development.*"[803]

But it is not just about concrete innovation incentives of third parties. The Commission also considers the innovation incentive of the dominant undertaking and third parties in general:

> "*The existence of {an obligation to supply} — even for a fair remuneration — may undermine undertakings' incentives to invest and innovate and, thereby, possibly harm consumers. The knowledge that they may have a duty to supply against their will may lead dominant undertakings — or undertakings who anticipate that they may become dominant — not to invest, or to invest less, in the activity in question. Also, competitors may be tempted to free ride on investments made by the dominant undertaking instead of investing themselves.*"[804]

Accordingly, the preservation of innovation incentives may also be considered as an efficiency:

> "*The Commission will consider claims by the dominant undertaking that a refusal to supply is necessary to allow the dominant undertaking to realise an adequate return on the investments required to develop its input business, thus generating incentives to continue to invest in the future, taking the risk of failed projects into account. The Commission will also consider claims by the dominant undertaking that its own innovation will be negatively affect-*

802 Margin squeeze refers to the situation that an undertaking charges a price for the product or technology in question that does not allow competitors on the downstream market to trade profitably on a lasting basis, see Priority Guidance, para 80.

803 Priority Guidance, para 87.

804 Priority Guidance, para 75.

ed by the obligation to supply, or by the structural changes in the market conditions that imposing such an obligation will bring about, including the development of follow-on innovation by competitors."[805]

The Commission's approach shows that it is not only about a specific follow-on innovation of a third party but rather about the conservation of innovation incentives in the industry. Such assessment necessarily must take into account the innovation capacity of the market players. The significance of market shares is low when it comes to innovation incentives that presuppose the ability to perform research and development.

Even though the Commission's Priority Guidance is not a binding law,[806] it may indicate how Article 102 TFEU shall be applied. All in all, the competitive position in innovation may determine the market position of an undertaking. This is even more the case with respect to behavior influencing innovation incentives.

(b) Factors determining market power

According to the European Court of Justice, market dominance is defined as follows:

> *"The dominant position {...} relates to a position of economic strength enjoyed by an undertaking which enables it to prevent effective competition being maintained on the relevant market by affording it the power to behave to an appreciable extent independently of its competitors, its customers and ultimately of the consumers. Such position does not preclude some competition, which it does where there is a monopoly or a quasi-monopoly, but enables the undertaking which profits by it, if not to determine, at least to have an appreciable influence on the conditions under which that competition will develop, and in any case to act largely in disregard of it so long as such conduct does not act to its detriment."*[807]

---

805 Priority Guidance, para 89.

806 See *Section II) A) 3) (d)*.

807 ECJ, Judgment of 13.02.1979, Case 85/76, ECLI:EU:C:1979:36, Summary 4, para 38-39, *Hoffmann-La Roche*; settled case law since ECJ, Judgment of 14.02.1978, Case 27/76, ECLI:EU:C:1978:22, Summary 2, para 65-66, *United Brands*; recently in ECJ, Judgment of 06.12.2012, Case C-457/10 P, ECLI:EU:C:2012:770, para 175, *AstraZeneca*.

The Commission relies on a similar approach.[808] Two factors are decisive: the ability to behave independently and the ability to prevent effective competition.[809]

The European Court of Justice further finds that "*a dominant position derives from a combination of several factors which, taken separately, are not necessarily determinative.*"[810] Generally, market power can be assessed by means of market structure, company structure and market behavior[811].[812]

The starting point for the analysis of market dominance is the market structure. The structure of a market is mainly determined by the number of competitors and the size of their respective market shares.[813] Market shares above 50% constitute very large market shares and may serve as evidence of a dominant position.[814] Market shares between 70% and 80% are even a clear indication of the existence of a dominant position.[815] The Commission finds that "*dominance is not likely if the undertaking's market share is below 40% in the relevant market.*"[816] However, there may be specific cases where undertakings may be considered dominant with a market

808 Priority Guidance, para 10.

809 *Schroeter/Bartl* in von der Groeben/Schwarze/Hatje, Europäisches Unionsrecht, Art. 102 AEUV para 73.

810 ECJ, Judgment of 14.02.1978, Case 27/76, ECLI:EU:C:1978:22, para 66, *United Brands*.

811 The criterion of market behavior will not be further elaborated as it is not important in the scope of innovation competition but rather focuses on pricing policy; for further information see *Bergmann/Fiedler* in Loewenheim/Meessen/Riesenkampff/Kersting/Meyer-Lindemann, Kartellrecht, Art. 102 AEUV para 141 et seq; *Fuchs* in Immenga/Mestmäcker, Wettbewerbsrecht EU, Art. 102 AEUV para 108 et seq.

812 *Bergmann/Fiedler* in Loewenheim/Meessen/Riesenkampff/Kersting/Meyer-Lindemann, Kartellrecht, Art. 102 AEUV para 117; *Fuchs* in Immenga/Mestmäcker, Wettbewerbsrecht EU, Art. 102 AEUV para 86; *Bulst* in Bunte, Kartellrecht, Art. 102 AEUV para 44.

813 *Bulst* in Bunte, Kartellrecht, Art. 102 para 45.

814 GC, Judgment of 01.07.2010, Case T-321/05, ECLI:EU:T:2010:266, para 242-243, *AstraZeneca*; ECJ, Judgment of 03.07.1991, Case C-62/86, ECLI:EU:C:1991:286, para 60, *AKZO*.

815 GC, Judgment of 01.07.2010, Case T-321/05, ECLI:EU:T:2010:266, para 243, *AstraZeneca*; CFI, Judgment of 12.12.1991, Case T-30/89, ECLI:EU:T:1991:70, para 92, *Hilti*; CFI, Judgment of 30.09.2003, Joined Cases T-191/98 and T-212/98 to T-214/98, ECLI:EU:T:2003:245, para 907, *Atlantic Container Line*.

816 Priority Guidance, para 14.

share below 40%,[817] for example when the market is highly fragmented.[818] Market shares below 25% will very unlikely lead to a dominant position.[819]

Usually, the market structure assessment is supplemented by the analysis of the structure of the company concerned.[820] Generally, technological advantages over competitors resulting from special experience, knowledge and skills in the manufacture of products or the provision of services may create or strengthen market dominance.[821] Such technological advantages may be reflected in the scale of research and development activities and the capacities allocated to them.[822] In some cases, technological advancement may even in itself create dominance.[823] However, the respective case law rather refers to specific technological capacities that can be directly linked to downstream product market activity.

In *Commercial solvents*, the ECJ found that an undertaking could be considered market dominant if it is the only market player with established processes and methods to produce certain chemicals on an industrial

---

817 Priority Guidance, para 14.

818 ECJ, Judgment of 15.12.1994, Case C-250/92, ECLI:EU:C:1994:413, para 48, *DLG/Gøttrup-Kliem*, CFI, Judgment of 17.12.2003, Case T-219/99, ECLI:EU:C:2003:343, para 224, *British Airways*.

819 *Bergmann/Fiedler* in Loewenheim/Meessen/Riesenkampff/Kersting/Meyer-Lindemann, Kartellrecht, Art. 102 AEUV para 126.

820 In an earlier judgment, the ECJ found that in order to find out whether an undertaking is market dominant, first its structure and then the situation on the said market should be assessed, ECJ, Judgment of 14.02.1978, Case 27/76, ECLI:EU:C:1978:22, para 67, *United Brands*; however, this approach has not been used in practice, cf. *Bulst* in Bunte, Kartellrecht, Art. 102 para 60; see also ECJ, Judgment of 13.02.1979, Case 85/76, ECLI:EU:C:1979:36, para 49, *Hoffmann-La Roche*: "*It is in the light of the preceding considerations that Roche's shares of each of the relevant markets, complemented by those factors which in conjunction with the market shares make it possible to show that there may be a dominant position, must be evaluated.*"

821 *Bergmann/Fiedler* in Loewenheim/Meessen/Riesenkampff/Kersting/Meyer-Lindemann, Kartellrecht, Art. 102 AEUV para 136; see also ECJ, Judgment of 13.02.1979, Case 85/76, ECLI:EU:C:1979:36, para 48, *Hoffmann-La Roche*, mentioning "*the technological lead of an undertaking over its competitors*" as a relevant factor for assessing dominance.

822 *Bergmann/Fiedler* in Loewenheim/Meessen/Riesenkampff/Kersting/Meyer-Lindemann, Kartellrecht, Art. 102 AEUV para 136; see also *Schröter/Bartl* in von der Groeben/Schwarze/Hatje, Europäisches Unionsrecht, Art. 102 AEUV para 109.

823 *Bergmann/Fiedler* in Loewenheim/Meessen/Riesenkampff/Kersting/Meyer-Lindemann, Kartellrecht, Art. 102 AEUV para 136; *Fuchs* in Immenga/Mestmäcker, Wettbewerbsrecht EU, Art. 102 AEUV para 103.

scale.[824] In *United Brands*, the ECJ also took into account technical knowledge to determine the market position of an undertaking. The Court finds:

> *"In the field of technical knowledge and as a result of continual research UBC keeps on improving the productivity and yield of its plantations by improving the draining system, making good soil deficiencies and combating effectively plant disease. It has perfected new ripening methods in which its technicians instruct the distributor/ripeners of the Chiquita Banana. That is another factor to be borne in mind when considering UBC's position since competing firms cannot develop research at a comparable level and are in this respect at a disadvantage compared with the applicant."*[825]

In *Michelin*, the ECJ relied upon advantages in research and a wide product range:

> *"{…} it should first be observed that in order to assess the relative economic strength of Michelin MV and its competitors on the Netherlands market the advantages which those undertakings may derive from belonging to groups of undertakings operating throughout Europe or even the world must be taken into consideration. Amongst those advantages, the lead which the Michelin group has over its competitors in the matters if investment and research and the special extent of its range of products, to which the Commission referred to in its decision, have not been denied. In fact in the case of certain types of tyre the Michelin Group is the only supplier on the market to offer them in its range."*[826]

In *Tetra Pak I*, the Commission based its assessment of market dominance partly on the possession of a specific aseptic-filling technique for milk.[827]

In *AKZO*, a highly developed marketing organization and knowledge were emphasized:

> *"Moreover, the Commission rightly pointed out that other factors confirmed AKZO' s predominance in the market. In addition to the fact that AKZO regards itself as the world leader in the peroxides market, it should be observed*

---

824 ECJ, Judgment of 06.03.1974, Joined cases 6/73 and 7/73, ECLI:EU:C:1974:18, para 9-18, *Commercial solvents*.

825 ECJ, Judgment of 14.02.1978, Case 27/76, ECLI:EU:C:1978:22, para 82-84, *United Brands*.

826 ECJ, Judgment of 09.11.1983, Case 322/81, ECLI:EU:C:1983:313, para 55 and Summary 9, *Michelin*.

827 Cf. CFI, Judgment of 10.07.1990, Case T-51/89, ECLI:EU:T:1990:41, para 7, *Tetra Pak*.

that, as AKZO itself admits, it has the most highly developed marketing organization, both commercially and technically, and wider knowledge than that of their competitors with regard to safety and toxicology {…}."[828]

In the *SIV* case, the General Court explicitly referred to technological lead with respect to the assessment of a dominant position of two undertakings:

"*There is nothing, in principle, to prevent two or more independent economic entities from being, on a specific market, united by such economic links that, by virtue of that fact, together they hold a dominant position vis-à-vis the other operators on the same market. This could be the case, for example, where two or more independent undertakings jointly have, through agreements or licences, a technological lead affording them the power to behave to an appreciable extent independently of their competitors, their customers and ultimately of their consumers.*"[829]

In *Eurofix-Bauco/Hilti*, the Commission further mentioned the research and development position of an undertaking as a factor determining market power:

„*In addition to the strength derived from its market share and the relative weakness of its competitors, Hilti has other advantages that help reinforce and maintain its position in the nail gun market: {…} Hilti has an extremely strong research and development position and is one of the leading companies worldwide not only in nail guns but also other fastening technologies, {…}.*"[830]

All in all, strength in research and development may well be considered in the assessment of market dominance. While some of the decisions of Union Courts and the Commission focus on specific technologies used to produce specific products (*Commercial solvents* and *Tetra Pak I*), there are also considerations on the research and development capacity of an undertaking, for example in *United Brands*, *Michelin*, *AKZO*, *SIV* and *Eurofix-Bauco/Hilti*. However, even though innovation capacity is taken into account,

828 ECJ, Judgment of 03.07.1991, Case C-62/86, ECLI:EU:C:1991:286, para 61, *AKZO*.

829 CFI, Judgment of 10.03.1992, Joined cases T-68/89, T-77/89 and T-78/89, ECLI:EU:T:1992:38, para 358, *SIV*; note that there is a difference between the permissibility of the cooperation and the assessment of a joint dominant position.

830 European Commission, Decision of 22.12.1987, 88/138/EEC, OJ L 65, 11.03.1988, p. 19-44, IV/30.787 and 31.488, para 69, *Eurofix-Bauco/Hilti*.

there are no criteria mentioned for assessing such capacity or strength in research and development. In addition, whereas market dominance has been established with respect to the possession of specific technologies necessary to compete on downstream markets, innovation capacity as such has only be used to supplement the assessment of market dominance already established by means of high market shares or other factors. There has been no case yet where market dominance of an undertaking was exclusively or mainly established by way of its research and development capacity as such.

Most importantly, in the cases mentioned above, technological advance is always analyzed with respect to specific identifiable markets. But harm to competition and innovation may also occur before the emergence of identifiable markets or beyond specific existing markets.[831] An undertaking's position in innovation competition, and therefore its ability to act independently of competitors and customers, may not correctly be reflected with respect to specific markets. That does not mean there is no market position of the undertaking concerned at all, but, as mentioned in *Dow/DuPont*, undertakings may be "*more important innovation competitors at industry level than their downstream market shares {…} suggest*"[832] and thus also have an impact on incentives to innovate. So far, there has not been an assessment of an undertaking's position in innovation competition in European case law on Article 102 TFEU.

The difference between the innovation competition approach as developed in *Dow/DuPont* and the current case law may well be illustrated by the *SIV* case. This case refers to agreements or licenses that result in a technological lead of two undertakings. In that regard, reference can be made to the findings with respect to restrictive agreements in *Section III) A) 2) and 3)*. Specific R&D or technology transfer agreements may impact certain existing or future product or service markets, but they are unlikely to lead to a general impact on the overall level of innovation. Put differently, an important innovator may license one of its thriving technologies and therefore impact the market on which the technology is used. However, with respect to further innovation based on the licensed technology, it is only the important innovator that is addressee of a possible compulsory license and not the cooperation partner. Only the owner of the license may (possibly) hinder future innovation, not the cooperation itself. With

831 See examples at the beginning of this *Section III) B)*.

832 Headline of Dow/DuPont Decision Section 8.7; see also Dow/DuPont Decision Headline of Section 8.7.2.

respect to the abuse of a dominant position, it is also not within the scope of innovation competition to preserve competition through innovation with respect to certain markets but rather to secure further innovation incentives. It is, accordingly, not about a specific market but about the innovation incentive, which may be decreased through the behavior of an important innovator.

(c) Innovation-driven competitive pressure in German law

A hint on how to incorporate innovation competition aspects in the scope of market dominance can be found in German law. In the course of the 9th amendment of the Act against Restraints of Competition ("ARC"),[833] the German legislator has introduced new rules on how to assess the market position of an undertaking. The new Section 18 (3a) paragraph 5 ARC states:

> *"In particular in the case of multi-sided markets and networks, in assessing the market position of an undertaking account shall also be taken of: {…} innovation-driven competitive pressure."*

The rule has been established to cover disruptive effects in platform and network markets. However, it is not restricted to such use (this is implied by the wording "in particular").[834] The German legislator explains:

> *"Paragraph 5 mentions the aspects of the effects of innovation potential in the digital economy, which must be taken into account in the required overall assessment. Market positions of platforms and networks in the Internet can theoretically be more easily acquired by competitors due to the dynamic developments prevailing there, in part as a result of simple technological innovations or short-term changes in user expectations. The competitive pressure resulting from the innovative power of Internet-based offerings enables*

833 Entered into force on 9 June 2017.

834 *Podszun* even finds that it is unlikely that disruption will happen in platform or network markets, due to strong networks effects that prevent disruptive changes in market position. He finds it more likely that disruptions happen in traditional markets, *Podszun*, Deutscher Bundestag, Ausschussdrucksache 18(9)1092, 19.01.2017, Stellungnahme als Sachverständiger im Wirtschaftsausschuss des Deutschen Bundestages zur Vorbereitung der Anhörung am 23.01.2017, Die 9. Novelle des Gesetzes gegen Wettbewerbsbeschränkungen (GWB) (hereinafter "Stellungnahme 9. GWB-Novelle"), p. 49-50.

disruptive changes that can lead to the vulnerability of even a company's strong market position. However, it is not easy to decide whether, within the forecast period of the antitrust authorities, shifts in existing market positions are likely to occur that already rule out the assumption of market dominance. Therefore, in each individual case a careful examination is necessary to determine whether there is not only an abstract, temporally too vague contestability of the market position of an undertaking. Would alone the prospect that a dominant position might be eliminated at some point in the future lead to the denial of dominance, the allegation of abuse of that position would per se be excluded from examination."[835]

(1) Application in practice

The new provision aims at covering likely shifts in existing market positions due to innovative changes. The competitive pressure taken into account shall not only be abstract, but there must also be sings that the market position is contestable due to existing innovation efforts. Authorities, courts and commentators in literature have interpreted Section 18 (3a) paragraph 5 ARC in this sense.

Podszun finds that the mere speculation by a court that innovations may change the market position in the future should not lead to denying a company market power and, thus, grant a monopoly return for the

835 BT-Drs. 18/10207, p. 51; author's translation from: *„Nummer 5 erwähnt den in der erforderlichen Gesamtbetrachtung zu berücksichtigenden Aspekt der Wirkungen von Innovationspotential in der digitalen Ökonomie. Marktpositionen etwa von Plattformen und Netzwerken im Internet können durch die dort vorherrschenden dynamischen Entwicklungen infolge teilweise einfacher, technologischer Innovationen oder sich kurzfristig ändernder Nutzervorstellungen theoretisch eher von Wettbewerbern angegriffen werden. Der Wettbewerbsdruck aufgrund der Innovationskraft internetbasierter Angebote beinhaltet die Möglichkeiten von disruptiven Veränderungen, die zur Angreifbarkeit auch einer starken Marktposition eines Unternehmens führen können. Allerdings ist es nicht einfach zu entscheiden, ob innerhalb des kartellbehördlichen Prognosezeitraums Verschiebungen bestehender Marktstellungen mit einiger Wahrscheinlichkeit eintreten, die schon die Annahme einer Marktbeherrschung ausschließen. In jedem Einzelfall ist daher eine sorgfältige Prüfung notwendig, ob nicht nur eine abstrakte, zeitlich zu vage Angreifbarkeit der Marktposition vorliegt. Würde allein die Aussicht, dass eine marktbeherrschende Position irgendwann wegfallen könnte, zur Verneinung der Marktbeherrschung führen, bliebe der Vorwurf einer missbräuchlicher Ausnutzung dieser Stellung per se einer Prüfung entzogen.“*

remaining period of time.[836] The mere finding that innovations can shake up a market position and innovation potential can limit market power does not help in practice.[837]

Esser/Höft find that it is not decisive if there is a concrete contestability of the market position, but rather whether a possible contestability can already be observed in the current competitive behavior.[838] If so, there is no scope for independent behavior in the meaning of a dominant position.[839]

The Federal Cartel Office ("FCO") has used the concept of innovation-driven competitive pressure in two merger cases and in the abuse of dominance decision *Facebook*.

The *Parship/Elitepartner*[840] decision was issued before the 9th ARC amendment and the formal introduction of innovation-driven competitive pressure but already used a similar concept. The FCO took a stand on the dynamics of the Internet and found that such dynamics could not rule out market power in online markets in general abstract terms.[841] Rather, concrete evidence of such dynamics within the forecast period of merger control would be required. An abstract vulnerability that can be expected at any given point in time would not be sufficient.[842] The FCO found that in the case at hand there was, indeed, such pronounced and concretely identifiable evidence on dynamics challenging the market position of the merging parties[843] and, accordingly, cleared the merger.

In contrast, in *CTS Eventim/Four Artists*[844], the FCO found that there was no innovation-driven competitive pressure in the meaning of the newly-introduced Section 18 (3a) paragraph 5 ARC. Like in *Parship/Elitepartner*, the FCO relied on concrete evidence for a dynamic or disruptive process

836 *Podszun*, Stellungnahme 9. GWB-Novelle, p. 50.

837 *Podszun*, Stellungnahme 9. GWB-Novelle, p. 50.

838 *Esser/Höft*, NZKart 2017, 259, 264.

839 *Esser/Höft*, NZKart 2017, 259, 264.

840 FCO, Decision of 22.10.2015, B6-57/17, BeckRS 2016, 1137, *Online-Dating-Plattform*.

841 FCO, Decision of 22.10.2015, B6-57/17, BeckRS 2016, 1137, para 176, *Online-Dating-Plattform*.

842 FCO, Decision of 22.10.2015, B6-57/17, BeckRS 2016, 1137, para 176, *Online-Dating-Plattform*.

843 FCO, Decision of 22.10.2015, B6-57/17, BeckRS 2016, 1137, para 178-183, *Online-Dating-Plattform*; see also *Tamke*, NZKart 2018, 503, 507.

844 FCO, Decision of 23.11.2017, B6-35/17, BeckRS 2017, 143034, *CTS Eventim/Four Artists*.

within the forecast period.[845] The FCO found that it was not apparent that market entry of innovative solutions was likely and those solutions could be expected to achieve significant market success within the forecast period, which would threaten CTS's market position.[846] CTS was even held to have considerable scope to fend off innovations from competitors.[847] The FCO finally prohibited the merger.

The FCO's decision concerning innovation-driven competitive pressure in the *CTS Eventim/Four Artists* case was confirmed by court.[848] The Higher Regional Court of Düsseldorf explicitly points out:

> "*The innovative strength of competitors may limit the scope for entrepreneurial action of the market leader; conversely, it may also contribute to the creation or strengthening of a dominant position if the company in question is able to exert innovation-driven competitive pressure on its rivals. {…} Rather, what is needed is strong and meaningful evidence to support the assumption that the market position under assessment can be effectively constrained by technical or other, for example product-related, innovations. In the field of merger control, the forecast period of three to five years at most is to be taken into account.*"[849]

845 FCO, Decision of 23.11.2017, B6-35/17, BeckRS 2017, 143034, para 198, *CTS Eventim/Four Artists*.

846 FCO, Decision of 23.11.2017, B6-35/17, BeckRS 2017, 143034, para 202, *CTS Eventim/Four Artists*.

847 FCO, Decision of 23.11.2017, B6-35/17, BeckRS 2017, 143034, para 205, *CTS Eventim/Four Artists*.

848 Higher Regional Court Düsseldorf, Decision of 05.12.2018, VI-Kart 3/18 (V), NZKart 2019, p. 53-59, para 100-102; Higher Regional Court Düsseldorf, Decision of 03.04.2019, VI-Kart 2/18 (V), NZKart 2019, p. 282-286, para 140-142.

849 Higher Regional Court Düsseldorf, Decision of 05.12.2018, VI-Kart 3/18 (V), NZKart 2019, p. 53-59, para 101; Higher Regional Court Düsseldorf, Decision of 03.04.2019, VI-Kart 2/18 (V), NZKart 2019, p. 282-286, para 141; author's translation from: *„Die Innovationskraft der Wettbewerber kann den unternehmerischen Verhaltensspielraum des Marktführers begrenzen; umgekehrt kann es aber auch zur Entstehung oder Verstärkung einer marktbeherrschenden Position beitragen, wenn das betreffende Unternehmen einen innovationsgetriebenen Wettbewerbsdruck auf seine Konkurrenten ausüben kann. {...} Erforderlich sind vielmehr belastbare und aussagekräftige Anhaltspunkte für die Annahme, dass die zur Beurteilung stehende Marktposition mithilfe technischer oder sonstiger, beispielsweise produktbezogener Innovationen wirksam begrenzt werden kann. Im Bereich der Fusionskontrolle ist dabei auf den Prognosezeitraum von regelmäßig drei bis maximal fünf Jahren abzustellen."*

Finally, the FCO assessed innovation-driven competitive pressure in detail in the *Facebook* case. Facebook was alleged of having abused its dominant position in the social network market.[850] The FCO first points towards differences between merger control and abuse of dominance. The FCO finds:

> *"Here – in contrast to merger control above all – it is not about the question to what extent innovation-driven competition of undertakings is undermined, but about to what extent innovations can relativize the market power of an undertaking."*[851]

With respect to the situation in merger control, the FCO explicitly refers to the Dow/DuPont Decision.[852]

Concerning the standard required to include innovation-driven competitive pressure into the assessment, the FCO states:

> *"For a decisive relativization of a market position that can be considered as being strong according to further market power criteria, concrete evidence of a dynamic or disruptive process, which may also originate from markets other than the relevant market, is required in each individual case. An abstract vulnerability that can be expected at some point in time is not sufficient. This applies above all to the control of abuse of dominance, which is based on the current situation."*[853]

In its assessment, the FCO recurred to past market developments and came to the conclusion that there has not been any pressure on Facebook's mar-

850 FCO, Decision of 06.02.2019, B6-22/16, BeckRS 2019, 4895, *Facebook*; see also Higher Regional Court Düsseldorf, Decision of 26.08.2019, VI-Kart 1/19 (V), NZKart 2019, p. 495-501.

851 FCO, Decision of 06.02.2019, B6-22/16, BeckRS 2019, 4895, para 501, *Facebook*; author's translation from : *„Dabei geht es hier – anders als vor allem in der Fusionskontrolle – nicht um die Frage, inwieweit innovationsgetriebener Wettbewerb von Unternehmen gefährdet wird, sondern darum, inwieweit Innovationen die Marktmacht eines Unternehmens relativieren können.“*

852 FCO, Decision of 06.02.2019, B6-22/16, BeckRS 2019, 4895, para 501, fn. 481, *Facebook.*

853 FCO, Decision of 06.02.2019, B6-22/16, BeckRS 2019, 4895, para 503, *Facebook*; author's translation from: *„Für eine entscheidende Relativierung einer nach weiteren Marktmachtkriterien vorliegenden starken Marktposition sind vielmehr in jedem Einzelfall konkrete Anhaltspunkte für einen dynamischen oder disruptiven Prozess erforderlich, der auch aus anderen Märkten als dem relevanten Markt stammen kann. Eine abstrakte, zu irgendeinem Zeitpunkt zu erwartende Angreifbarkeit reicht nicht. Dies gilt vor allem für die Missbrauchsaufsicht, die auf die gegenwärtige Situation abstellt.“*

ket position by means of innovation so far.[854] This finding is not changed by Facebook's own investment in research and development, because market power may not be relativized by the fact that an undertaking has to react at all to innovation efforts of competitors.[855]

> *"On the contrary, the ability to immediately ward off competitive advances from outside is also an expression of market power in the Internet sector, especially with regard to the provisions of Section 18 (3a) ARC. The decisive factor here is the pressure that can actually be exerted on the market position by competitors in the area of innovation. However, this pressure is only weakly pronounced if the innovation activity, which can certainly be observed, cannot ultimately have any effect by means of rapid defense."*[856]

(2) Appraisal

From case law, it comes clear that Section 18 (3a) paragraph 5 ARC requires concrete evidence of a dynamic or disruptive process. In fact, the FCO seems to rely on evidence suggesting market entry of innovative solutions or shifts in consumer behavior already observable. Innovation-driven competitive pressure may limit market power as well as create or strengthen a dominant position.

With respect to abuse of dominance constellations, the FCO emphasizes the difference from merger control. However, the fact that it is about relativization of market power and that the current situation (in contrast to a forecast period) is decisive in assessing abuse of dominance, does not render the criteria in the cited Dow/DuPont Decision inapplicable. In fact, as mentioned above,[857] innovation capacity and innovation incentives are

---

854 FCO, Decision of 06.02.2019, B6-22/16, BeckRS 2019, 4895, para 504, 521, *Facebook.*

855 FCO, Decision of 06.02.2019, B6-22/16, BeckRS 2019, 4895, para 516, 517, *Facebook.*

856 FCO, Decision of 06.02.2019, B6-22/16, BeckRS 2019, 4895, para 517, *Facebook*; author's translation from: "*Vielmehr ist – insbesondere auch im Hinblick auf die Regelung des § 18 Abs. 3a GWB – auch die Fähigkeit, wettbewerbliche Vorstöße von außen sofort abzuwehren, Ausdruck von Marktmacht im Bereich des Internet. Denn entscheidend ist hier der Druck, der tatsächlich von Wettbewerbern im Bereich der Innovationen auf die Marktposition ausgeübt werden kann. Dieser ist jedoch nur schwach ausgeprägt, wenn die durchaus feststellbare Innovationstätigkeit durch schnelle Abwehr letztlich keine Wirkung entfalten kann.*"

857 See *Section II) C) 3).*

factors that can be assessed at the time of the behavior in question and do not occur in the far future.

As the FCO rightly points out, the decisive factor is whether pressure can actually be exerted on the market position by competitors in the area of innovation. However, this pressure does not depend on developments in the future. An important innovator, by its mere existence, may exert a constant pressure on the market position of competitors. It is not about the innovation activity but about the ability to innovate and thus to prevent companies with high market shares from acting independently of competitors and customers. In that sense, *Esser/Höft* are right in finding that it is decisive whether a possible contestability of a market position can already be observed in the current competitive behavior.

On the other hand, *Podszun* makes the valid point that the mere finding that innovation may change market positions does not make operable the criterion of innovation-driven competitive pressure. In fact, what is missing are concrete steps for assessment. It seems unlikely that the forward-looking approach requiring concrete disruptive processes correctly reflects the pressure innovation may exert on existing market players. One should rather focus on the ability and incentive to perform research and development activities as a more suitable measure to assess current market conditions. This approach is indeed foreshadowed in the grounds of the Law, that refer to the competitive pressure resulting from "*innovative power*"[858]. The Higher Regional Court of Düsseldorf seems to take a similar view when focusing on the "*innovative strength*"[859] of competitors instead of concrete innovation activities.

Having said this, there are two considerations that must be taken into account with respect to the German provision. First of all, the wording "competitive pressure" in Section 18 (3a) paragraph 5 ARC suggests a restriction rather than a creation of dominance. Innovation-driven pressure may be exerted by competitors, thus restricting the scope of action of the market dominant undertaking. However, the creation or strengthening of a dominant position not only depends on the competitive pressure an undertaking may exert on other undertakings in the industry (thus preventing effective competition) but also on its ability to act independently. That is not sufficiently reflected in Section 18 (3a) paragraph 5 ARC.

---

858 BT-Drs. 18/10207, page 51; see fn. 835.

859 Higher Regional Court Düsseldorf, Decision of 05.12.2018, VI-Kart 3/18 (V), NZKart 2019, p. 53-59, para 101; Higher Regional Court Düsseldorf, Decision of 03.04.2019, VI-Kart 2/18 (V), NZKart 2019, p. 282-286, para 141; see fn. 849.

In addition, Section 18 (3a) paragraph 5 ARC potentially covers all kinds of possible behavior, not just that related to innovation. With respect to actions of undertakings aiming at existing markets, it is indeed questionable whether the mere innovation capacity of another undertaking is sufficient to limit market dominance. This aspect will be further analyzed in *Section III) B) 3)*.

All in all, those two aspects indeed limit the scope for assessment under German law of the mere ability and incentive to innovate as a factor determining market power. Even though the German provision points into the direction of the concept of innovation competition as developed in *Dow/DuPont*, there are still major differences. For innovation capacity and incentive to play an important role in the assessment of abuse of dominance, there have to be specific criteria for determining such capacity and incentives, there needs to be a theoretic background linking innovation capacity to market power and such assessment may have to be limited to specific forms of potentially abusive behavior.

2) Incorporating innovation competition into Article 102 TFEU

Obviously, the theory of harm in *Dow/DuPont* and its underlying rationale cannot be transferred to abuse of dominance on a one-to-one basis. In abuse of dominance settings, there is no behavior leading to the communitization of R&D assets such as in case of a merger. However, one may reconsider that *Dow/DuPont* focuses on the behavior of important innovators. In that Decision, the Commission for the first time spelled out criteria to assess the importance of an undertaking with respect to innovation incentives. When assuming that a merger of two important innovators may lead to decreased innovation incentives, one may as well argue that internal growth leading to the same result as a merger in terms of innovation capacity may also have an effect on those innovation incentives. In contrast to external growth (that is, a merger or other kind of transaction), internal growth as such may not be prohibited in European Law.[860] However, an internally grown dominant undertaking may be subject to certain behavioral rules.

With that in mind, transferring the logic in *Dow/DuPont* to abuse of dominance settings may result in the following hypothesis:

860 Priority Guidance, para 1. This is different in the U.S. where Section 2 Sherman Act prohibits the attempt to monopolize.

> "It may be considered an abuse of dominance in the meaning of Article 102 TFEU if an important innovator engages in practices decreasing innovation incentives."

Or put differently:

> "With respect to behavior impacting innovation incentives, market dominance shall be assessed on the basis of innovation capacity."

In addition, one may also think of a kind of innovation defense of market dominant undertakings with a low innovation potential. Their behavior potentially impacting innovation incentives may be assessed differently in case there are other important innovators in the industry.

All in all, if innovation is an important parameter of competition[861] as well as one of the European Union goals[862], then authorities should start to focus on the important innovator.

(a) The rationale behind Dow/DuPont and Article 102 TFEU: assessment criteria

Whereas the Dow/DuPont Decision deals with the combination of two important innovators, Article 102 TFEU rather concerns one important innovator, possibly decreasing innovation incentives of third undertakings. Accordingly, the increase of cannibalization concerns or a possible alignment on the product market may not be used as determining factors in an abuse of dominance case. Cannibalization is unlikely to be increased in case of unilateral conduct of an already dominant undertaking. Also, there is no alignment of two players on product markets that could have an effect on innovation incentives. All in all, it is not about the innovation incentives of the dominant undertaking. As mentioned above, the mere internal growth leading to dominance is not prohibited and can therefore not serve as a starting point for enforcement action of a competition authority. In the setting of abuse of dominance, it is rather about the innovation incentive and ability of third undertakings. Those incentives should be protected.

---

861 See recently European Commission, Decision of 18.07.2018, C(2018) 4761 final, OJ C 402, 28.11.2019, p. 19-22, Case AT.40099, p. 196 et seq, 222 et seq, 257 et seq, 299 et seq, *Google Android*; see also *Section II) A) 3)*.

862 See *Section II) A) 2)*.

Innovation ability and incentives of undertakings may most likely be influenced by behavior of an important innovator. At this point, *Dow/DuPont* comes into play as the decision offers specific criteria for defining an important innovator. These criteria have been explained in *Section II) C) 1)*. First of all, markets must be contestable on the basis of innovation. In the case of behavior restricting third parties' innovation incentives there may a presumption on such contestability on the basis of innovation. Otherwise, the dominant undertaking would likely not try to prevent innovation from competitors. In addition, an important innovator must generally be able to market innovative products. This includes the assets to perform the entire research and development process from basic research until marketing, that is personnel, knowledge, facilities and so on. The general ability to innovate may be reflected in the past development of high-quality patents and commercially successful innovative products. The patent and product assessment carried out in *Dow/DuPont*[863] may apply accordingly.

When assessing the market power of an undertaking, the Commission usually takes into account expansion or market entry.[864] In that regard, the assessment in *Dow/DuPont* covering barriers to entry with respect to innovation may be transferred.[865] An increase in appropriability as well as other efficiencies may be used in the context of justification of a certain potentially abusive behavior.

(b) Oligopolistic market structure

The Commission sets up the requirement of an oligopolistic market structure in *Dow/DuPont*.[866] In fact, in case of a merger it is doubtful if the economic foundation for *Dow/DuPont* may claim validity beyond oligopoly cases.[867] One may wonder whether there is also the need for an oligopolistic market structure when addressing the abusive behavior of important innovators.

However, as mentioned above, the Commission's theory of harm and its underlying rationale in *Dow/DuPont* cannot be transferred to abuse

---

863 See Dow/DuPont Decision, para 2428 et seq.
864 Priority Guidance, para 16, 17.
865 See *Section II) B) 3)*.
866 Dow/DuPont Decision, para 2007, 2019; see *Section II) C) 1)*.
867 Dow/DuPont Decision, para 3244; *Section II) C) 6)*; see also *Federico/Langus/Valletti*, Horizontal Mergers and Product Innovation, p. 1.

of dominance cases on a one-by-one basis. In this regard, it is important to distinguish addressee, action and effect of the innovation competition assessment in merger control from those of abuse of dominance cases.

The addressee of an innovation competition assessment is the important innovator. This holds true for merger cases as well as for abuse of dominance. Whereas both merging parties may be considered important innovators, in the scope of Article 102 TFEU it is only important whether the potentially abusing undertaking is an important innovator.

The relevant action in merger settings is the merger itself. In abuse of dominance cases, there are specific positive actions resulting in an abuse that are at the center of the assessment.

Finally, the effect in merger cases is a decrease of innovation incentives in the industry, namely by reducing rivalry between the merging parties. Potentially abusive practices of important innovators, in contrast, impact innovation incentives of third parties that are competitors and trading partners. In the latter case, it is thus not a general change in the market structure that leads to a decrease in innovation incentives but particular practices of an important innovator directly impacting third parties.

In summary, a merger between two important innovators in an oligopoly may decrease innovation incentives vis-à-vis competitors. Abusive conduct of an important innovator may lead to a decrease in innovation ability and incentive vis-à-vis third parties (competitors and trading partners). In the latter case, the effect is not dependent on an oligopolistic market structure. Rather, the important innovator may directly influence innovation incentives of market participants independent of the market structure. The reduction of innovation incentives is not due to a decrease of competitive pressure in the industry but results from targeted action.

(c) SIEC test versus dominant position

The assessment standard in merger control is the significant impediment to effective competition (the so-called "SIEC test"). The creation or strengthening of a dominant position is an example of one such significant impediment. Article 2 (3) EC Merger Regulation states:

> "*A concentration which would significantly impede effective competition, in the common market or in a substantial part of it, in particular as a result of the creation or strengthening of a dominant position, shall be declared incompatible with the common market.*"

In contrast, the provision on abuse of dominance only relates to a dominant position and not to any further impediment of competition. Article 102 TFEU reads:

> *"Any abuse by one or more undertakings of a dominant position within the internal market or a substantial part of it shall be prohibited as incompatible with the internal market in so far as it may affect trade between Member States. {…}."*

In its innovation competition assessment in *Dow/DuPont*, the Commission explicitly relies on the SIEC test[868] and not on the creation of a dominant position. The SIEC test has been newly introduced in merger assessment in 2004 in order to cover unilateral effects in oligopolistic markets.[869] However, it has been argued that the new standard also facilitates the assessment of effects of mergers on innovation as it does not necessarily require the definition of relevant markets.[870]

This is different in the scope of Article 102 TFEU. Article 102 TFEU is dependent on the assessment of existing markets and the dominant position of an undertaking on that market. But the criteria for assessment of an important innovator may nevertheless be used in the context of abuse of dominance. First of all, as mentioned above,[871] there is no need for an oligopoly in those settings. The behavior of the important innovator is directed towards a specific trading partner regardless of the market structure. Accordingly, the SIEC test, necessary for assessing effects in case there is no market dominance but there are nevertheless anticompetitive effects,[872] is not required in such cases.

In contrast, the concept of an important innovator may well be incorporated into the assessment of market dominance. The relevant market is defined as usual.[873] What changes is the assessment of the dominant position. With respect to certain anticompetitive practices,[874] it is not the market share on existing markets that is decisive but rather the undertak-

---

868 See for example Dow/DuPont Decision, para 1988, 2006, 2007.

869 Recital 25 EC Merger Regulation; *Körber* in Immenga/Mestmäcker, Wettbewerbsrecht Fusionskontrolle, Art. 2 FKVO para 183; *Drexl*, Anti-Competitive Stumbling Stones, p. 20.

870 *Drexl*, Anti-Competitive Stumbling Stones, p. 20.

871 *Section III) B) 2) (b)*.

872 *Körber* in Immenga/Mestmäcker, Wettbewerbsrecht Fusionskontrolle, Art. 2 FKVO para 183.

873 See the relevant criteria in the Market Definition Notice.

874 See *Section III) B) 3)*.

ing's importance as innovator. For example in refusal to deal situations with respect to licenses or other input relevant for innovation activities, it may not be relevant in terms of competition policy whether the refusing undertaking has a high market share. Even when assuming that the technology it possesses is a very important technology, it may nevertheless not have high shares on the technology market yet because it has recently been introduced or because the technology is rather important for follow-on innovations and not yet in the existing form. In that case, the important innovator may be required to license or supply its technology or other input. This example will be further elaborated in *Section III) B) 3) (b) (1)*.

(d) Dynamic aspects in Article 102 TFEU

The definition of the relevant market and the market power of an undertaking may differ in case of a merger and in case of the assessment of abuse of dominance. Merger control and Article 102 TFEU pursue different objectives. Whereas Article 102 TFEU is oriented towards the past and allows for a retroactive control of the behavior of market participants, merger control focuses on the analysis of the future market structure.[875] In contrast to the assessment of abuse of dominance, that may only take into account the actual situation and has to be based on objectively ascertainable facts, market definition in merger control requires a prediction of future market conditions.[876] The latter includes considerations on the dynamics of the market and the expected technical development.[877]

While in case of a merger what matters is how the market will look like in the near future (and how it would have looked like without the merger),[878] Article 102 TFEU requires market dominance at the time of the

875 CFI , Judgment of 13.07.2006, Case T-464/04, ECLI:EU:T:2006:216, para 251 et seq, *Impala*; *Körber* in Immenga/Mestmäcker, Wettbewerbsrecht Fusionskontrolle, Einleitung zur FKVO para 11 and Art. 2 FKVO para 20, 21; *Bergmann/Fiedler* in Loewenheim/Meessen/Riesenkampff/Kersting/Meyer-Lindemann, Kartellrecht, Art. 102 AEUV para 37.

876 *Bergmann/Fiedler* in Loewenheim/Meessen/Riesenkampff/Kersting/Meyer-Lindemann, Kartellrecht, Art. 102 AEUV para 37; *Jung* in Grabitz/Hilf/Nettesheim, Das Recht der Europäischen Union, Art. 102 AEUV para 34.

877 *Bergmann/Fiedler* in Loewenheim/Meessen/Riesenkampff/Kersting/Meyer-Lindemann, Kartellrecht, Art. 102 AEUV para 37; *Körber* in Immenga/Mestmäcker, Wettbewerbsrecht Fusionskontrolle, Art. 2 FKVO para 21.

878 *Körber* in Immenga/Mestmäcker, Wettbewerbsrecht Fusionskontrolle, Art. 2 FKVO para 21.

potentially abusive behavior. Unlike the U.S. provision Section 2 Sherman Act, which contains a general prohibition of monopolization that includes the attempt to monopolize,[879] the acquisition of a dominant position does not as such fall within the scope of Article 102 TFEU. [880]

Effects on innovation are considered to be dynamic effects taking place in the future.[881] In this regard, it may be difficult to incorporate them into the static assessment of Article 102 TFEU. However, as mentioned in *Section II) C) 3)*, the assessment in *Dow/DuPont* covers static short-term effects rather than long-term dynamic effects. It is about the decrease of innovation incentives at the time of the implementation of the transaction and not about the innovative product or service developed in the future.

This is even more the case with respect to the assessment of the important innovator. The innovation capacity of an undertaking is a static factor that can be analyzed at the time of the behavior in question. What's more, in the case of abuse of dominance, starting point for competition policy intervention is not the final innovation but a third undertaking's ability and incentive to innovate. This ability and incentive may depend on the current behavior of the important innovator at hand. What matters are not developments in the future but static parameters for assessing market dominance. Accordingly, the criteria set up in *Dow/DuPont* may be transferred to the static assessment of abuse of dominance.

3) Kinds of abusive behavior that interrelate with innovation capacity

After defining the relevant market and determining whether an undertaking has a dominant position on that market, the third step in the assessment under Article 102 TFEU is the analysis of whether there is an abusive behavior. It must be acknowledged that innovation capacity as a means of determining market dominance is not fit for every kind of abusive behavior. In fact, behavior concerning price-setting on an existing market is unlikely to have any negative impact on competition if performed by an undertaking with low market shares but high innovation capacity.[882]

879 *Fuchs* in Immenga/Mestmäcker, Wettbewerbsrecht EU, Art. 102 AEUV para 40.

880 *Dreher* finds that in case of a decision bringing a continuing abusive conduct to an end, market dominance may also have to be examined from a forward-looking perspective, *Dreher*, ZWeR 2009, 149, 170.

881 See *Section II) C) 3)*.

882 An exception may be excessive prices in refusal to deal situations, see *Section III) B) 3) (b) (3)*.

In that setting, competitors with high market shares are able to constrain the pricing behavior of the important innovator. This may be different with respect to behavior directly influencing innovation incentives of third undertakings.[883]

In general, the specific kind of abusive behavior is an important factor in the assessment of the existence of a dominant position.[884] The special responsibility of dominant undertakings correlates with a view to the legitimate interests of those who are affected by the market strategy of a company in a way that would not be possible if competition were sufficiently effective.[885] Conversely, when assuming that innovation capacity may lead to market dominance, this has implications for the kind of behavior considered to be abusive.

(a) Definition of abusive behavior

The European Court of Justice defines an abuse in the scope of Article 102 TFEU as follows:

> "*The concept of abuse is an objective concept relating to the behaviour of an undertaking in a dominant position which is such as to influence the structure of a market where, as a result of the very presence of the undertaking in question, the degree of competition is weakened and which, through recourse to methods different from those which condition normal competition in products or services on the basis of the transactions of commercial operators, has the effect of hindering the maintenance of the degree of competition still existing in the market or the growth of that competition.*"[886]

---

883 *Federico/Scott Morton/Shapiro* find that there may be antitrust violations „*in cases where the challenged conduct disrupts the competitive process by impeding the incentive or ability of rivals to innovate*", *Federico/Scott Morton/Shapiro*, Antitrust and Innovation, p. 25; however, the theory of harm in *Dow/DuPont* rather points to a general reduction of incentives to innovate not just that of actual or potential rivals.

884 *Mestmäcker/Schweitzer*, Europäisches Wettbewerbsrecht, § 17 para 38; see also *Fuchs* in Immenga/Mestmäcker, Wettbewerbsrecht EU, Art. 102 AEUV para 78, 80; *Bishop/Walker*, The Economics of EC Competition Law, para 3-053.

885 Cf. *Mestmäcker/Schweitzer*, Europäisches Wettbewerbsrecht, § 17 para 38.

886 ECJ, Judgment of 13.02.1979, Case 85/76, ECLI:EU:C:1979:36, para 91, *Hoffmann-La Roche*; established case law based on ECJ , Judgment of 21.02.1973, Case 6/72, ECLI:EU:C:1973:22, Summary 12 and para 26, *Continental Can*; see also ECJ, Judgment of 03.07.1991, Case C-62/86,

The European Court of Justice focuses on the maintenance of the degree of competition still existing on the market. A dominant undertaking has a "*special responsibility not to allow its conduct to impair genuine undistorted competition on the common market.*"[887]

As mentioned in *Section II) A) 3) (a)*, the Commission not only has a duty to preserve innovation as a stand-alone objective of the Treaties, but innovation itself is a means of competition. The theory of "creative destruction" by *Schumpeter* implies that the constant process of taking market share from competitors by means of introducing innovative products or services is a basic driver of competitive markets.

Accordingly, the preservation of innovation incentives that maintain the degree of genuine and undistorted competition on the market is generally in line with the European Court of Justice's definition of the objectives of the provision of abuse of dominance.

(b) Kinds of abusive behavior impacting innovation incentives

Not all kinds of behavior generally considered to be abusive are related to the innovation capacity of an undertaking. In fact, if an important innovator engages in practices impacting prices (such as predatory or excessive pricing), this may have an effect on the resources of competitors or trading partners that can be invested in R&D activities. However, said behavior does not depend on the position of an undertaking as innovator. An undertaking with high market shares is much more likely to impact competition on the relevant market through its pricing behavior than a firm with small market shares and high R&D potential. In fact, an important innovator is unlikely to even be able to excessively raise its prices vis-à-vis trading partners or to set prices below cost level without immediately being driven out of the market.

This is different with respect to behavior directly pointing at the ability and incentives to innovate of competitors and trading partners. The latter are most likely to depend on input of an undertaking being strong in

---

ECLI:EU:C:1991:286, para 69, *AKZO*; ECJ, Judgment of 19.04.2012, Case C-549/10 P, ECLI:EU:C:2012:221, para 17, *Tomra*; ECJ, Judgment of 16.07.2015, Case C-170/13, ECLI:EU:C:2015:477, para 45, *Huawei Technologies*.

887 ECJ, Judgment of 09.11.1983, Case 322/81, ECLI:EU:C:1983:313, para 57, *Michelin*; ECJ, Judgment of 27.03.2012, Case C-209/10, ECLI:EU:C:2012:172, para 23, *Post Danmark I*; ECJ, Judgment of 06.09.2017, Case C-413/14 P, ECLI:EU:C:2017:632, para 135, *Intel*; see also Priority Guidance, para 9.

R&D in order to further develop their own products and services. Different kinds of potentially abusive behavior are worth considering in this context.

(1) Refusal to supply

In general, even a dominant undertaking is free to choose its trading partners.[888] This follows from the principles of freedom of contract and property.[889] However, under specific circumstances, a refusal to supply may constitute an abuse of a dominant position under Article 102 TFEU. In those settings, an undertaking may be obliged to enter into a contractual relationship. With respect to the licensing of intellectual property rights, the European Court of Justice has set up assessment criteria on when to grant a compulsory license in its *IMS Health* decision:

> *"It is clear {...} that, in order for the refusal by an undertaking which owns a copyright to give access to a product or service indispensable for carrying on a particular business to be treated as abusive, it is sufficient that three cumulative conditions be satisfied, namely, that that refusal is preventing the emergence of a new product for which there is a potential consumer demand, that it is unjustified and such as to exclude any competition on a secondary market."*[890]

In the subsequent *Microsoft* decision, the General Court somehow lowered the standard and found that instead of a new product, the mere limitation of technological development was sufficient for an abuse of dominance.[891]

The Commission had found that Microsoft abused its dominant position by refusing to supply its competitor Sun with interoperability information for the purpose of developing and distributing work group server

---

888 Priority Guidance, para 74.

889 See Opinion of Advocate General Jacobs delivered on 28.05.1998, Case C-7/97, ECLI:EU:C:1998:264, para 56, *Bronner*.

890 ECJ, Judgment of 29.04.2004, Case C-418/01, ECLI:EU:C:2004:257, para 38, *IMS Health*; see also para 52 of that decision.

891 CFI, Judgment of 17.09.2007, Case T-201/04, ECLI:EU:T:2007:289, para 647, 665, *Microsoft*; see for an assessment of the *Microsoft* decision in terms of extension of a dominant position by preventing "follow-on" innovation: *Federico/Scott Morton/Shapiro*, Antitrust and Innovation, p. 29-32.

operating system products.[892] According to the Commission, such information would be necessary for competitors to be able to provide new and enhanced products.[893] Microsoft was held to have a dominant position in the PC operating system market as well as in the work group server operating system market.[894]

With respect to the impact of Microsoft's obligation to supply on innovation, the Commission concluded:

> "*However, a detailed examination of the scope of the disclosure at stake leads to the conclusion that, on balance, the possible negative impact of an order to supply on Microsoft's incentives to innovate is outweighed by its positive impact on the level of innovation of the whole industry (including Microsoft).*"[895]

Apparently in *Microsoft*, as in *Dow/DuPont*, the Commission focused on innovation at industry level.[896] However, what remains unclear is the interrelation between Microsoft's dominant position on the operating system market and the impact of its behavior on innovation incentives. Even though there is no need for a strict causality between dominance and abusive behavior,[897] it is nonetheless necessary that there is a normative link between a dominant position and the anti-competitive effects caused by the conduct in question.[898] The mere fact that an undertaking has high market shares does, as such, not say anything about its ability to decrease innovation incentives. It may well be that Microsoft was, at the time

892 European Commission, Decision of 24.05.2004, C(2004) 900 final, OJ L 32, 06.02.2007, p. 23-28, Case COMP/C-3/37.792, (summary decision), para 2, *Microsoft*.

893 European Commission, Decision of 24.05.2004, C(2004) 900 final, OJ L 32, 06.02.2007, p. 23-28, Case COMP/C-3/37.792, (summary decision), para 18, *Microsoft*.

894 European Commission, Decision of 24.05.2004, C(2004) 900 final, OJ L 32, 06.02.2007, p. 23-28, Case COMP/C-3/37.792, (summary decision), para 15, 17, *Microsoft*.

895 European Commission, Decision of 24.03.2004, C(2004) 900 final, OJ L 32, 06.02.2007, p. 23-28, Case COMP/C-3/37.792, para 783, *Microsoft*.

896 This should not be confused with the fact that in *Dow/DuPont*, the Commission tried to preserve the level of rivalry in the industry whereas in Microsoft, the focus was on the individual behavior of *Microsoft* vis-à-vis other players in the industry; see to this point *Section III) B) 2) (b)*.

897 ECJ , Judgment of 21.02.1973, Case 6/72, ECLI:EU:C:1973:22, para 27, *Continental Can*; *Fuchs* in Immenga/Mestmäcker, Wettbewerbsrecht EU, Art. 102 AEUV para 136.

898 *Fuchs* in Immenga/Mestmäcker, Wettbewerbsrecht EU, Art. 102 AEUV para 136.

of the Commission decision, also the most important innovator in the industry.[899] But the *Microsoft* decision lacks any assessment of innovation capacity of Microsoft and its competitors.

Innovation capacity may not only be relevant in cases of an actual refusal to supply but also in case of "constructive refusal"[900]. Generally, delaying or otherwise degrading the supply of a product or imposing unreasonable conditions in return for the supply may amount to such "constructive refusal".[901] In that specific setting, excessive pricing may also play a role. There is no difference between actual and constructive refusal with respect to its impact on innovation incentives. In either case, an important innovator may cause harm by withdrawing its innovative solution that is a basis for follow-on research and development.

(2) Misuse of regulatory framework

Recently, there have been a number of cases on the misuse of regulatory procedures by market dominant undertakings.[902] AstraZeneca was held to have abused its dominant position by misrepresenting certain dates vis-à-vis patent offices in order to extend the period of patent protection for one of its medicines.[903] The General Court found that such conduct may also reduce incentives for other pharmaceutical companies to engage in innovation activities:

> *"Nor can the applicants object that a finding of an abuse of a dominant position in cases where misleading representations have been made to patent offices for the purposes of obtaining intellectual property rights to which an*

---

899 In fact, *Federico/Scott Morton/Shapiro* find that the *„largest firms are often the most successful innovators precisely because innovation has allowed them to acquire a strong position in the market"*, *Federico/Scott Morton/Shapiro*, Antitrust and Innovation, p. 2.

900 Priority Guidance, para 79.

901 Priority Guidance, para 79.

902 For an overview see European Commission, Report from the Commission to the Council and the European Parliament, Competition Enforcement in the Pharmaceutical Sector (2009-2017), European competition authorities working together for affordable and innovative medicines, p. 21-22.

903 European Commission, Decision of 15.06.2005, K(2005) 1757 final, OJ L 332, 30.11.2006, p. 24-25, Case COMP/A.37.507/F3, *AstraZeneca*; GC, Judgment of 01.07.2010, Case T-321/05, ECLI:EU:T:2010:266, *AstraZeneca*; ECJ, Judgment of 06.12.2012, Case C-457/10 P, ECLI:EU:C:2012:770, *AstraZeneca*.

> *undertaking is not entitled, or to which it is entitled for a shorter period, would result in a 'freeze' on patent applications and would run counter to the public interest in encouraging innovation. It is quite clear that, where established, such behaviour is indeed contrary to the public interest, as weighed up and applied by the legislator. As the Commission observes, such misuse of the patent system potentially reduces the incentive to engage in innovation, since it enables the company in a dominant position to maintain its exclusivity beyond the period envisaged by the legislator."*[904]

As with the refusal to supply situations mentioned above, also in the case of abusive extension of patent protection what matters is whether the acting undertaking is an important innovator. If a firm with a high innovation capacity (reflected in important patents and successful introduction of innovative products in the past) engages in behavior impacting innovation incentives of other companies, this will have a severe impact on innovation in the industry. It is, in addition, not mandatory that a patent holder always have a market dominant position with respect to its patent.[905] There may be several patented products that target the same market. Whereas the patent focuses on the mode of action, market definition is based on substitutability from the perspective of the consumer.[906]

(3) Discrimination

Innovation capacity may also be an important parameter in assessing anticompetitive discrimination. Article 102 (2) lit c) TFEU states that an abuse of a dominant position may also consist in "*applying dissimilar conditions to equivalent transactions with other trading parties, thereby placing them at a competitive disadvantage*".

---

904 GC, Judgment of 01.07.2010, Case T-321/05, ECLI:EU:T:2010:266, para 367, *AstraZeneca*.

905 *Drexl* finds: „*Since competition in innovation occurs outside of markets, market dominance should not be a requirement for defensive patenting to harm this form of dynamic competition.*", *Drexl*, Anti-Competitive Stumbling Stones, p. 37. However, another way of solving the problem would be to use innovation capacity as a criterion to measure market dominance.

906 Market Definition Notice, para 7.

With respect to the criterion of a "competitive disadvantage", the European Court of Justice has held:

> *"In view of the foregoing, the answer to the questions referred is that the concept of 'competitive disadvantage', for the purposes of subparagraph (c) of the second paragraph of Article 102 TFEU, must be interpreted to the effect that, where a dominant undertaking applies discriminatory prices to trade partners on the downstream market, it covers a situation in which that behaviour is capable of distorting competition between those trade partners. A finding of such a 'competitive disadvantage' does not require proof of actual quantifiable deterioration in the competitive situation, but must be based on an analysis of all the relevant circumstances of the case leading to the conclusion that that behaviour has an effect on the costs, profits or any other relevant interest of one or more of those partners, so that that conduct is such as to affect that situation."*[907]

An effect on the ability and incentive of trading partners to innovate may also constitute such an effect on "any other relevant interest". As clarified by the European Court of Justice's judgment, the prohibition of discrimination mainly prevents the distortion of competition between downstream trading partners.[908] Such competition may, however, also consist in marketing innovative products. If innovation is a parameter of competition, then it should also play a role in discrimination settings.

This finding can be associated with refusal to supply situations:[909] It may decrease innovation incentives if undertakings are unable to have access to an innovative solution necessary for further research. But it may just as well hinder innovation (and in addition also innovation competition) if only few out of several undertakings are supplied with the innovative solution. In the latter setting, there is not only an impact on the ability to innovate of some of the trading partners, but the discrimination may also

---

907 ECJ, Judgment of 19.04.2018, Case C-525/16, ECLI:EU:C:2018:270, para 37, *MEO*.

908 ECJ, Judgment of 15.03.2007, Case C-95/04 P, ECLI:EU:C:2007:166, para 144, *British Airways*; CFI, Judgment of 09.11.2009, Case T-301/04, ECLI:EU:T:2009:317, para 192, *Clearstream*; see also *Fuchs* in Immenga/Mestmäcker, Wettbewerbsrecht EU, Art. 102 AEUV para 387; *Huttenlauch* in Loewenheim/Meessen/Riesenkampff/Kersting/Meyer-Lindemann, Kartellrecht, Art. 102 AEUV para 203; *Mestmäcker/Schweitzer*, Europäisches Wettbewerbsrecht, § 18 para 21.

909 See *Section III) B) 3) (b) (1)*.

lead to less rivalry, since there are fewer companies to perform research and development.

(4) Treatment of those and other kinds of conduct

There may be other kinds of conduct by important innovators that can be considered abusive. It is crucial that the important innovator use its power over innovative solutions to decrease innovation activities of other undertakings. This may either take the form of explicit or implicit refusal of access or other strategies to prevent innovation activities within the innovator's own area of research and development (or even beyond).

Those cases may often involve innovations protected by IP rights, but they are not limited to that. There may well be innovative solutions that do not fall within the scope of IP protection that are nonetheless necessary for further ability, and thus incentive, to innovate.

However, it is essential in cases involving innovations developed by important innovators that there is always a balancing exercise with respect to the innovator's own innovation incentives. The Commission rightly points out in its Priority Guidance that an obligation to supply may undermine the dominant undertakings' incentives to innovate.[910] An undertaking that is aware of such duty to supply may not invest or invest less in research and development activities.[911]

The Commission analyses the impact on innovation incentives of the dominant undertaking as efficiencies:

> *"The Commission will consider claims by the dominant undertaking that a refusal to supply is necessary to allow the dominant undertaking to realise an adequate return on the investments required to develop its input business, thus generating incentives to continue to invest in the future, taking the risk of failed projects into account. The Commission will also consider claims by the dominant undertaking that its own innovation will be negatively affected by the obligation to supply, or by the structural changes in the market conditions that imposing such an obligation will bring about, including the development of follow-on innovation by competitors.*
> *However, when considering such claims, the Commission will ensure that the conditions set out in Section III D are fulfilled. In particular, it falls*

910 Priority Guidance, para 75.
911 Priority Guidance, para 75.

on the dominant undertaking to demonstrate any negative impact which an obligation to supply is likely to have on its own level of innovation. If a dominant undertaking has previously supplied the input in question, this can be relevant for the assessment of any claim that the refusal to supply is justified on efficiency grounds."[912]

In Section III D of the Priority Guidance, the Commission establishes general criteria for the assessment of efficiencies in an abuse of dominance setting. Efficiencies must be sufficient to guarantee that no net harm to consumers arises.[913] The Commission sets up four cumulative conditions:[914]

1. Efficiencies have been or are likely to be realized as a result of the conduct (this includes technical improvements or reduction in cost);
2. The conduct is indispensable to realize the efficiencies;
3. The efficiencies outweigh the negative effects of the conduct in question, namely on competition and consumer welfare;
4. The conduct does not eliminate effective competition.

With respect to the last condition, the Commission finds:

"*Rivalry between undertakings is an essential driver of economic efficiency, including dynamic efficiencies in the form of innovation. In its absence the dominant undertaking will lack adequate incentives to continue to create and pass on efficiency gains.*"[915]

It is noteworthy that the criteria set up by the Commission with respect to its assessment under Article 102 TFEU slightly differ from those used in merger analysis.[916] Efficiencies in merger control have to benefit consumers, be merger-specific and verifiable.[917] The main difference is that efficiencies in the assessment of abuse of dominance do not necessarily have to directly benefit consumers. They rather have to outweigh the negative effects. But those can also arise at the level of innovation itself and do

912 Priority Guidance, para 89-90.
913 Priority Guidance, para 30.
914 Priority Guidance, para 30; those conditions are based on ECJ, Judgment of 15.03.2007, C-95/04 P, ECLI:EU:C:2007:166, para 86, *British Airways*; ECJ, Judgment of 27.03.2012, Case C-209/10, ECLI:EU:C:2012:172, para 42, *Post Danmark I*; see recently ECJ, Judgment of 06.09.2017, Case C-413/14 P, ECLI:EU:C:2017:632, para 140, *Intel*.
915 Priority Guidance, para 30.
916 For a detailed discussion on efficiencies in merger analysis see *Section II) H) 5)*.
917 Horizontal Merger Guidelines, para 78.

not necessarily have to directly impact consumers. Indeed, the European Court of Justice held that the Commission's assessment has to determine

> "*whether the exclusionary effect arising from such a system, which is disadvantageous for competition, may be counterbalanced, or outweighed, by advantages in terms of efficiency which also benefit the consumer.*"[918]

However, this does not mean that there must be a direct measurable effect on consumer welfare. The European Court of Justice also found that

> "*it is for the dominant undertaking to show that the efficiency gains likely to result from the conduct under consideration counteract any likely negative effects on competition and consumer welfare in the affected markets*".[919]

The latter rather refers to the specific negative effect arising from the dominant undertakings' conduct. If this conduct directly affects consumers, then the efficiencies must outweigh that consumer harm. However, if the negative effects mainly occur at a level beyond existing markets,[920] as is the case with respect to innovation incentives, then it must be sufficient if the efficiencies also indirectly influence consumer harm.

The Commission also refrains from using its notion of verifiability in merger control, relating to clearly identifiable and quantifiable effects not too far in the future,[921] in abuse of dominance cases.

As a result, the efficiency approach in the Priority Guidance is far more suitable for assessing innovation effects than the one used in the Horizontal Merger Guidelines. Efficiencies may for example lie in the prevention of free riding of competitors on the investments made by the dominant undertaking in research and development instead of investing themselves.[922] Conduct of the dominant undertaking that limits free riding may well fulfill the four cumulative conditions set up in the Priority Guidance.

---

918 ECJ, Judgment of 15.03.2007, C-95/04 P, ECLI:EU:C:2007:166, para 86, *British Airways*; ECJ, Judgment of 27.03.2012, Case C-209/10, ECLI:EU:C:2012:172, para 41, *Post Danmark I*; see recently ECJ, Judgment of 06.09.2017, Case C-413/14 P, ECLI:EU:C:2017:632, para 140, *Intel*.

919 ECJ, Judgment of 27.03.2012, Case C-209/10, ECLI:EU:C:2012:172, para 42, *Post Danmark I*.

920 Even though indirectly influencing the market position of an undertaking; this is comparable to financial strength or vertical integration.

921 Horizontal Merger Guidelines, para 86.

922 Cf. Priority Guidance, para 75.

In addition, rules on the burden of proof in abuse of dominance cases are different from those in merger control. Whereas the Horizontal Merger Guidelines state:

> *"It is, therefore, incumbent upon the notifying parties to provide in due time all the relevant information necessary to demonstrate that the claimed efficiencies are merger-specific and likely to be realised. Similarly, it is for the notifying parties to show to what extent the efficiencies are likely to counteract any adverse effects on competition that might otherwise result from the merger, and therefore benefit consumers."*[923]

In contrast, the Priority Guidance on Article 102 TFEU reads:

> *"It is incumbent upon the dominant undertaking to provide all the evidence necessary to demonstrate that the conduct concerned is objectively justified. It then falls to the Commission to make the ultimate assessment of whether the conduct concerned is not objectively necessary and, based on a weighing-up of any apparent anti-competitive effects against any advanced and substantiated efficiencies, is likely to result in consumer harm."*[924]

As a result, in abuse of dominance cases, it is on the Commission to balance possible positive and negative effects on innovation incentives. This is also the only possible way, given that in this setting the innovation incentives of third parties must be taken into account. The necessary data on innovation plans and activities of those third parties are impossible to obtain for a market dominant undertaking.[925]

In addition, as mentioned in the context of the Dow/DuPont Decision,[926] innovation efficiencies are different from price efficiencies. Contrary to the Commission's statement in its Priority Guidance that rivalry sets incentives to create and pass on efficiency gains, the passing on of innovation efficiencies does not depend on competitive pressure.[927] Before engaging in research and development activities, an undertaking will deal with the overall profitability of such activities. In the event that the undertaking anticipates, for example, a high degree of free riding of competitors and trading partners on its innovation due to a likely obligation to supply,

923 Horizontal Merger Guidelines, para 87.

924 Priority Guidance, para 31.

925 See *Section III) B) 4) (a)*.

926 See *Section II) H) 5)*.

927 This has to be distinguished from the finding that rivalry drives innovation; while the latter is true with respect to the overall incentive to innovate it does not say anything about passing on of innovation efficiencies.

it will refrain from performing research. But this is independent of rivalry in the industry.

4) Powers of the Commission with respect to important innovators

Where the Commission finds an abuse of dominance, it has several options for issuing a response.[928] They are laid down in Regulation 1/2003[929]. As a first pillar, the Commission has the power to affect the behavior of undertakings. According to Article 7 (1) of Regulation 1/2003, the Commission may find that there is an infringement of Article 102 TFEU. In case there is a legitimate interest, the Commission may also find that there has been an infringement committed in the past. The authority may require the undertakings to bring the infringement to an end and for this purpose impose remedies. The Commission may further impose interim measures according to Article 8 of Regulation 1/2003 and accept commitments by the undertakings concerned according to Article 9 of Regulation 1/2003.

As a second pillar, the Commission may impose penalties, namely fines according to Article 23 of Regulation 1/2003 and periodic penalty payments according to Article 24 of Regulation 1/2003. In particular, Article 23 (2) lit a) of Regulation 1/2003 enables the Commission to impose fines on undertakings if they intentionally or negligently infringe Article 101 or 102 TFEU.

Abusive behavior of an important innovator leading to a decrease in innovation incentives of other undertakings is not easy to assess. There are several uncertainties in the assessment[930] and, most importantly, the analysis requires numerous and mostly confidential data. In *Dow/DuPont*, the Commission analyzed innovation capabilities of the players in the industry, patents and active ingredients shares as well as innovation and con-

---

928 As set out in *Section III) A) 3)*, the innovation competition approach is not applicable in Article 101 TFEU settings. If one would assume that the rationale in *Dow/DuPont* was applicable in restriction by effect cases, the reasoning on the following pages would apply accordingly. The innovation competition approach in *Dow/DuPont* is independent of the object of any agreement or concerted practice, for example on restricting own or third party innovation activities. It therefore cannot be used in restriction by object cases, see *Section III) A) 1)*.

929 Fn. 688.

930 See *Section II) H) 7)*.

centration tendencies in the entire industry.[931] Extensive market surveys were conducted. The constraint of third parties on Dow's and DuPont's innovation activities required a "*deep dive into the competitor's pipelines and related innovation capabilities.*"[932]

With this in mind, one may wonder if the Commission may use all of its powers in cases involving important innovators and their impact on innovation incentives. This is particularly doubtful with respect to the imposition of fines according to Article 23 (2) lit a) of Regulation 1/2003.

(a) Fines and procedural principles

Fines in EU competition law are recognized as "*having a character similar to criminal law*"[933]. This is not undisputed as Article 23 (5) of Regulation 1/2003 explicitly mentions that fining decisions shall not be of a criminal law nature. It is general opinion that the wording relates to the fact that the Member States did not transfer criminal law competences to the Union in the Treaties and that Article 23 (5) of Regulation 1/2003 has therefore rather a clarifying function.[934]

In any case, the legal classification of fines under the ECHR is important for the distinction between administrative and criminal sanctions.[935] Even though the European Union has not yet acceded to the ECHR, the fundamental rights as guaranteed therein and the fundamental freedoms resulting from the constitutional traditions of the Member States (that have all acceded to the ECHR) constitute general principles of the European

---

931 Cf. *Section II) B) 3)*.

932 *Esteva Mosso*, Innovation in EU Merger Control, p. 11.

933 Opinion of Advocate General Kokott, delivered on 28.02.2013, Case C-681/11, ECLI:EU:C:2013:126, para 40, *Schenker*; the ECJ consistently applies principles of criminal law in competition law, for example the presumption of innocence, ECJ, Judgment of 08.07.1999, Case C-199/92 P, ECLI:EU:C:1999:358, para 149, 140, *Hüls*, or the *ne bis in idem* principle, ECJ, Judgment of 14.02.2012, Case C-17/10, ECLI:EU:C:2012:72, para 94, *Toshiba Corporation*; *Schwarze*, EuR 2009, 171, 173, 180.

934 Cf. *Nowak* in Loewenheim/Meessen/Riesenkampff/Kerstin/Meyer-Lindemann, Kartellrecht, Art. 23 Kartellverfahrensordnung para 50; *Feddersen* in Grabitz/Hilf/Nettesheim (2009), Das Recht der Europäischen Union, Art. 23 VO 1/2003 para 18; *Kienapfel* in von der Groeben/Schwarze/Hatje, Europäisches Unionsrecht, Art. 23 VO 1/2003 para 10; *Schwarze*, EuR 2009, 171, 181.

935 *Kienapfel* in von der Groeben/Schwarze/Hatje, Europäisches Unionsrecht, Art. 23 VO 1/2003 para 10.

Union's law according to Article 6 (3) TEU. The European Union is not formally bound by the ECHR, but the European Court of Justice uses the ECHR as a source of legal knowledge.[936] The authority of the ECHR is further strengthened by the rule of interpretation of Article 6 (1) TEU in conjunction with Article 52 (3) CFR.[937] Article 52 (3) CFR states:

> "*In so far as this Charter contains rights which correspond to rights guaranteed by the Convention for the Protection of Human Rights and Fundamental Freedoms, the meaning and scope of those rights shall be the same as those laid down by the said Convention. {…}.*"

Article 48-50 CFR contain provisions on criminal charges/offences.

The European Court of Human Rights has elaborated upon the criteria for determining the concept of a "criminal charge" in the meaning of Article 6 (1) ECHR , which is to be understood autonomously under the European Convention on Human Rights.[938]

The European Court of Human Rights set up three main criteria for the assessment: "*{I}t is first necessary to know whether the provision(s) defining the offence charged belong, according to the legal system of the respondent State, to criminal law, disciplinary law or both concurrently.*"[939] Second, "*{t}he very nature of the offence is a factor of great import.*"[940] Third, the degree of severity of the penalty that the person risks incurring has to be taken into consideration.[941] The European Court of Human Rights finds:

> "*In a society subscribing to the rule of law, there belong to the "criminal" sphere deprivations of liberty liable to be imposed as a punishment, except those which by their nature, duration or manner of execution cannot be appreciably detrimental. The seriousness of what is at stake, the traditions of the Contracting States and the importance attached by the Convention to respect for the physical liberty of the person all require that this should be so {…}.*"

---

936 *Geiger* in Geiger/Khan/Kotzur, EUV/AEUV, Art. 6 EUV para 23, 26.

937 *Geiger* in Geiger/Khan/Kotzur, EUV/AEUV, Art. 6 EUV para 23, 26.

938 *Kienapfel* in von der Groeben/Schwarze/Hatje, Europäisches Unionsrecht, Art. 23 VO 1/2003 para 11.

939 European Court of Human Rights, Judgment of 08.06.1976, No 5100/71 ect., ECLI:CE:ECHR:1976:0608JUD000510071, para 82, *Engel et al/Netherlands.*

940 European Court of Human Rights, Judgment of 08.06.1976, No 5100/71 ect., ECLI:CE:ECHR:1976:0608JUD000510071, para 82, *Engel et al/Netherlands.*

941 European Court of Human Rights, Judgment of 08.06.1976, No 5100/71 ect., ECLI:CE:ECHR:1976:0608JUD000510071, para 82, *Engel et al/Netherlands.*

Based on the above criteria, it is not clear whether a fine under Article 23 of Regulation 1/2003 is of criminal nature.[942] As mentioned above, the legal system of the European Union states that fines are not of criminal law nature. The same is true for most Member States.[943] In addition, a fine is not a deprivation of liberty that has been mentioned by the European Court of Human Rights as an example for a severe penalty.

However, the European Court of Human Rights[944] as well as the General Court[945] meanwhile assume that fines are to be considered a "criminal charge" in the meaning of Article 6 (1) ECHR. According to the European Court of Human Rights, antitrust fines do not belong to "hardcore criminal law" and "*consequently, the criminal-head guarantees will not necessarily apply with their full stringency {...}.*"[946] It may for example be compatible with Article 6 (1) ECHR for criminal penalties to be imposed by an administrative or non-judicial body.[947]

The view of the European Court of Human Rights and the General Court is to be agreed with. Antitrust fines have indeed to be considered as "criminal charge" or having a character similar to criminal law. The mere fact that a legislator states that a provision is of non-criminal nature cannot as such determine the autonomous interpretation of the ECHR. Otherwise, a legislator could easily undermine the special guarantees on fair trials in criminal proceedings in Article 6 (2) and (3) ECRH by simply

---

942 Cf. *Kienapfel* in von der Groeben/Schwarze/Hatje, Europäisches Unionsrecht, Art. 23 VO 1/2003 para 11.

943 *Kienapfel* in von der Groeben/Schwarze/Hatje, Europäisches Unionsrecht, Art. 23 VO 1/2003 para 11, fn. 35 mentions Ireland and England as states that treat antitrust violations as criminal.

944 European Court of Human Rights, Judgment of 23.11.2006, No 73053/01, ECLI:CE:ECHR:2006:1123JUD007305301, para 43, *Jussila/Finland*; European Court of Human Rights, Judgment of 27.09.2011, No 43509/08, ECLI:CE:ECHR:2011:0927JUD004350908, para 39 et seq, *Menarini Diagnostics/Italy.*

945 The General Court finds that even though antitrust fines are not of criminal nature, they can be considered as a criminal charge within the meaning of Article 6 (1) ECHR; the General Court further applies the criminal law principles of *nemo tenetur* and *in dubio pro reo*, GC, Judgment of 13.07.2011, Case T-138/07, ECLI:EU:T:2011:362, para 52, 54, 146 et seq, *Schindler*.

946 European Court of Human Rights, Judgment of 23.11.2006, No 73053/01, ECLI:CE:ECHR:2006:1123JUD007305301, para 43, *Jussila/Finland*.

947 European Court of Human Rights, Judgment of 24.02.1994, No 12547/86, ECLI:CE:ECHR:1994:0224JUD001254786, para 48, *Bendenoun/France*; European Court of Human Rights, Judgment of 23.11.2006, No 73053/01, ECLI:CE:ECHR:2006:1123JUD007305301, para 43, *Jussila/Finland*.

saying that a rule is not of criminal nature.[948] Likewise, a penalty may be severe even if it does not include a deprivation of liberty. A fine of up to 10 % of the global group turnover that may amount up to several billion Euros[949] is definitely a severe consequence for an undertaking. Such a fine may have a far-reaching effect on the freedom to operate of the undertaking concerned because it may be deprived of any investment options.

A classification of fines as coercive administrative measure[950] is not convincing. A fine of several million or even billion Euros would in most cases be disproportionate to the enforcement of the administrative order. This high amount clearly has a sanctioning effect. In addition, the existence of periodic penalty payments in Article 24 of Regulation 1/2003 shows that there is a special provision for coercive administrative measures.

It is, accordingly, general opinion that basic principles of criminal law claim validity in the case of antitrust proceedings of the Commission.[951] Even though they may not apply with their full stringency, the authoritative content must be preserved. Otherwise, the concept of a "criminal charge" would be rendered meaningless.

One of the basic principles of criminal law is the principle of *nullum crimen, nulla poena sine lege certa* (principle of legal certainty). This principle ensures that the perpetrator can foresee its criminal liability and the consequences of the act when it is committed and is, thus, deterred from committing the prohibited act by the threat of punishment.[952] The

948 The classification in national law is thus according to the European Court of Human Rights of minor importance compared to the other two criteria set up in the *Engel* judgment, European Court of Human Rights, Judgment of 21.02.1984, No 8544/79, ECLI:CE:ECHR:1984:0221JUD000854479, para 52, *Öztürk/Germany*; see also *Kienapfel* in von der Groeben/Schwarze/Hatje, Europäisches Unionsrecht, Art. 23 VO 1/2003 para 11, fn. 34.

949 The Commission fined Google 4.3 billion Euros in an antitrust case, European Commission, Decision of 18.07.2018, C(2018) 4761 final, OJ C 402, 28.11.2019, p. 19-22, Case No AT.40099, *Google Android*.

950 Cf. *Kienapfel* in von der Groeben/Schwarze/Hatje, Europäisches Unionsrecht, Art. 23 VO 1/2003 para 11.

951 *Feddersen* in Grabitz/Hilf/Nettesheim (2009), Das Recht der Europäischen Union, Art. 23 VO 1/2003 para 18-21; *Kienapfel* in von der Groeben/Schwarze/Hatje, Europäisches Unionsrecht, Art. 23 VO 1/2003 para 13 et seq; *Nowak* in Loewenheim/Meessen/Riesenkampff/Kersting/Meyer-Lindemann, Kartellrecht, Art. 23 Kartellverfahrensordnung para 51; *Dannecker/Biermann* in Immenga/Mestmäcker, Wettbewerbsrecht EU, Vor Art. 23 VO 1/2003 para 39.

952 *Dannecker/Biermann* in Immenga/Mestmäcker, Wettbewerbsrecht EU, Vor Art. 23 VO 1/2003 para 45.

principle of legality in Article 49 CFR points in the same direction.[953] As mentioned above, the decisive factor here is the classification as criminal charge within the meaning of the ECHR.[954]

Legal certainty *"requires the law to define clearly offences and the penalties sanctioning them."*[955] Further, *"the clarity of the law is assessed having regard not only to the wording of the relevant provision but also to the information provided by settled, published case law."*[956]

It is doubtful whether fines imposed upon an important innovator for hindering innovation of other parties will ever fulfill those criteria. It may well be that the legal aspects for assessing innovation capacity and incentives may be established through case law or even explicit guidance by the Commission. However, it will remain impossible for the undertakings concerned to obtain the data necessary to perform the factual assessment.

Market shares in existing markets are usually factually easy to assess.[957] Information on the total volume of products or revenues on a market can be found in industry reports. On that basis, an undertaking can easily calculate its own share of that total volume. This is different with respect to innovation capacity. Research and development assets as well as plans are confidential business information that is usually not published. Information inquiries to competitors on that matter are likely to violate Article 101 (1) TFEU, because they reduce strategic uncertainty and enable the undertakings to be aware of the market strategies of their competitors.[958]

953 ECJ, Judgment of 20.12.2017, Case C-102/16, ECLI:EU:C:2017:1012, para 50-52, *Vaditrans*; ECJ, Judgment of 10.11.2011, Case 405/10, ECLI:EU:C:2011:722, para 48, *Garenfeld*; ECJ, Judgment of 12.12.1996, Cases C-74/95 and C-129/95, ECLI:EU:C:1996:491, para 25; CFI, Judgment of 05.05.2006, Case T 279/02, ECLU:EU:T:2006:103, para 66, *Degussa*; *Jarass*, Charta der Grundrechte der Europäischen Union, Art. 49 para 11.

954 See Article 52 (3) CFR.

955 ECJ, Judgment of 17.06.2010, C-413/08 P, ECLI:EU:C:2010:346, para 94, *Lafarge*; see also ECJ, Judgment of 22.05.2008, C-266/06 P, ECLI:EU:C:2008:295, para 39, *Evonik Degussa*; *Dannecker/Biermann* in Immenga/Mestmäcker, Wettbewerbsrecht EU, Vor Art. 23 VO 1/2003 para 45.

956 ECJ, Judgment of 17.06.2010, C-413/08 P, ECLI:EU:C:2010:346, para 94, *Lafarge*, referring to European Court of Human Rights, Judgment of 27.09.1995, No. 15312/89, ECLI:CE:ECHR:1995:0927JUD001531289, para 25, *G v France*; see also ECJ, Judgment of 22.05.2008, C-266/06 P, ECLI:EU:C:2008:295, para 40 et seq, *Evonik Degussa*; *Dannecker/Biermann* in Immenga/Mestmäcker, Wettbewerbsrecht EU, Vor Art. 23 VO 1/2003 para 45.

957 The legal market definition may be more complicated; however, legal certainty may be developed through case law.

958 Cf. Horizontal Cooperation Guidelines, para 58, 60, 62, 66.

The exchange of individualized data on future prices and quantities is considered a restriction by object.[959] Even though the information on R&D capabilities is not directly related to price, an exchange may nevertheless lead to a collusive outcome if innovation instead of price is the factor determining competition in a given industry. The Commission finds that "*if companies compete with regard to R&D it is the technology data that may be most strategic for competition.*"[960]

Even if the exchange of information on R&D capabilities and projects does not lead to a restriction by object, it may still result in anticompetitive effects also prohibited under Article 101 (1) TFEU. In its Horizontal Cooperation Guidelines, the Commission points out:

> "*Sharing of strategic data can give rise to restrictive effects on competition because it reduces the parties' decision-making independence by decreasing their incentives to compete. Strategic information can be related to prices (for example, actual prices, discounts, increases, reductions or rebates), customer lists, production costs, quantities, turnovers, sales, capacities, qualities, marketing plans, risks, investments, technologies and R&D programmes and their results.*"[961]

Besides the high risk of violating Article 101 (1) TFEU by asking competitors for data on R&D capacities and projects, undertakings do not have any legal right to obtain that information. In fact, competitors will almost certainly be reluctant to disclose any information on their confidential research projects.

As a result, even though it may be legally clarified how to analyze an abuse of dominance with respect to innovation incentives, it will be impossible for undertakings to make the factual assessment themselves.[962] In any case, the principle of direct applicability of Article 102 TFEU[963] would require such self-assessment. It is, therefore, not possible for an undertaking to assess whether it is an important innovator (compared to other undertakings) or if its behavior decreases innovation incentives of competitors or trading partners. The relevant undertakings cannot foresee their liability at the time of their action and be deterred from committing the

959 Horizontal Cooperation Guidelines, para 74.
960 Horizontal Cooperation Guidelines, para 86.
961 Horizontal Cooperation Guidelines, para 86.
962 *Dreher* mentions the information problem in determining the secret know-how potential of an undertaking, *Dreher*, ZWeR 2009, 149, 159.
963 Article 1 (3) of Regulation 1/2003.

prohibited act. The standard of legal certainty requiring the law to clearly define offences is not met. This is regardless of further clarification by case law. Even though the provision can be defined clearly in legal terms, undertakings are not able to factually assess its preconditions. Imposing a fine on an important innovator for decreasing innovation incentives of other undertakings would violate the principle of legal certainty.

Alternatively, fines imposed upon an important innovator would likely conflict with the principle of *nulla poena sine culpa* (no punishment without fault). It is not undisputed whether the principle of fault is a general principle of law.[964] In any case, the European Court of Justice has taken it as a given principle at EU level[965] and it is a principle common to the Constitutions of the EU Member States.[966] The principle of innocence is included in Article 48 of the CFR: "*Everyone who has been charged shall be presumed innocent until proved guilty according to law.*" This implies that "guilt" or "fault" is an important prerequisite for a criminal charge. In addition, Article 23 (1) and (2) of Regulation 1/2003 explicitly point out that a fine may only be imposed in case of intentional or negligent behavior.

In the practice of the Commission and the Union Courts, there is no clear line between intentional and negligent anticompetitive behavior.[967] Generally, an error of facts has the effect of excluding intent.[968] However, if that error is committed negligently, a fine may be imposed for negligent behavior.[969] A behavior is negligent

964 *Dannecker/Biermann* in Immenga/Mestmäcker, Wettbewerbsrecht EU, Vor Art. 23 VO 1/2003 para 61.

965 Opinion of Advocate General Kokott, delivered on 28.02.2013, Case C-681/11, ECLI:EU:C:2013:126, para 41, *Schenker*; the ECJ finds that there are two principles typical of criminal law, "namely the principles *nulla poena sine culpa* and *in dubio pro reo*", ECJ, Judgment of 18.11.1987, Case 137/85, ECLI:EU:C:1987:493, para 14, Maizena; see also ECJ, Judgment of 11.07.2002, Case C-210/00, ECLI:EU:C:2002:440, para 35, 44, *Käserei Champignon Hofmeister*.

966 Opinion of Advocate General Kokott, delivered on 28.02.2013, Case C-681/11, ECLI:EU:C:2013:126, para 41, *Schenker;* Opinion of Advocate General Van Gerven, delivered on 15.09.1993, Case C-116/92, ECLI:EU:C:1993:357, para 18, *Charlton*.

967 CFI, Judgment of 21.02.1995, Case T-29/92, ECLI:EU:T:1995:34, para 361, *SPO*; ECJ, Order of 25.03.1996, C-137/95 P, ECLI:EU:C:1996:130, para 51 et seq, *SPO*.

968 *Dannecker/Biermann* in Immenga/Mestmäcker, Wettbewerbsrecht EU, Vor Art. 23 VO 1/2003 para 204; Opinion of Advocate General Mayras delivered on 29 October 1975, Case 26/75, ed. 1975, 1367, 1382 et seq, *General Motors*.

969 *Dannecker/Biermann* in Immenga/Mestmäcker, Wettbewerbsrecht EU, Vor Art. 23 VO 1/2003 para 204.

> *"where the author of the infringement, although acting without any intention to perform an unlawful act, has not foreseen the consequences of his action in circumstances where a person who is normally informed and sufficiently attentive could not have failed to foresee them."*[970]

Thus, the question has to be whether an error on the innovation capacity and R&D projects of competitors or trading partners can be considered as being committed negligently.

As mentioned above, undertakings will usually not have any (lawful) access to the number and quality of R&D assets or projects[971] of other industry players. As a result, "*a person who is normally informed and sufficiently attentive*" would still not be able to assess and foresee whether the undertaking concerned is an important innovator compared to other undertakings in the industry. Intentionality or negligence, as a basis for imposing a fine, would likely always be missing in cases concerning an important innovator.

Even though the basic principles associated with criminal law will, according to the European Court of Human Rights, not necessarily apply with their full stringency to antitrust fines, it seems hard to believe that it is lawful to impose a high fine on an undertaking that cannot foresee its liability and therefore does not act intentionally or negligently. The basic rationale behind the principle of legal certainty and the principle of fault – that is, that the addressee of a provision must be able to deliberately prevent a sanction based on a clear decision-making basis – must also apply in case of an antitrust fine.

---

970 Opinion of Advocate General Mayras, delivered on 29.10.1975, Case 26/75, ECLI:EU:C:1975:141, Reports of Cases 1975, 1367, at p. 1389 et seq, *General Motors* with reference to the legislation of the Member States; *Dannecker/Biermann* in Immenga/Mestmäcker, Wettbewerbsrecht EU, Vor Art. 23 VO 1/2003 para 198; in an earlier case, the ECJ found that the company UBC "*adopted measures which it know or ought to have known contravened the prohibition set out in {Article 102 TFEU}. {…} The Commission therefore had good reasons to find that UBC's infringements were at the very least negligent.*", ECJ, Judgment of 14.02.1978, Case 27/76, ECLI:EU:C:1978:22, para 300-301, *United Brands*; Advocate General Mayras seems to concretize the meaning of what a company "ought to have known".

971 Projects that are in planning or early discovery stage; it is, in contrast, common in certain industries to benchmark pipeline projects of competitors; this is particularly possible if there are patent applications at an early stage of the R&D process.

(b) Other Commission powers

With respect to other powers of the Commission, particularly the power to require an undertaking to bring the infringement to an end and to impose remedies, the general principle of legal certainty is the point of reference. This principle is, beyond its existence in criminal law, a general principle of law recognized in all Member States.[972] The European Court of Justice finds that "*Community legislation must be certain and its application foreseeable by those subject to it.*"[973] In case of finding and termination of an infringement according to Article 7 of Regulation 1/2003, the formal Commission decision provides for legal certainty. Imposed measures have to be clearly defined so that they can build the basis for enforcement action.[974] The Commission decision sets out the consequences for the addressee with regard to its future conduct.[975] In that regard, it is precisely foreseeable for the addressee of the decision whether its behavior is compatible with Article 102 TFEU.[976]

Aside from the right to realize concentrations,[977] there are other forms of company behavior that fall within the scope of Article 16 CFR (Freedom to conduct a business) and Article 17 CFR (Right to property).[978] Article 16 CFR covers, for example, the free use of an undertaking's

---

972 CFI, Judgment of 27.09.2006, Case T-43/02, ECLI:EU:T:2006:270, para 71 et seq, *Jungbunzlauer*; *Dannecker/Biermann* in Immenga/Mestmäcker, Wettbewerbsrecht EU, Vor Art. 23 VO 1/2003 para 44; Soltész/Steinle/Bielesz, EuZW 2003, 202, 205.

973 ECJ, Judgment of 15.12.1987, Case 325/85, ECLI:EU:C:1987:546, para 18, *Ireland/Commission*.

974 *Ritter/Wirtz* in Immenga/Mestmäcker, Wettbewerbsrecht EU, Art. 7 VO 1/2003 para 38.

975 ECJ, Judgment of 31.03.1993, Joined cases C-89/85, C-104/85, C-114/85, C-116/85, C-117/85 and C-125/85 to C-129/85, ECLI:EU:C:1993:120, para 184-185, *Ahlström*; *Dalheimer* in Grabitz/Hilf/Nettesheim (2009), Das Recht der Europäischen Union, Art. 7 VO 1/2003 para 8; *Breit* in von der Groeben/Schwarze/Hatje, Europäisches Unionsrecht, Art. 7 VO 1/2003 para 10.

976 *Dreher* finds that, opposed to fining decision, in case of a forward-looking decision to put an end to an abusive conduct, the question of market dominance may also be examined from a forward-looking perspective, *Dreher*, ZWeR 2009, 149, 170.

977 See *Section II) H) 7) (a)*.

978 Cf. for a fining decision: *Schwarze*, EuR 2009, 171, 180.

economic, technical and financial resources,[979] the freedom of contract[980] and the right to business secret[981]. Article 17 (2) CFR explicitly mentions the protection of intellectual property.[982] All of those dimensions of the fundamental rights may be affected by a Commission decision ordering an important innovator to disclose information, to enter into contracts or to take other forms of action to raise innovation incentives and ability of third parties.

As opposed to the situation of a merger, where future expectations of the undertakings concerned may be changed,[983] a Commission order on a dominant undertaking may alter the undertaking's existing business strategy. It is, therefore, decisive that there is a careful balancing assessment taking into account the innovation incentives and fundamental rights of the important innovator as well as of competitors and trading partners.

5) Conclusion

In conclusion, the two statements established at the beginning of this Section must be answered in the affirmative. With respect to behavior impacting innovation incentives of competitors or trading partners, market dominance shall be assessed on the basis of innovation capacity. In that regard, the concept of the important innovator as developed in *Dow/ DuPont*, should be incorporated in the assessment of market dominance.

It is crucial to note that innovation capacity and ability only serve as a basis for market dominance with respect to behavior influencing innovation incentives of third parties. Behavior of important innovators directly relating to market prices does not constitute an abuse of dominance within the scope of the abovementioned theory. Special attention must be paid to

---

979 ECJ, Judgment of 27.03.2014, Case C-314/12, ECLI:EU:C:2014:192, para 49, *UPC*; *Jarass*, Charta der Grundrechte der Europäischen Union, Art. 16 para 10.

980 ECJ, Judgment of 22 .01.2013, Case C-283/11, ECLI:EU:C:2013:28, para 42, *Sky Österreich*; Judgment of 18.07.2013, Case C-426/11, ECLI:EU:C:2013:521, para 32, *Alemo-Herron*; Judgment of 17.10.2013, C-101/12, ECLI:EU:C:2013:661, para 25, *Schaible*; *Jarass*, Charta der Grundrechte der Europäischen Union, Art. 16 para 10.

981 ECJ, Judgment of 23.09.2004, Joined cases C-435/02 and C-103/03, ECLI:EU:C:2004:552, para 49, *Springer*; *Jarass*, Charta der Grundrechte der Europäischen Union, Art. 16 para 10.

982 For further explanation see *Jarass*, Charta der Grundrechte der Europäischen Union, Art. 17 para 10.

983 See *Section II) H) 7) (b)*.

efficiencies, namely the own research and development incentives of the important innovator.

Conversely, based on the same principles, an undertaking with high market shares that is not an important innovator may defend itself by means of the innovation capacity of other industry players. In that kind of "innovation defense", an undertaking may be considered as not being dominant with respect to behavior directly impacting innovation incentives of competitors or trading partners. However, attention must be paid to the fact that a firm with high market shares may at the same time be an important innovator. Accordingly, the criteria for assessment may be altered but this does not necessarily change the outcome.

In any case, fines may likely not be imposed on important innovators. In most cases, it will be impossible for undertakings to assess their own innovative strength in relation to that of third parties. Information on innovation assets and planned research and development projects is almost entirely confidential. A fine imposed on an important innovator would therefore violate the principle of legal certainty and the principle of fault. However, it may be possible for the Commission to set up a decision finding and terminating an infringement.

All in all, it may be considered an abuse of dominance in the meaning of Article 102 TFEU if an important innovator engages in practices decreasing innovation incentives.

C) Allocation of the result in primary law

Based on the above assessment, the concept of *Dow/DuPont* can be used in the scope of Article 102 TFEU but not in the scope of Article 101 TFEU. Aside from the specific rationale of the Dow/DuPont Decision and its application in the scope of cooperation and unilateral behavior, this result can also be based on the general differences between Article 101 and 102 TFEU and their relation to merger control.

1) Function of Article 101 and 102 TFEU in the internal market

Article 101 and 102 TFEU both serve the same objective as set out in Article 3 (3) TEU and Protocol No (27): the maintenance of a system of effective and undistorted competition within the internal market.[984] However, both Articles pursue this objective in different ways.[985] Whereas Article 101 TFEU seeks to prevent the cooperative synchronization of entrepreneurial autonomy of action, Article 102 TFEU opposes the exercise of such autonomy of action by a market-dominant undertaking which can no longer be controlled by competition.[986] Even though one and the same behavior may violate Article 101 TFEU as well as Article 102 TFEU, there needs to be an additional structural element for an agreement to constitute an abuse of a market dominant position.[987] In contrast, an agreement or concerted practice is not a prerequisite for a violation of Article 102 TFEU.

2) Development of the EC Merger Regulation

Before the introduction of the first EC Merger Regulation[988], there were no general provisions on the control of the creation or strengthening of a dominant position through mergers.[989] The European Court of Justice established a control via Article 102 TFEU of certain mergers strengthen-

---

984 ECJ, Judgment of 21.02.1973, Case 6/72, ECLI:EU:C:1973:22; para 25, *Continental Can*; CFI, Judgment of 10.07.1990, Case T-51/89, ECLI:EU:T:1990:41, para 22, *Tetra Pak I*; *Jung* in Grabitz/Hilf/Nettesheim, Das Recht der Europäischen Union, Art. 102 AEUV para 22.

985 ECJ, Judgment of 21.02.1973, Case 6/72, ECLI:EU:C:1973:22; para 25, *Continental Can*; CFI, Judgment of 10.07.1990, Case T-51/89, ECLI:EU:T:1990:41, para 22, *Tetra Pak I*; *Jung* in Grabitz/Hilf/Nettesheim, Das Recht der Europäischen Union, Art. 102 AEUV para 22.

986 *Jung* in Grabitz/Hilf/Nettesheim, Das Recht der Europäischen Union, Art. 102 AEUV para 22; see also *Weiß* in Calliess/Ruffert, EUV/AEUV, Art. 102 AEUV para 2; *Schröter/Bartl* in von der Groeben/Schwarze/Hatje, Europäisches Unionsrecht, Art. 102 AEUV para 36.

987 Cf. *Jung* in Grabitz/Hilf/Nettesheim, Das Recht der Europäischen Union, Art. 102 AEUV para 22; the Court of First Instance found in Tetra Pak: „*The additional element lies in the very context of the case — in the fact that Tetra Pak's acquisition of the exclusive licence had the practical effect of precluding all competition in the relevant market.*“, CFI, Judgment of 10.07.1990, Case T-51/89, ECLI:EU:T:1990:41, para 24, *Tetra Pak I*.

988 Council Regulation (EEC) No 4064/89 of 21 December 1989 on the control of concentrations between undertakings, OJ L 395, 30.12.1989, p. 1-12, entered into force in 1990; replaced by the current EC Merger Regulation in 2004.

989 *Huttenlauch* in Loewenheim/Meessen/Riesenkampff/Kersting/Meyer-Lindemann, Kartellrecht, Art. 102 AEUV para 251; there have been special merger control rules for undertakings from the coal and steel sector in Art. 66 of the Treaty establishing the European Coal and Steel Community.

ing a dominant position in its *Continental Can*[990] decision. The European Court of Justice found that Article 102 TFEU[991]

> "*is not only aimed at practices which may cause damage to consumers directly, but also at those which are detrimental to them through their impact on an effective competition structure*"[992].

According to the Court,

> "*{a}buse may therefore occur if an undertaking in a dominant position strengthens such position in such a way that the degree of dominance reached substantially fetters competition, i.e. that only undertakings remain in the market whose behaviour depends on the dominant one.*"[993]

However, since the abovementioned approach only allows for the control of mergers strengthening an already existing dominant position (not of mergers that create dominance for the first time), the first EC Merger Regulation was introduced. The Regulation shall allow for a systematic control of concentrations between undertakings[994] and take into account the significant increase in cross-border mergers in the EU.[995] The development of the EC Merger Regulation already shows the close interrelationship of merger control and Article 102 TFEU.

3) Interrelation between Article 101 and 102 TFEU and the EC Merger Regulation

With a view to the above development of the EC Merger Regulation, it is not surprising that Article 102 TFEU and Article 2 (3) EC Merger Regulation are closely related. Both have as a centerpiece the "dominant position". Article 2 (3) EC Merger Regulation is broader and also includes

---

990 ECJ, Judgment of 21.02.1973, Case 6/72, ECLI:EU:C:1973:22, *Continental Can*.

991 At that time Article 86 of the EC Treaty.

992 ECJ, Judgment of 21.02.1973, Case 6/72, ECLI:EU:C:1973:22, para 26, *Continental Can*.

993 ECJ, Judgment of 21.02.1973, Case 6/72, ECLI:EU:C:1973:22, para 26, *Continental Can*.

994 See the preamble of Council Regulation (EEC) No 4064/89 of 21 December 1989 on the control of concentrations between undertakings, OJ L 395, 30.12.1989, p. 1-12.

995 Cf. *Hacker* in von der Groeben/Schwarze/Hatje, Europäisches Unionsrecht, A. Einleitung zur Fusionskontrollverordnung, para 1.

a significant impediment to effective competition beyond the creation or strengthening of a dominant position. Article 102 TFEU requires an additional abusive behavior. However, both provisions have a strong focus on a particular market structure.

Article 101 TFEU instead focuses on the behavior of two or more independent undertakings (or associations of two or more independent undertakings). Article 101 TFEU may be used in a merger setting in case of a joint venture that coordinates the behavior of the parent companies. Article 2 (4) EC Merger Regulation reads:

> "*To the extent that the creation of a joint venture constituting a concentration pursuant to Article 3 has as its object or effect the coordination of the competitive behaviour of undertakings that remain independent, such coordination shall be appraised in accordance with the criteria of Article 81(1) and (3) of the Treaty, with a view to establishing whether or not the operation is compatible with the common market.*"

This shows quite well that the substantive overlap between merger policy and Article 101 TFEU is of behavioral nature.

This does not mean that market conditions are irrelevant for the application of Article 101 TFEU. In fact, market shares may have an effect on the appreciability[996] of a restriction by effect or on whether it is block exempted[997]. But whereas the market structure may have an impact on the assessment under Article 101 TFEU, certain market conditions are not a prerequisite for the application of that Article as such.

4) Innovation competition and Article 101 and 102 TFEU

The innovation competition approach in *Dow/DuPont* serves the purpose of securing a competitive allocation/distribution of research and development resources allowing for free innovation competition.[998] It concerns the market/innovation structure in an industry. Therefore, the innovation

---

996 See Communication from the Commission – Notice on agreements of minor importance which do not appreciably restrict competition under Article 101 (1) of the Treaty on the Functioning of the European Union (De Minimis Notice), OJ C 291, 30.08.2014, p. 1-4.

997 Most block exemption Regulations contain specific market share thresholds.

998 Cf. *Section II) C) 3)*.

competition approach may be of use in settings with a strong structural component such as in the scope of Article 102 TFEU.

Indeed, in case certain structural aspects are important with a view to the EC Merger Regulation, it is likely that those aspects also play a role in an assessment under Article 102 TFEU. Having said this, there need to be adjustments as mentioned in *Section III) B) 2)* to meet the particularities of Article 102 TFEU.

In contrast, the approach in *Dow/DuPont* is not about a particular behavior (beyond the merger as such). Indeed, the Commission's rationale explicitly ignores any observable research and development activities. The mere communitization of research and development assets and capabilities leads to reduced innovation incentives. In the case of a permanent reallocation of assets, Article 101 TFEU would not even be applicable because there would be no ongoing coordination of two undertakings. The mere sale of a research and development asset does not restrict the freedom to operate of the participating undertakings. The rationale in the Dow/DuPont Decision that a merger of two out of a limited number of important innovators is – under certain circumstances – likely to reduce innovation incentives does not say anything about the coordination of two independent undertakings. In case two or more independent undertakings coordinate their research and development activities, the approach in Dow/DuPont is no longer necessary.[999] All in all, there is indeed a difference if two companies such as Dow and DuPont merge or if they cooperate. Whereas in the first case research and development assets are reallocated, in the second case the structural setting remains unchanged.

5) Conclusion

The innovation competition approach in *Dow/DuPont* is about the structural allocation of research and development assets and capabilities. This approach is of use in the structural setting of Article 102 TFEU, focusing to some extent on the market position of a single undertaking. However, innovation competition is not about the coordination of two or more independent undertakings. Therefore, the rationale in *Dow/DuPont* cannot be applied in the scope of Article 101 TFEU. This result shows the differences between structural and behavioral aspects of competition policy. Whereas Article 101 and 102 TFEU and the merger control rules all point

---

999 See *Section III) A) 3)*.

towards securing free trade within the internal market, the provisions have different starting points to reach this goal.

IV) Summary

Competition and innovation are two pillars of the internal market. Whereas innovation is an objective in the EU Treaties as such, it also is an important parameter of competition. The European Commission therefore must take into account innovation in its competition policy and decisions. This may include a competitive allocation of research and development resources allowing for free innovation competition. The Dow/DuPont Decision has to be assessed against this background.

A) *Innovation Competition in Dow/DuPont*

1) Rationale in *Dow/DuPont*

The Commission's theory of harm in *Dow/DuPont* consists of the following points:[1000]

- As a result of the transaction, lines of research or early pipeline products in certain innovation spaces are likely to be discontinued, deferred or redirected.
- The transaction is likely to significantly reduce innovation competition and thus ultimately product innovation in the whole industry.

This finding is based on the underlying rationale:

> *"Economic principles indicate that a merger between two out of a limited number of significant innovators is likely to reduce product innovation when appropriability is high (that is, when IPRs are effective), and when there are no merger-specific efficiencies associated with the merger."*[1001]

Four conditions must be fulfilled for a merger to lead to the abovementioned harm to product innovation:

1. The parties of the transaction must be close and important innovators. This implies that the respective market is contestable on the basis of innovation. Furthermore, the parties must be able to successfully bring to market an innovation (this usually implies that they are vertically

1000 Dow/DuPont Decision, para 2014, 3056, 3057.
1001 Dow/DuPont Decision, para 2042.

integrated and in the possession of sufficient financial resources). In addition, they must be close innovation competitors, targeting the same research goals.
2. There must be a limited number of innovators in the industry. This requires that there be an oligopolistic market structure and high barriers to entry.
3. Appropriability must be high pre-merger. This is the case when IP rights are effective or other strategies enable the innovator to capture the value of an innovation.
4. There must be no merger-specific efficiencies. The combination of complementary assets, economies of scale or cost efficiencies, *inter alia*, may outweigh negative effects on innovation.

The Commission treats effects on innovation competition as standard unilateral effects under the Horizontal Merger Guidelines. In order to perform the innovation competition assessment, the Commission analyzes the industry structure and developments as well as the different innovation players. The Commission uses various factors to determine the parties' strength as innovators – for example, expertise and assets; R&D input targets; output in the form of new and successful AIs; and the strength of the patent portfolios. In addition, the Commission narrows down the analysis with respect to certain innovation spaces.

The Commission's findings are mainly based on three economic mechanisms through which a merger can reduce innovation:

1. A merger can affect innovation competition. This refers to the effect of cannibalizing profits of the other party through the introduction of a new product or, more broadly speaking, the "*negative externality*"[1002] that an innovator imposes on its competitors. The cannibalization effect is internalized post-merger, "*adding to the opportunity cost of innovation and thus depressing the innovation incentive.*"[1003] Post-merger, one party no longer gains profits from a competing firm but from the merging partner when introducing a new product.
2. Innovation incentives may also be affected by changes in current and future product market competition that typically occur with a merger.[1004] The Commission finds that "*the effect of a less intense product market competition on innovation is potentially ambiguous.*"[1005] Neverthe-

1002 Annex 4, para 17.
1003 Annex 4, para 6.
1004 Annex 4, para 7.
1005 Annex 4, para 7.

less, even though less intense product market competition may, under certain circumstances, incentivize innovation, this effect is unlikely to outweigh the loss of innovation competition mentioned above.[1006]

3. The Commission identifies two important efficiencies increasing innovation incentives that may come along with a merger: a possible lower risk of imitation by other market players (increasing the innovator's possibility to appropriate the value of the innovation) and the ability for process innovations to be applied over a larger scale.[1007]

2) Protective purpose and time horizon

The innovation competition assessment in *Dow/DuPont* aims at protecting the innovation incentives of the merging parties and other industry players. It is a key to understanding *Dow/DuPont* that the Commission does not (and cannot) aim at protecting the research and development process or the final product/future competition.

With respect to innovation, there are three possible starting points for competition policy:

4. The innovation incentive, meaning the impulse to start or continue research and development, including the general ability to perform such activities.
5. The innovation effort or the innovation activity – that is, the actual process of performing research and development in the sense of specific discovery and development actions.
6. The final product or competition on a future market which requires research and development success and, with respect to competition in future markets, several undertakings successfully introducing new products.

The best arguments speak in favor of innovation incentives as a protective purpose of Commission action. Since research and development is a stochastic process, policy cannot set incentives to raise the likelihood of a successful result, meaning the innovative product. The uncertain interrelation between research and development and the innovative product is not at all affected by competition policy. The success of innovation activities is by no means changed through an increase in rivalry. The stochastic research and development process does not become deterministic in a

1006 Annex 4, para 8.
1007 Annex 4, para 9.

less concentrated and more competitive surrounding. In other words, it does not become more likely that research is successful if market features change.

The same is true with respect to innovation activities: The activities themselves are not influenced by changes in market concentration. They would be in the case of regulatory intervention or other actions that would directly terminate the respective innovation activity. However, even in the case of a more concentrated market, undertakings would be free to continue their research and development activities. The question is rather if they would do so, meaning if their incentives to perform R&D would be changed through shifts in the market features. According to the Commission's assessment in *Dow/DuPont*, those incentives may be changed with a view to cannibalization (or broader innovation competition) concerns. If an undertaking fears that it will cannibalize more of its own sales (as is the case post-merger), its incentive to perform R&D will decrease, not the possibility to continue the R&D activity. In conclusion, the protective purpose of Commission action regarding competition policy must be to maintain innovation incentives.

Those incentives may be decreased immediately after the implementation of the transaction as a result of reduced innovation competition, both with respect to innovation spaces as well as concerning innovation at industry level. It is not important at what time future products may have been introduced, as after the initial incentive to start research, the actual success of that research does not depend on competition policy or market structure. The assessment of innovation competition in *Dow/DuPont* is not about long-time dynamic effects, but rather adopts a static view of the competitive pressure leading to innovation incentives at the time of the Transaction. This approach is most comparable to the concept of allocative efficiencies and focuses on the optimal distribution of innovation assets.

3) Innovation competition and innovation spaces

The Commission treats innovation as a parameter of competition rather than a market on its own. In addition, the concept of innovation spaces – that are targeted innovation efforts towards a goal broader than a specific product – does not imply a market definition as well. Innovation spaces are rather a means of concretizing innovation activities in specific parts of the industry. The Commission supplements its assessment of innovation competition in the industry with a "deep-dive" into specific areas of innovation in order to capture the full picture. Innovation spaces can be understood as a link between innovation activities on industry level and the final product market, showing the direction of research and development. This finding is based on the Commission's conclusion that it may not be able to precisely identify the activities in innovation spaces that are likely to be discontinued, deferred or redirected.[1008] If the Commission would use innovation spaces as markets, it could not leave open the respective activities if it concludes that there is actual competitive harm leading to Commission intervention.

Taken together, these points suggest that innovation is not a market on its own, but rather a factor that influences the market position of an undertaking on a different level. Innovation spaces concretize the activities on that level, completing the picture of the respective innovation conditions. Consequentially, the Commission does not assess specific products or pipelines, but rather focuses on competitive pressure with respect to research and development activities in general.

4) The approach in *Dow/DuPont* is novel and necessary

As is usually the case with innovations, the theory of harm in *Dow/DuPont* did not come out of the blue but rather had predecessors in other Commission decisions. However, this has been the first time that the Commission expressed concerns on mere innovation incentives without clear interrelation to product markets. The innovation spaces do not replace a product market, most of all because the Commission did not provide any evidence or assessment on which of the innovation spaces could possibly be harmed. Most importantly, in *Dow/DuPont* there has been for the first time a theoretical background and a legal and economic assessment of innovation competition. The Commission's rationale that a merger between two out of a limited number of innovators in a market characterized by oligopolistic market structure and high barriers to entry as well as high appropriability may depress innovation incentives has no example in preceding decisions. All in all, even though the Commission's concern may have been grounded in prior case law, in *Dow/DuPont*, there is for the first time a manifest theory of harm and the explanation of an underlying rationale. There is a novel "theory" in the meaning of a definition and

1008 Dow/DuPont Decision, para 3024, 3025.

explanation of innovation concerns beyond specific product markets or observable research activities.

There are some commonalities with the Innovation Market Analysis that has been introduced in the United States in 1995 by *Gilbert* and *Sunshine*.[1009] However, the most important difference between the two approaches lies in the incorporation of innovation concerns into the legal framework. Whereas *Gilbert* and *Sunshine* analyze innovation as a market on its own, the Commission explicitly refers to innovation competition as a means that affects the market position of the merging parties. In addition, *Gilbert* and *Sunshine* still focus on specific research and development activities that are directed to future products, and not so much on a reduction of innovation incentives at industry level.

As mentioned above, innovation is an objective of the EU Treaties and also a decisive factor in the competitive process. Therefore, the European Commission must fully take into account factors that influence innovation when releasing decisions. This means that research and development shall not only be protected once it has started and is directed towards a specific product or product market, but that innovation must be secured in a comprehensive way, including the mere incentives to perform research and development. Even though innovation concerns have been part of traditional concepts – such as the potential competition doctrine and the future markets concept – , those concepts have only covered part of the innovation process. The concept of innovation competition, as developed in *Dow/DuPont*, incorporates the mere innovation capacity and the innovation incentive beyond any specific (future) product or existing research activity. Whereas traditional concepts do not at all include the initiation of innovation activities (their scope begins way after the basic and broad research has started), the innovation competition approach focuses on the innovation incentives as a protective goal. It is not about the final product but about the competitive pressure to generally start R&D.

5) Under certain circumstances, a link between innovation and competition may be established to the requisite legal standard

Until now, there has not been a definite theoretical or empirical finding on the precise interrelation between competition and innovation incentives. However, the Commission did not reach the conclusion in *Dow/*

1009 See *Gilbert/Sunshine*, 63 Antitrust Law Journal (1995), 569.

DuPont that there was such a definite relationship between market concentration and innovation incentives in general. The Commission rather developed a theory of harm for a specific case, namely a merger between important innovators in a close oligopoly with high barriers to entry and a high level of appropriability. Under those circumstances, there is economic literature supporting the Commission's findings.

Case law requires the Commission to ensure that the economic principles and theories used are accurate, reliable, consistent and complete. The Commission must rely on the most likely outcome and provide a cogent assessment of the economic background. This implies that there does not have to be one-hundred percent security as to the underlying economic findings. It is the peculiarity of the normative that – even in the case that there is no definite empirical or theoretical finding supporting a decision – the law must find a solution to existing problems.

It is important to distinguish the facts of the specific *Dow/DuPont* case from the general underlying theory. Whereas it is the goal of this thesis to scrutinize the underlying theory of harm in *Dow/DuPont* and assess whether this theory can be applied in scenarios other than a merger setting as well, it is not about a critique of the specific case. Admittedly, since the theory has been developed in a case, it cannot completely be separated from the underlying facts. However, the accuracy, reliability, consistency and completeness of the specific features of the crop protection industry and the economic data submitted in *Dow/DuPont* are irrelevant for the general validity of the Commission's approach.

To date, economic literature has not established a general link between market concentration and innovation. However, certain criteria have been established that may serve as a basis for whether a merger will lead to reduced innovation incentives in a specific case. Among those criteria are the level of appropriability, barriers to entry, the number of players in an industry and whether products are differentiated or not. In the Dow/DuPont Decision, the Commission has taken into account all of those features. The most important factor, the possibility of appropriating the value of an innovation, is even explicitly mentioned in the Commission's theory of harm. When appropriability is high, *Schumpeter's* finding – that competition is likely to decrease innovation incentives since firms fear spillovers in a competitive environment –[1010] loses much of its impact.

The Commission's assessment in *Dow/DuPont* concerning a possible link between market concentration and innovation incentives is accurate,

1010 *Schumpeter*, Capitalism, Socialism and Democracy, especially p. 87-107.

reliable, consistent and complete. With respect to the specific setting, the relevant literature has been considered. In its Annex 4, the Commission also deals with divergent economic views. One may have a look at the counterfactual: not considering innovation concerns in an innovation driven scenario means considering them negatively. In other words, it is impossible to exclude a merger's impact on innovation by simply ignoring innovation competition. If the Commission decided to refrain from assessing innovation concerns, this could lead to even greater harm to research and development incentives.

Concerning the specific market features in *Dow/DuPont*, the Commission has made efforts to support its theory of harm with all economic findings available. This must be sufficient in light of the normativity of legal decisions. The mere fact that there is no one-hundred-percent scientific certainty about a specific result does not prevent an authority from adopting a decision.

6) Other factors impacting innovation must be taken into account

Whereas price level depends to a high degree on market concentration and the level of competition, innovation may also be incentivized by other factors. For a complete assessment of innovation competition, those factors must not only be taken into account but also must be put in relation to market concentration.

In *Dow/DuPont*, regulatory issues and resistance of crops have been mentioned as additional factors impacting innovation incentives. The Commission found that those factors were not altered by the transaction and were therefore not important in the innovation assessment of the transaction. However, it is not important for factors countervailing possible anti-competitive effects to be altered through a merger as long as their effect is sufficiently strong pre-merger. In traditional merger assessment, the Commission considers buyer power or the extent of entry barriers as countervailing factors. However, buyer power or entry barriers are usually also not changed through a specific merger. Thus, the Commission must assess the significance of factors such as regulation or resistance in the crop protection industry and relate it to the negative effects arising from reduced competitive pressure.

7) The treatment of efficiencies must be altered with respect to innovation

Aside from the link between market concentration and innovation and the weighing of other innovation incentivizing factors, one of the main points in the discussion has been the assessment of efficiencies in *Dow/DuPont.*

Traditionally, efficiencies must benefit consumers, be merger-specific and verifiable. Furthermore, the burden of proof for efficiencies lies with the parties of a transaction.

In *Dow/DuPont*, the Commission found that the efficiencies brought forward by the parties did not fulfill the traditional criteria. They would take place in the long term based on a complex chain of events. The parties had not submitted any concrete evidence on either the time-frame or the passing on to consumers.

First, there are good arguments for an ex officio assessment of efficiencies in cases relating to innovation competition. The burden of proof should not be with the parties. This is because efficiencies are already part of the underlying theory of harm:

> "*Economic principles indicate that a merger between two out of a limited number of significant innovators is likely to reduce product innovation when appropriability is high (that is, when IPRs are effective), and when there are no merger-specific efficiencies associated with the merger.*"[1011]

This indicates that the competitive harm (reduction of product innovation or rather reduction of incentives to product innovation) will only occur if there are no efficiencies. Without the assessment of efficiencies, there cannot be an ascertainment as to the possible negative effects on innovation. The mere assessment of the limited number of significant innovators in a specific market setting with high appropriability does not lead to the conclusion that innovation incentives are reduced. Even though there is, under specific circumstances, a link between market concentration and innovation incentives, the final assessment of a reduction of the very innovation incentives relies on the incorporation of possible innovation-enhancing effects. Unlike concentration on product markets that has a high likelihood of leading to increased prices, this is not automatically the case with respect to innovation.

Imagine the parties not bringing forward any efficiency claims (for whatever reason) even though post-merger there would be extremely large cost efficiencies and a high reduction of knowledge spillover. In that case,

1011 Dow/DuPont Decision, para 2042.

if a Commissions' merger assessment does not take into account those effects by itself (without the parties invoking it), it would lead to a completely flawed outcome, even eminently decreasing innovation incentives. This refers to the potentially ambiguous relationship between market concentration and innovation incentives. Whereas market concentration will in general lead to higher prices, the link between concentration in innovation and innovation incentives is only valid under specific circumstances. Those circumstances include the absence of innovation-specific efficiencies.

The difference between price and innovation efficiencies may be illustrated with respect to cost savings: One of the thoughts behind the Commission's theory of harm is that increased cannibalization post-merger may lead to decreased innovation incentives. This is due to the fact that the merged entity is likely to capture sales from own products. Thus, innovation does not "pay out" because it does not lead to a greater stream of revenues. However, if there are sufficient cost efficiencies with respect to R&D, innovation activities may be profitable, as they outweigh the captured sales from a company's own products. In that respect, cost efficiencies not only counteract lost returns to innovation but also prevent losing returns in the first place. It should be kept in mind that the reasoning behind cannibalization and its relation to innovation incentives is not that a firm wants to prevent taking sales from own products but rather that it wants to prevent losing revenues. It is not in the specific interest of a firm to protect old products, but to maximize income.

Things are different with respect to price: In general, a higher market share may give the merged entity the ability to increase prices or limit production without losing income. Aside from cost savings there need to be additional factors that put pressure on the merged firm to not raise prices. Apart from those additional factors, the merged entity would have no incentive to pass on cost savings to consumers. This means that the decision to raise prices is to a large extent determined by competitive pressure from third parties. Even if there remain other players on the market, the merged entity may still have an incentive to raise prices if those players do not sufficiently restrict that incentive. In case of innovation incentives, such third party pressure is not required. The decision to innovate is driven by the prospect to raise income. Any additional income will be sufficient to decide to innovate. This means that even if the competitive pressure of third parties is low, there will still be innovation incentives as long as a new product will gain any revenues from other market participants.

The ability to raise prices and the passing on of cost efficiencies depend on different preconditions. This is not the case with respect to innovation incentives: the reduction of rivalry and the increase of cost efficiencies are two sides of the same action, namely a merger. There are no additional factors that determine whether innovation incentives are increased or decreased. Whereas with respect to prices, there is harm in the first place that may be outweighed by other factors, there is no presumption that an increase in concentration will lead to a decrease in innovation incentives independent of efficiencies. The same reasoning applies with respect to other efficiencies such as the increase of appropriability. They are an imminent part of a merger and – regardless of any additional factors like competitive pressure of third parties – influence the basic company decision to increase or decrease innovation activities.

For that reason, the burden of proof that traditionally lies with the parties must be shifted to the Commission concerning innovation competition. Since innovation-enhancing effects cannot be separated from innovation-depressing effects, the Commission must incorporate both in its assessment regardless of the parties invoking possible benefits. Otherwise, the Commission's outcome with respect to innovation incentives would not only be incomplete but bears the risk of being manifestly wrong.

Second, the traditional criteria for assessing efficiencies are not fit for innovation competition. This is particularly the case for the requirement that efficiencies must benefit consumers. In fact, it seems impossible that in an assessment based on concentration of innovation competitors and importance of innovators, there may be any factor directly affecting consumers in a market. The protective goal of Commission action is the innovation incentive – and not the final innovative product. In that respect, it cannot be expected of the parties to submit findings concerning any effect on the innovation outcome. Accordingly, when the harm may be a decrease in innovation incentives, possible efficiencies also must relate to those very innovation incentives and not to the final consumer.

In addition, it seems unlikely that the standard of the Horizontal Merger Guidelines concerning verifiability may be fulfilled. The Horizontal Merger Guidelines require that

> *"the efficiencies are likely to materialise, and be substantial enough to counteract a merger's potential harm to consumers. {...} Where reasonably possible, efficiencies and the resulting benefit to consumers should therefore be quantified."*[1012]

1012 Horizontal Merger Guidelines, para 86.

A consumer benefit can, by its very nature, not be substantiated for a setting beyond existing markets. Second, it may be difficult to precisely quantify, for example, the level of appropriability post-merger. Hence, it must be sufficient to prove that there will be higher appropriability and that this will likely outweigh an increased concentration with respect to innovation.

As far as efficiencies are concerned, the standard in the Horizontal Merger Guidelines is only partly fit to cover innovation competition. Whereas is seems likely to show that effects are merger-specific, it is impossible to quantify benefits for consumers. The level of verifiability must be adjusted to the specific efficiency.

8) *Dow/DuPont* is anchored in primary law

The novel approach in *Dow/DuPont* is in line with the European Treaties. Innovation is one of the objectives of the TEU and TFEU. Innovation and competition are both pillars of the internal market. In addition, innovation is an important driver of competition. The Commission's comprehensive approach in the Dow/DuPont Decision is therefore anchored in the provisions of the Treaties. The Commission has to take into account innovation incentives when issuing merger decisions in order to be in line with the objectives of the Treaties. It is not sufficient for the preservation of innovation to take into account research and development activities with respect to defined markets, but there is the need to secure the entire innovation process from the basic incentive to the final marketed product. The Commission therefore only puts into practice what is stated in primary law. *Dow/DuPont* does not mark a shift in the triangle of the internal market, the competition rules and the rules on innovation but realizes its full potential.

B) *Innovation Competition and the scope of its application in EU Competition Law*

1) Restrictive agreements according to Article 101 TFEU

(a) Starting points for an assessment under Article 101 TFEU

The Commission's innovation competition approach in *Dow/DuPont* affects the position of an undertaking. The Commission does not define an own innovation market but rather uses the innovation capacity of an undertaking to determine its innovative strength in relation to upstream or downstream markets. With respect to Article 101 (1) TFEU, the position of companies in innovation competition may thus determine whether an agreement between them has a restrictive effect. In addition, one may think of an exemption according to Article 101 (3) TFEU due to improved production of goods or promotion of technical or economic progress without eliminating competition.

Up to date, the innovation competition approach has not found its way into legislation or Guidelines on Article 101 TFEU. The notion of "competition in innovation" – as mentioned in the R&D BER, the Horizontal Cooperation Guidelines and the Technology Transfer Guidelines – is different from the innovation competition approach in *Dow/DuPont*.

First of all, competition in innovation seems to still be closely related to the Innovation Market Analysis by *Gilbert* and *Sunshine*. The Horizontal Cooperation Guidelines seem to apply usual market assessment criteria to innovation. In contrast, innovation competition as developed in *Dow/DuPont* does not relate to specific products or markets but to innovation incentives in general.

Second, "R&D poles" as mentioned in the Guidelines do not correlate with "innovation spaces" in the Dow/DuPont Decision. This is for two reasons: According to their treatment in the Horizontal Cooperation Guidelines, R&D poles relate to specific products. The Guidelines define R&D poles as efforts directed towards a certain new product or technology. In contrast, innovation spaces can be defined as the spaces in which goals broader than a specific product are targeted. In addition, R&D poles require existing research and development activity. According to the Horizontal Cooperation Guidelines, there must be R&D efforts with a "similar timing", and only targeted activities can have a certain timing. Also, the examples in the Guidelines exclusively rely on existing research and development activities towards specific products. The same is true with respect to the Technology Transfer Guidelines that deal with "innovation aiming at creating new products".

(b) No application of the innovation competition approach in case of R&D cooperation

One may think of transferring the concept behind *Dow/DuPont* to R&D cooperation. Taking into account the rationale behind *Dow/DuPont*, this would lead to the following hypothesis:

> "An R&D cooperation between two out of a limited number of significant innovators is likely to reduce the incentives for product innovation when appropriability is high and when there are no cooperation-specific efficiencies."

However, the hypothesis cannot be verified. There is no reduction of innovation incentives through an R&D cooperation. There are major differences between structural changes through a merger and a temporary cooperation.

First of all, the incentive to start R&D with respect to a specific research activity is embodied in the R&D agreement itself. Obviously, the parties want to start innovation activities. Otherwise, they would not have engaged in setting up a joint project. Accordingly, the parties of an R&D agreement do have the incentive to conduct innovation activities. This is not necessarily the case in a merger setting, because there may be other reasons for merging than joint R&D performance.

This intuitive finding is substantiated by an analogy to the mechanisms driving innovation incentives as elaborated in *Dow/DuPont*: the cannibalization mechanism, the product market mechanism and appropriability.

In a merger setting, the increase in cannibalization concerns may lead to a reduction of innovation incentives. However, with respect to R&D cooperation, this concern is not valid. The respective companies have already assessed possible cannibalization mechanisms and have obviously come to the conclusion that it is profitable for them to perform R&D. Moreover, cannibalization is not increased because the amount of products or pipeline products that could be cannibalized does not grow by means of an R&D cooperation. There remain two independent industry players with their respective own product and research portfolio. That product and research portfolio is not affected by the cooperation. If at all, the negative externality imposed on one another is internalized only for the specific cooperation project in question. With respect to that project, however, the parties already decided that it is profitable to them to perform R&D. In addition, the parties retain the option to terminate cooperation in case it is no longer profitable for them. If there is a fear of cannibalizing own products or research activities, the respective undertaking could decide to terminate either its own efforts or the cooperation. This decision will depend on the specifics in the individual case and does not presume a general reduction in R&D activities. The cannibalization concern does not support the finding that R&D cooperation reduces innovation incentives.

The same is true with respect to the product market channel. Market power on product markets may incentivize research and development activities because of a higher impact on pricing of the final product. Two undertakings are able to coordinate their price setting, resulting in higher revenues. This leads to better exploitation of the final result of R&D. This is as true for mergers as it is for R&D cooperation if the parties decide to jointly exploit the final results. However, the decision of whether the product market channel promises a high level of revenues has already been made at the stage of entering into an R&D agreement. It is at least not altered through the cooperation.

Appropriabilty may only serve as a decisive factor if the level is not already high pre-cooperation. In case of effective IP rights or marketing strategies, it may not affect the innovation incentive. If appropriability is low, cooperation may even increase innovation incentives.

There is also no indication that R&D cooperation leads to a slowdown of research and development activities. It is true that it is no longer possible to gain a competitive advantage over the R&D cooperation partner once the cooperation has started. But the decision on competitive advantages is made before entering into the agreement. Further, it seems rather unlikely for an undertaking to decide on establishing an R&D cooperation just to slow down the research process if it could have accelerated the process outside the cooperation (and thus taken sales from its competitor). Again, whereas after a merger the decision to perform R&D is taken within the newly merged entity, in case of a cooperation two independent legal entities decide on how to perform R&D. They will each decide on the way most profitable to them. If there is a competitive advantage in separately performing R&D, this will be the way taken. If it is more profitable to cooperate, the undertakings will decide on setting up an R&D agreement. Accordingly, in a free market, the R&D cooperation itself is the competitive advantage.

It is far from clear that cooperation actually reduces the need to constantly innovate. The parties remain competitors. They will decide on continuing the cooperation. In case a cooperation is no longer efficient, it may be terminated. This is a major difference compared to a merger that cannot easily be undone after its implementation.

There are also no indications that the mere existence of an R&D cooperation will prevent third parties from performing R&D in the same sector. Whereas the merging parties have fewer incentives to start and maintain research and development post-merger, the innovation incentives of the cooperating parties are not changed through the conclusion of an R&D agreement. This difference also influences third parties' research and development. In a merger setting the reduced incentives of the merging parties lead to a general decrease in competitive pressure on the innovation level. The merging parties have less incentives to perform R&D. Accordingly, they are also less likely to introduce new products and exert competitive pressure on rivals. This in turn leads to third parties' reduced innovation incentives since they do not have to fear the merged entity to cannibalize their sales. All in all, innovation incentives decrease in the industry (or at least in certain innovation spaces). But this effect does not arise in a cooperation setting. As mentioned above, the innovation incentive of the cooperating parties does not decrease through the R&D agreement. Since the general intensity of competitive pressure on the innovation level is not altered, third parties' research and development incentives remain the same. In conclusion, an R&D cooperation is unlikely to decrease innovation incentives of the cooperating undertakings as well as those of third parties.

It is true that the number of independent research and development activities may be decreased. This may limit the number of possible solutions to a problem. However, this argument would counteract any kind of concentration or cooperation regardless of possible pro-innovation effects. In addition, the focus on the mere number of independent approaches ignores any pro-competitive effects of cooperation. Accordingly, the number of independent research and development projects cannot be considered as being a decisive factor for the legitimacy of R&D cooperation at a very early stage. In the case that certain research activities are already directed towards specific markets, this may be different. However, at this point in time, there is no need for the innovation competition approach. The concepts of potential competition and future markets are sufficient to cover effects on competition in identifiable markets.

(c) No application of the innovation competition approach in cooperation settings in general

The concept of innovation competition as developed in *Dow/DuPont* does not fit into the specific setting of cooperation. First of all, in case of a cooperation the parties remain independent market players. Even though they may align their research and development activities with respect to certain targets, they decide independently whether and how to begin and continue the cooperation. Secondly, cannibalization as the major rationale behind *Dow/DuPont* is not increased through cooperation. The number of products or research activities that could be cannibalized does not increase in case of a cooperation. Those two points claim general validity in the case of a cooperation. As opposed to a merger, cooperating parties remain structurally independent. This means that there is always the possibility of terminating a cooperation. In addition, the number of products or services that can be cannibalized generally does not increase for each cooperating party.

This is also true for technology transfer agreements. In contrast to R&D agreements, technology transfer takes place chronologically before the decision to start innovation activities. The primary purpose of licensing agreements is to enable the licensee to use the technology for the production of goods or services. Nonetheless, since a technology is an "asset", a licensing agreement may have an impact on the innovation capacity of an undertaking. The licensed technology may increase the ability and therefore also the incentive of the licensee to innovate. In case of an exclusive license, the setting is far more structural because the licensee has the licensed technology at its disposal.

But in case of technology transfer, there is no communitization comparable to a merger. The licensed technology is not actually communitized in the sense of being a jointly exploited asset. Depending on the characteristics of the specific arrangement, one, both or even more parties can use the licensed technology. However, their decisions on how to use the technology for the purpose of further research and development are usually independent. There is no "concentration" of decision-making processes.

The initial question – if the principles set out in *Dow/DuPont* must apply accordingly if Dow and DuPont had set up a research and development cooperation instead of merging – must be answered in the negative. The differences between mergers and cooperation do not allow for a transfer of the innovation competition approach.

2) Abuse of a dominant position according to Article 102 TFEU

(a) Starting points for the assessment under Article 102 TFEU

Innovation competition as mentioned in *Dow/DuPont* may alter or determine the market position of an undertaking and thus supplement the concept of market dominance under Article 102 TFEU. This does not mean that an innovation market shall be established, but that power in an existing product market may not only depend on market shares but also on the innovation capacity of an undertaking.

There have been attempts to include technological advantages of an undertaking in the assessment of market dominance. While some of the decisions of Union Courts and the Commission focus on specific technologies used to produce specific products, there are also considerations on the research and development capacity of an undertaking. However, even though innovation capacity is taken into account, there are no criteria mentioned for assessing such capacity or strength in research and development. Most importantly, technological advance is always analyzed with respect to specific identifiable markets. But harm to competition and innovation may also occur before the emergence of identifiable markets or beyond specific existing markets.

(b) The notion of an "important innovator" developed in Dow/DuPont may be used to determine market dominance

Dow/DuPont focuses on the behavior of important innovators. In that Decision, the Commission for the first time spelled out criteria to assess the importance of an undertaking with respect to innovation incentives. When assuming that a merger of two important innovators may lead to decreased innovation incentives, one may as well argue that internal growth leading to the same result as a merger in terms of innovation capacity may also have an effect on those innovation incentives. If innovation is an important parameter of competition as well as one of the European Union goals, then authorities should start to focus on the important innovator.

With that in mind, transferring the logic in *Dow/DuPont* to abuse of dominance settings may result in the following hypothesis:

> "It may be considered an abuse of dominance in the meaning of Article 102 TFEU if an important innovator engages in practices decreasing innovation incentives."

Or put differently:

> "With respect to behavior impacting innovation incentives, market dominance shall be assessed on the basis of innovation capacity."

Whereas the Dow/DuPont Decision deals with the combination of two important innovators, Article 102 TFEU rather concerns one important innovator, possibly decreasing innovation incentives of third undertakings. Abusive conduct of an important innovator may lead to a decrease in innovation ability and incentive vis-à-vis third parties (competitors and trading partners). In the latter case, the effect is not dependent on an oligopolistic market structure. Rather, the important innovator may directly influence innovation incentives of market participants independent of the market features. The reduction of innovation incentives is not due to a decrease in competitive pressure in the industry but results from targeted action. For that reason, the principles on the important innovator as developed in *Dow/DuPont* may be used beyond the SIEC test and incorporated into the assessment of a market dominant position.

Article 102 TFEU is oriented towards the past and allows for a retroactive control of the behavior of market participants. As mentioned above, the assessment in *Dow/DuPont* covers static short-term effects rather than long-term dynamic effects. It is about the decrease in innovation incentives at the time of the implementation of the transaction and not about the innovative product or service developed in the future. In that regard, the rationale behind *Dow/DuPont* may well be incorporated into the static assessment under Article 102 TFEU. This is even more the case with respect to the assessment of the important innovator. The innovation capacity of an undertaking is a static factor that can be analyzed at the time of the behavior in question. What's more, in the case of abuse of dominance, the starting point for competition policy intervention is not the final innovation but a third undertaking's ability and incentive to innovate. This ability and incentive may depend on the current behavior of the important innovator at hand.

(c) The importance of innovation capacity in abuse of dominance cases is restricted to certain kinds of abusive behavior

It must be acknowledged that innovation capacity as a means of determining market dominance is not fit for every kind of abusive behavior. In fact, behavior concerning price-setting on an existing market – even though this may influence the resources of competitors or trading partners that can be invested in research and development – is unlikely to have any negative impact on competition if performed by an undertaking with low market shares but high innovation capacity. In that setting, competitors with high market shares are able to constrain the pricing behavior of the important innovator. This is different with respect to behavior directly influencing innovation incentives of third undertakings.

It should be considered abusive if an important innovator uses its power over innovative solutions to decrease the innovation activities of other undertakings. This may either take the form of explicit or implicit refusal of access or other strategies to prevent innovation activities within the innovator's own area of research and development (or even beyond).

Those cases may often involve innovations protected by IP rights, but they are not limited to that. There may well be innovative solutions that do not fall within the scope of IP protection that are nonetheless necessary for further ability, and thus incentive, to innovate. In any case, refusal to supply constellations, the misuse of regulatory framework (for example with respect to patent protection) or discrimination are likely candidates for the application of the concept of the important innovator.

However, it is essential in cases involving innovations developed by important innovators that there is always a balancing exercise with respect to the innovator's own innovation incentives. The traditional efficiency assessment in abuse of dominance cases is far better suited for covering innovation aspects than that under merger control. The main difference from merger control is that efficiencies in the assessment of abuse of dominance do not necessarily have to directly benefit consumers. Furthermore, in abuse of dominance cases, it is on the Commission to balance possible positive and negative effects on innovation incentives. Efficiencies may for example lie in the prevention of free riding of competitors on the investments made by the dominant undertaking in research and development instead of investing themselves.

(d) The powers of the Commission may be restricted in settings involving important innovators

The Commission may not impose fines on important innovators hindering innovation incentives of competitors or trading partners. This is due to the fact that the principle of legal certainty is not fulfilled in those cases. Legal certainty may not only be provided by the wording of a provision but also by settled case law. Even though it may well be that the legal aspects for assessing innovation capacity and incentives are established through case law or even explicit guidance by the Commission, it will remain impossible for the undertakings concerned to obtain the data necessary to perform the factual assessment.

In contrast to market volume (that may be obtained through industry reports), research and development assets as well as plans are confidential business information that is usually not published. Information inquiries to competitors on that matter are likely to violate Article 101 (1) TFEU, because they reduce strategic uncertainty and enable the undertakings to be aware of market strategies of their competitors. Besides the high risk of violating Article 101 (1) TFEU by asking competitors for data on R&D capacities and projects, undertakings do not have any legal right to obtain that information. In fact, competitors will almost certainly be reluctant to disclose any information on their confidential research projects.

The same result may be obtained with respect to the principle of fault. Since the undertakings are not able to assess whether they are an important innovator with respect to innovation assets and ability, they will not act intentionally or negligently. For those reasons, the Commission cannot impose fines on important innovators decreasing innovation incentives of third parties.

Things are different with respect to other Commission powers. In case of finding and termination of an infringement according to Article 7 of Regulation 1/2003, the formal Commission decision provides for legal certainty. The Commission decision sets out the consequences for the addressee with respect to its future conduct. In that regard, it is precisely foreseeable for the addressee of the decision whether its behavior is compatible with Article 102 TFEU.

(e) The criteria set up in Dow/DuPont for determining an important innovator may be used in the context of abuse of dominance

All in all, the two hypotheses must be answered in the affirmative. It may be considered an abuse of dominance if an important innovator engages in practices directly decreasing the innovation incentives of competitors or trading partners. In those settings, market dominance shall be assessed on the basis of innovation capacity. The criteria set up in *Dow/DuPont* should serve as a basis for the assessment.

Conversely, based on the same principles, an undertaking with high market shares that is not an important innovator may defend itself by means of the innovation capacity of other industry players. In that kind of "innovation defense", an undertaking may be considered as not being dominant with respect to behavior directly impacting innovation incentives of competitors or trading parties. However, attention must be paid to the fact that a firm with high market shares may at the same time be an important innovator.

3) Allocation of the result in primary law

Based on the above assessment, the concept of *Dow/DuPont* can be used in the scope of Article 102 TFEU but not in the scope of Article 101 TFEU. Besides the specific rationale of the Dow/DuPont Decision and its application in the scope of cooperation and unilateral behavior, this result can also be based on the general differences between Article 101 and 102 TFEU and their relation to merger control.

The innovation competition approach in *Dow/DuPont* is about the structural allocation of research and development assets and capabilities. This approach is of use in the structural setting of Article 102 TFEU, focusing to some extent on the market position of a single undertaking. However, innovation competition is not about the coordination of two or more independent undertakings. Innovation competition points towards the conditions for market behavior, not the market behavior itself. Therefore, the rationale in *Dow/DuPont* cannot be applied in the scope of Article 101 TFEU. This result shows the differences between structural and behavioral aspects of competition policy. Whereas Article 101 and 102 TFEU and the merger control rules all point towards securing free trade within the internal market, the provisions have different starting points to reach this goal.

Bibliography

Aghion, Philippe/Harris, Christopher/Howitt, Peter/Vickers, John: Competition, Imitation and Growth with Step-by-Step Innovation, 68 Review of Economic Studies (2001), Issue 3, p. 467-492.

Aghion, Philippe/Bloom, Nick/Blundell, Richard/Griffith, Rachel/Howitt, Peter: Competition and innovation: an inverted-U relationship, 120 Quarterly Journal of Economics (2005), Issue 2, p. 701-728.

Amelio, Andrea/Buettner, Thomas/Hariton, Cyril/Koltay, Gabor/Papandropoulos, Penelope/Sapi, Geza/Valletti,Tommaso M./Zenger, Hans: Recent Developments at DG Competition: 2017/2018, 53 Review of Industrial Organization (2018), No 4, p. 653-679.

Argyres, Nicholas S./ Silverman, Brian S.: R&D, Organization Structure, and the Development of Corporate Technological Knowledge, 25 Strategic Management Journal (2004), Issue 8-9, p. 929-958.

Arrow, Kenneth J.: Economic Welfare and the Allocation of Resources for Invention, in: Universities-National Bureau Committee for Economic Research, Committee on Economic Growth of the Social Science Research Council: The Rate and Direction of Inventive Activity: Economic and Social Factors, Princeton 1962, p. 609-262.

Baker, Jonathan: Beyond Schumpeter vs. Arrow: How Antitrust Fosters Innovation, 74 Antitrust Law Journal (2007), p. 575-602.

Barney, Jay: Firm Resources and Sustained Competitive Advantage, 17 Journal of Management (1991), No 1, p. 99-120.

Barth, Uli: Innovationmärkte in der Fusionskontrolle. Eine rechtsvergleichende Untersuchung nach deutschem, europäischem und U.S.-amerikanischem Recht, Baden-Baden, 2004.

Basedow, Jürgen: Das Sozialmodell von Lissabon: Solidarität statt Wettbewerb?, EuZW 2008, p. 225.

Behrens, Peter: Der Wettbewerb im Vertrag von Lissabon, EuZW 2008, p. 193.

Bishop, Simon/Walker, Mike: The Economics of EC Competition Law: Concepts, Application and Measurement, 3rd edition, London 2010.

Callies, Christian/Ruffert, Matthias (editors): EUV/AEUV. Das Verfassungsrecht der Europäischen Union mit Europäischer Grundrechtecharta. Kommentar, 6th edition, Munich 2022.

Carlton, Dennis W./Gertner, Robert H.: Intellectual Property, Antitrust and Strategic Behavior, in: Jaffe, Adam B./Lerner, Josh (editors): Innovation Policy and the Economy, Volume 3, Cambridge, MA 2003, p. 29-59.

Cary, George S.: The European Commission's Flawed Understanding of Innovation Concerns, in: Kokott, Juliane/Pohlmann, Petra/Polley, Romina (editors), Europäisches, deutsches und internationals Kartellrecht. Festschrift für Dirk Schroeder, Cologne 2018, p. 183-201.

Chernenko, Marina: An innovative theory of innovation harm? An assessment of the European Commission's approach to innovation competition in merger review, 40 E.C.L.R. (2019), Issue I, p. 9-23.

Clark, John B.: The Real Dangers of the Trusts, 68 The Century Magazine (1904), No 6, p. 954-959.

Comanor, William S./Scherer, F.M.: Mergers and innovation in the pharmaceutical industry, 32 Journal of Health Economics (2013), p. 106-113.

d'Aspremont, Claude/Jacquemin, Alexis: Cooperative and Noncooperative R&D in Duopoly with Spillovers, 1988, available at: www.di.ens.fr/~aspremon/Claude/PDFs/dAsp88a.pdf; also published in 78 The American Economic Review (1988), No 5, p. 1133-1137.

Denicolò, Vincenzo/Polo, Michele: The innovation theory of harm: An appraisal, IEFE Working Paper No 103, March 2018, available at: papers.ssrn.com/sol3/papers.cfm?abstract_id=3146731.

Dreher, Meinrad: Die Kontrolle des Wettbewerbs in Innovationsmärkten. Marktabgrenzung und Marktbeherrschung in innovationsgeprägten Märkten, ZWeR 2009, p. 149-175.

Drexl, Josef: Anti-Competitive Stumbling Stones on the Way to a Cleaner World: Protecting Competition in Innovation without a Market, Max Planck Institute for Intellectual Property & Competition Law Research Paper No. 12-08; also published in 8 Journal of Competition Law and Economics (2012), Issue 3, p. 507-542.

Eikenberg, Henning: Der Europäische Forschungsraum: Ein Kompetenzproblem?, EuR 2008, p. 125-139.

Eikenberg, Henning: Plädoyer für eine Änderung der Gründungsverträge der EU: Die Vorschriften über Forschung, technologische Entwicklung und Raumfahrt, EuR 2015, p. 802-824.

Esser, Michael/Höft, Jan Christoph: Fusions- und Missbrauchskontrolle 4.0 – Die 9. GWB-Novelle als Antwort auf die Herausforderungen der Digitalisierung?, NZKart 2017, p. 259-264.

Esteva Mosso, Carles: Innovation in EU Merger Control. Remarks prepared for the 66th ABA Section of Antitrust Law Spring Meeting, Washington, 12 April 2018, https://ec.europa.eu/competition/speeches/text/sp2018_05_en.pdf.

Everling, Ulrich: Probleme der Rechtsangleichung zur Verwirklichung des europäischen Binnenmarktes, in: Baur, Jürgen F./Hopt, Klaus J./Mailänder, K. Peter (editors), Festschrift für Ernst Steindorff zum 70. Geburtstag am 13. März 1990, Berlin 1990, p. 1155-1171.

Farrell, Joseph/Shapiro, Carl: Antitrust Evaluation of Horizontal Mergers: An Economic Alternative to Market Definition, 10 The B.E. Journal of Theoretical Economics (2010), Issue 1, Article 9.

Federal Cartel Office (Bundeskartellamt): Innovationen – Herausforderungen für die Kartellrechtspraxis. Tagung des Arbeitskreises Kartellrecht. 5.10.2017. Hintergrundpapier: www.bundeskartellamt.de/SharedDocs/Publikation/DE/Diskussions_Hintergrundpapier/AK_Kartellrecht_2017_Hintergrundpapier.pdf?__blob=publicationFile&v=2.

Federico, Giulio: Horizontal Mergers, Innovation and the Competitive Process, October 2017, available at: papers.ssrn.com/sol3/papers.cfm?abstract_id=3049338 ; also published in 8 Journal of European Competition Law & Practice (2017), Issue 10, p. 668-677.

Federico, Giulio/Langus, Gregor/Valletti, Tommaso M.: A Simple Model of Mergers and Innovation, CESifo Working Paper Series No 6539, June 2017.

Federico, Giulio/Langus, Gregor/Valletti, Tommaso M.: Horizontal Mergers and Product Innovation, February 2018, available at: papers.ssrn.com/sol3/papers.cfm?abstract_id=2999178; also published in 59 International Journal of Industrial Organization (2018), p. 1-23.

Federico, Giulio/Scott Morton, Fiona/Shapiro, Carl: Antitrust and Innovation: Welcoming and Protecting Disruption, 24 May 2019, available at: papers.ssrn.com/sol3/papers.cfm?abstract_id=3393911; also published in 20 Innovation Policy and the Economy (2020), p. 125-190.

Geiger, Rudolf/Khan, Daniel-Erasmus/Kotzur, Markus (editors): EUV. AEUV. Vertrag über die Europäische Union. Vertrag über die Arbeitsweise der Europäischen Union. Kommentar, 6th edition, Munich 2017.

Glader, Marcus: Innovation Markets and Competition Analysis. EU Competition Law and US Antitrust Law, Cheltenham, UK and Northampton, MA, USA 2006.

Gilbert, Richard J.: Competition and innovation. Chapter 26 in Collins, Wayne Dale et al. (editors): Issues in Competition Law and Policy. ABA Antitrust Section, Chicago 2006.

Gilbert, Richard J.: Looking for Mr. Schumpeter: Where Are We in the Competition-Innovation Debate? in: Jaffe, Adam B./Lerner, Josh/Stern, Scott (editors): Innovation Policy and the Economy, Volume 6, Cambridge, MA 2006, p. 159-215.

Gilbert, Richard J./Newbery, David M.G.: Preemtive Patenting and the Persistence of Monopoly, 72 The American Economic Review (1982), No 3, p. 514-526.

Gilbert, Richard J./Greene, Hillary: Merging Innovation into Antitrust Agency Enforcement of the Clayton Act, 83 The George Washington Law Review (2015), Volume 6, p. 1919-1947.

Gilbert, Richard J./Sunshine, Steven C.: Incorporating Dynamic Efficiency Concerns in Merger Analysis: The Use of Innovation Markets, 63 Antitrust Law Journal (1995), p. 569-601.

Gilbert, Richard J./Sunshine, Steven C.: The Use of Innovation Markets: A Reply to Hay, Rapp and Hoerner, 64 Antitrust Law Journal (1995), p. 75-82.

Grabitz, Eberhard/Hilf, Meinhard/Nettesheim, Martin (editors): Das Recht der Europäischen Union. EUV/AEUV, Supplement 74, as at September 2021.

Grabitz, Eberhard/Hilf, Meinhard/Nettesheim, Martin (editors): Das Recht der Europäischen Union. EUV/AEUV, Supplement 40, as at October 2009 (referred to as "*Commentator* in Grabitz/Hilf/Nettesheim (2009)").

Grabitz, Eberhard: Über die Verfassung des Binnenmarktes, in: Baur, Jürgen F./ Hopt, Klaus J./Mailänder, K. Peter (editors), Festschrift für Ernst Steindorff zum 70. Geburtstag am 13. März 1990, Berlin 1990, p. 1229-1245.

Greenstein, Shane/Ramey, Garey: Market structure, innovation and vertical product differentiation, 16 International Journal of Industrial Organization (1998), Issue 3, p. 285-311.

Günther, Eberhard: Die Regelung des Wettbewerbs im Vertrag zur Gründung der Europäischen Wirtschaftsgemeinschaft, WuW 1957, p. 275-293.

von der Groeben, Hans/Schwarze, Jürgen/Hatje, Armin (editors): Europäisches Unionsrecht. Vertrag über die Europäische Union - Vertrag über die Arbeitsweise der Europäischen Union - Charta der Grundrechte der Europäischen Union. Kommentar, 7th edition, Baden-Baden 2015.

Hasselhorn, Ann Charlotte: Tagungsbericht zu den 2. Kölner Kartellrechtsgesprächen 2019: Innovation im Kartellrecht – Innovation des Kartellrechts, NZKart 2019, p. 546-548.

Haucap, Justus: Merger Effects on Innovation: A Rationale for Stricter Merger Control?, DICE Discussion Paper No 268. Dusseldorf 2017.

Haucap, Justus/Stiebale, Joel: How Mergers Affect Innovation: Theory and Evidence from the Pharmaceutical Industry, DICE Discussion Paper No 218, Dusseldorf 2016.

Hay, George A.: Innovations in Antitrust Enforcement, 64 Antitrust Law Journal (1995), p. 7-17.

Hayek, Friedrich A.: Recht, Gesetz und Freiheit. Eine Neufassung der liberalen Grundsätze der Gerechtigkeit und der politischen Ökonomie, Tübingen 2003.

Hayek, Friedrich A.: The Use of Knowledge in Society, 35 The American Economic Review (1945), No 4, p. 519-530.

Hoerner, Robert J.: Innovation Markets: New Wine in Old Bottles?, 64 Antitrust Law Journal (1995), p. 49-73.

Ibáñez Colomo, Pablo: Competition Law and Innovation: Where Do We Stand?, 9 Journal of European Competition Law & Practice (2018), Issue 9, p. 561-562.

Immenga, Ulrich/Mestmäcker, Ernst-Joachim (editors): Wettbewerbsrecht. Band 1. EU. Kommentar zum Europäischen Kartellrecht. Founded by Ulrich Immenga and Ernst-Joachim Mestmäcker, edited by Torsten Körber, Heike Schweitzer and Daniel Zimmer, 6th edition, Munich 2019.

Immenga, Ulrich/Mestmäcker, Ernst-Joachim (editors): Wettbewerbsrecht. Band 3. Fusionskontrolle. Kommentar zum Europäischen und Deutschen Kartellrecht. Founded by Ulrich Immenga and Ernst-Joachim Mestmäcker, edited by Torsten Körber, Heike Schweitzer and Daniel Zimmer, 6th edition, Munich 2020.

Italianer, Alexander: Prepared remarks on: Level-playing field and innovation in technology markets. Conference on Antitrust in Technology, 28 January 2013, Palo Alto (US), available at: ec.europa.eu/competition/speeches/text/sp2013_01_en.pdf.

Jarass, Hans D.: Charta der Grundrechte der Europäischen Union unter Einbeziehung der vom EuGH entwickelten Grundrechte, der Grundrechtsregelungen der Verträge und der EMRK. Kommentar, 4th edition, Munich 2021.

Jung, Nelson/Sinclair, Elizabeth: Innovation theories of harm in merger control: plugging a perceived enforcement gap in anticipation of more far-reaching reforms?, 40 E.C.L.R. (2019), Issue 6, p. 266-275.

Kern, Benjamin R.: Innovation Markets, Future Markets, or Potential Competition: How Should Competition Authorities Account for Innovation Competition in Merger Reviews?, January 2014, available at: papers.ssrn.com/sol3/papers.cfm?abstract_id=2380130; also published in 37 World Competition: Law and Economics Review (2014), No 2, p. 173-206.

Laitenberger, Johannes: EU-Wettbewerbsregeln, Binnenmarkt und 60 Jahre Römische Verträge – Herausforderungen in einer Welt im Wandel, NZKart 2017, p. 89-92.

Bunte, Hermann-Josef (editor): Kartellrecht. Kommentar, 14th edition, Cologne 2022.

Leber, Marius: Dynamische Effizienzen in der EU-Fusionskontrolle. Zum Prognoseproblem im Kartellrecht am Beispiel von Mobilfunkfusionen, Baden-Baden 2018.

Lippert, André: Abwägungsentscheidungen im Europäischen Wettbewerbsrecht, – Neuorientierung durch Verfassungsvertrag und Vertrag von Lissabon? –, DVBl 2008, p. 492-499.

Loewenheim, Ulrich/Meessen, Karl M./Riesenkampff, Alexander/Kersting, Christian/Meyer-Lindemann, Hans Jürgen (editors): Kartellrecht. Kommentar, 4th edition, Munich 2020.

Lopez, Angel L./Vives Xavier: Cross-ownership, R&D Spillovers, and Antitrust Policy, CESifo Working Paper Series No 5935, 2016.

Lopez, Angel L./Vives, Xavier: Overlapping Ownership, R&D Spillovers, and Antitrust Policy, May 2018, available at: blog.iese.edu/xvives/files/2018/06/Lopez-Vives-May-2018-forth.pdf; also published in 127 Journal of Political Economy (2019), Issue 5, p. 2394-2437.

Mestmäcker, Ernst-Joachim/Schweitzer, Heike: Europäisches Wettbewerbsrecht. 3rd edition, Munich 2014.

Monopolkommission: Wettbewerb 2018. XXII. Hauptgutachten der Monopolkommission gemäß § 44 Abs. 1 Satz 1 GWB, Baden-Baden 2018.

Montgomery, Cynthia A. (editor): Resource-Based and Evolutionary Theories of the Firm: Towards a Synthesis, Bosten/Dordrecht/London 1995.

Monti, Mario: A New Strategy for the Single Market. At the Service of Europe's Economy and Society. Report to the President of the European Commission José Manuel Barroso, Brussels, 9 May 2010.

Mooij, Benjamin/Rusu, Catalin S.: Innovation and EU Competition Law: In Need of a Narrative for Where the Money Is Put, 43 Legal Issues of Economic Integration (2016), p. 173-199.

Motta, Massimo/Tarantino, Emanuele: The Effect of a Merger on Investments, CEPR working paper No DP11550, 2016.

Motta, Massimo/Tarantino, Emanuele: The Effect of Horizontal Mergers, When Firms Compete in Prices and Investments, University of Mannheim, Working Paper Series, Working Paper 17-01, September 2017, available at: madoc.bib.uni-mannheim.de/42805/1/17-01_Motta,%20Tarantino.pdf.

Münchener Kommentar zum Wettbewerbsrecht, edited by Säcker, Franz Jürgen/Bien, Florian/Karpenstein, Ulrich/Ludwigs, Markus/Meier-Beck, Peter/Montag, Frank. Volume I. Europäisches Wettbewerbsrecht. 3rd edition, Munich 2020 {referred to as "*Commentator* in MüKo"}.

Münchener Kommentar zum Wettbewerbsrecht, edited by Säcker, Franz Jürgen/Bien, Florian/Karpenstein, Ulrich/Ludwigs, Markus/Meier-Beck, Peter/Montag, Frank. Volume I. Europäisches Wettbewerbsrecht. 2nd edition, Munich 2015 {referred to as "*Commentator* in MüKo 2015"}.

Petit, Nicolas: Innovation Competition, Unilateral Effects and Merger Policy, 29 January 2018, available at: papers.ssrn.com/sol3/papers.cfm?abstract_id=3113077 ; also published in 82 Antitrust Law Journal (2019), p. 873, 876-77.

Podszun, Rupprecht: Standard Essential Patents and the Antitrust Law in the Age of Standardisation and the Internet of Things: Shifting Paradigms, IIC 2019, p. 720-745.

Rapp, Richard T.: The Misapplication of the Innovation Market Approach to Merger Analysis, 64 Antitrust Law Journal (1995), p. 19-47.

RBB Economics: RBB Brief 54. An innovative leap into the theoretical abyss: Dow/DuPont and the Commission's novel theory of harm, July 2017, available at: www.rbbecon.com/publications/brief-54-an-innovative-leap-into-the-theoretical-abyss-dowdupont-and-the-commissions-novel-theory-of-harm/.

Reich, Norbert: Mindestharmonisierung im Verbraucherschutzrecht. Stellungnahme, in: Everling, Ulrich/Roth, Wulf-Henning (editors): Mindestharmonisierung im Europäischen Binnenmarkt. Rererate des 7. Bonner Europa-Symposiums vom 27. April 1996, Baden-Baden 1997, p. 175-179.

Ruffert, Matthias: Grund und Grenzen der Wissenschaftsfreiheit, in: Sommermann, Karl-Peter/Huster, Stefan/Schulte, Martin/Ruffert, Matthias et al. (editors), Kultur und Wissenschaft. Veröffentlichungen der Vereinigung der Deutschen Staatsrechtslehrer (VVDStRL), Volume 65, Berlin 2006, p.146-216.

Schwalbe, Ulrich/Zimmer, Daniel: Kartellrecht und Ökonomie. Moderne ökonomische Ansätze in der europäischen und deutschen Zusammenschlusskontrolle, 3rd edition, Frankfurt am Main 2021.

Schumpeter, Joseph A.: Capitalism, Socialism and Democracy, first published in the USA in 1942, edition used: Taylor & Franics e-Library, London and New York 2003.

Schwarze, Jürgen: Europäische Kartellbußgelder im Lichte übergeordneter Vertrags- und Verfassungsgrundsätze, EuR 2009, p. 171-199.

Schwarze, Jürgen/Becker, Ulrich/Hatje, Armin/Schoo, Johann (editors): EU-Kommentar, 4th edition, Baden-Baden 2019.

Shapiro, Carl: Competition and innovation. Did Arrow hit the bull's eye?, Chapter 7 of Lerner, Josh/Stern Scott (editors): The Rate and Direction of Inventive Activity Revisited, Chicago 2012, p. 361-404.

Soltész, Ulrich/Steinle, Christian/Bielesz, Holger: Rekordgeldbußen versus Bestimmtheitsgebot – Die Kartellverordnung auf dem Prüfstein höherrangigen Gemeinschaftsrechts, EuZW 2003, p. 202-210.

Spangler, Simon/Heppner, Marcus: Innovationen in der Fusionskontrolle nach Dow/ DuPont, PharmR 2018, p. 522-526.

Streinz, Rudolf (editor): EUV/AEUV. Vertrag über die Europäische Union. Vertrag über die Arbeitsweise der Europäischen Union. Charta der Grundrechte der Europäischen Union, 3rd edition, Munich 2018.

Streinz, Rudolf (editor): EUV/EGV. Vertrag über die Europäische Union und Vertrag zur Gründung der Europäischen Gemeinschaft, 1st edition, Munich 2003 (referred to as "*Commentator* in Streinz (2003)").

Tamke, Maren: Marktmacht in digitalen Märkten nach der 9. GWB-Novelle, NZKart 2018, p. 503-508.

Terhechte, Jörg Philipp: Die Europäische Union als Innovationsverbund – Innovationsverfassung und rechtliche Innovationen in der EU, EuR 2017, p. 3-30.

Thiede, Thomas/Müller, Christian: Die Entwicklung der europäischen Fusionskontrolle in den Jahren 2017 und 2018, EuZW 2019, p. 628-633.

Todino, Mario/van de Walle, Geoffroy/Stoican, Lucia: EU Merger Control and Harm to Innovation – A Long Walk to Freedom (from the Chains of Causation), 64 The Antitrust Bulletin (2019), Issue 1, p. 11-30.

Vedder, Christoph/Heinschel von Heinegg, Wolff (editors): Europäisches Unionsrecht. EUV/AEUV/GRCh/EAGV. Handkommentar, 2nd edition, Baden-Baden 2018.

Weitbrecht, Andreas/Mühle, Jan: Europäisches Kartellrecht 2009, EuZW 2010, p. 327-333.

Whinston, Michael: Comment on Chapter 7 of Lerner, Josh/Stern, Scott (editors): The Rate and Direction of Inventive Activity Revisited, Chicago 2012, p. 404-410.

Wiedemann, Gerhard (editor): Handbuch des Kartellrechts, 4th edition, Munich 2020.

Wirtz, Markus/Schulz, Max: Innovationswettbewerb in der Fusionskontrolle – *Bayer/Monsanto* und *Dow/DuPont*, NZKart 2019, p. 20-28.